Books by Charlie & Diane Winger

Highpoint Adventures –
The Complete Guide to the 50 State Highpoints

The Essential Guide to Great Sand Dunes
National Park & Preserve

The Trad Guide to Joshua Tree –
60 Favorite Climbs from 5.5 to 5.9

Book cover design by Diane Winger

Two Shadows

Two Shadows

For Barbara & Dave

The inspirational story of one man's triumph over adversity

Enjoy!

by Charlie Winger

Charlie Winger

Two Shadows : The inspirational story of one man's triumph over adversity /
Charlie Winger

ISBN 978-1-453-78678-9

The poem "Two Shadows" Copyright © Diane L. Winger, 1980
Inspired by conversations about the concept for this book

All photographs are from the Winger collection
or provided by friends and climbing partners,
except as noted.

Dedicated to everyone
who reached out to help me in so many ways
when I couldn't help myself.

*"The pessimist sees the difficulty in every opportunity;
the optimist the opportunity in every difficulty"*

L. P. Jacks

Two Shadows

by Diane Winger

Two shadows – in my life I've known
two shadows – one has faded, one has grown.
I'm on the top of the mountain.
At last my life is all my own,
above the shadows.

The old shadow – so many years ago –
was prison – and so few people know
the things I did as a young man.
The judge told me to go
into the shadow.

But somehow it was there I found my way
from the darkness into the light of day.
When I climbed out of the Hole
I kept on climbing every day
out of the shadow.

From the mountain, I see the prison far below
and my shadow falls where others may not go.
I made my life, chose my direction,
and I have so much to show –
out of the shadow.

One shadow lies ahead of me –
one shadow stretching far as I can see.
And from the top of the mountain,
it's so clear that it will be
my only shadow.

Contents

Acknowledgments
Forward
Introduction

In the Beginning

Climbing Adventures

Reality Check

---

* The first time a Term from the Glossary is used, it will be underlined like this.

♦♦♦

Acknowledgments

First and foremost, I need to thank my best supporter, my lovely and devoted wife, my partner of over thirty years, Diane. She has been a never-ending source of encouragement. Everyone needs a pillar of stability in their life and Diane is mine. She surreptitiously recorded many of my stories through the years, allowing me to gather together the bits and pieces critical to bringing life to some of these adventures. Her editing, graphic layout, and constructive criticism have been invaluable assets in the completion of this work. I could go on and on with my praise for Diane but perhaps just a few small words say what I wish to convey: "I love you."

Several friends have contributed to my efforts by proofreading selected chapters or "filling in the blanks" when I strayed off the beaten path. Your help has been appreciated and invaluable. I thank you one and all: Dave Cooper & Ginni Greer, Burt & Jo Falk, Sy & Joyce Fischer, Steve & Shane Holonitch, Alan Mosiman, Randy Murphy, Jim Scott, Jo Streep, and George Vandersluis & Mary Maurer.

Diane celebrates her personal highest elevation achieved
(at that time), 14,700 feet in Nepal

Forward

I never knew the first Charlie Winger. By the time I met Charlie in 1988 his metamorphosis was already accomplished. In fact, the Charlie I have known for over twenty years bears no resemblance to the person described in the early chapters of this book. That he was able to so completely turn his life around, from someone who was headed on a downward spiral from which no good outcome could be expected, to the positive role model he is today, is amazing.

In the following pages Charlie leads you through his "formative" early years, revealing a harsh introduction to the world. Rather than being molded by these early experiences, however, he chose to break the mold and live a positive and fulfilling life. Written in a frank and sometimes blunt style, Charlie's irrepressible sense of humor comes through strongly and helps lighten what could otherwise be a somber start to the book. His writing style is compelling and makes it difficult to put this book down.

The story of how Charlie put his early years behind him, became a successful businessman, and found fulfillment in climbing mountains should inspire all of us. As you read the chapters devoted to climbing, you will understand the passion that he has for this pastime – a passion that he has passed along to countless numbers of students and friends over the years.

Although this is an autobiography, the story Charlie tells in this book could be considered as an allegory for whatever personal summits we are attempting to scale. The mental fortitude, perseverance, and bonds of friendship needed to scale the peaks described here are no different than the qualities needed to excel in life in general. It is on the mountain that a person's true nature is laid bare. It has been said that character is revealed not by one's successes, but by how one responds to failure. Charlie shares with us both his successes and failures, and it is apparent that neither has done anything to diminish his indomitable spirit. It is this same spirit that has allowed him to "bounce back" (sorry Charlie) from the illness and fall that would have ended most other climbers' careers.

While I never knew the first Charlie, my life has been richer for knowing the second and counting him a friend. I look forward to reading many future chapters.

Dave Cooper
August 2010

Author of
Colorado Scrambles: Climbs Beyond the Beaten Path
and
Colorado Snow Climbs: A Guide for All Seasons
and contributing writer of "Trail Mix" column for
The Denver Post

http://davecooperoutdoors.com/

Introduction

I love entertaining people with climbing stories. Over the years, friends have encouraged me to write a book recounting my numerous adventures and misadventures. Most were unaware that there was another side of my life which was a story of its own. This is where the idea to write "Two Shadows" originated. One shadow was cast by the mountains I was climbing; the other shadow was cast by the prison walls of my past.

I decided to write this book in the hope that it would serve as an inspiration to others that it is possible to pull oneself up out of the quagmire of hopelessness and live a happy, productive life with a future.

This is the story of my life.

I was a total mess as a teenager, but with education, hard work, and the help of others, I was able to turn my life around and achieve success as an adult. I'm proud of what I have accomplished since those dark early days.

This narrative figuratively and literally has some very low points and some very high points — from a life of crime to a successful computer technology career and a discovered passion for mountain climbing; from the depths of hopeless despair to the exhilaration of achieving success in life — one step at a time.

I'm a mountaineer, so I relate to things that I can climb. Starting to write my story was like making that first difficult move in rock or ice climbing. Once you get past that move and get off the ground, you can focus on the climb itself and just allow events to flow and ebb as they may. You'll never know how far you can go if you don't make that first move. And, like climbing, the analysis of one's life story has risks and is best taken just one move at a time or else it, too, can be overwhelming.

Writing this book has been very cathartic for me. Until now, I had never tried to analyze my life — probably for good reason. I'm genuinely ashamed and embarrassed when I look back at my early years.

For me, parts of what I've written are a confessional, others an emotional release. I've faced some extremely painful memories. Yet, I emerged from those early times with my sense of humor intact. A bit off-the-wall, to be sure, but intact.

Some of the events I've recounted here are comic, some are tragic, and some are quite graphic. While others were enjoying high school and proms and football games or going to college, I was at a different kind of school, learning how to pick locks, steal things, and generally be a criminal. Graduation was either being paroled or getting off probation.

It is not my intent in this book to glamorize crime or boast about the criminal deeds I did in my early years, but rather to set the tone of the depths to which I had fallen and how long and difficult the odyssey to today has been.

I'm going to take you on a journey that starts in the tenements and alleys of pre-World War II Chicago through jails, reformatories, and the hell that was prison. From solitary confinement to the jungles of the Amazon, the heights of the Himalayas, the isolation of the desert Southwest, and many points in between. It's a journey I'm not always particularly proud of, but we can't go back and change history no matter how hard we try. Some things are better left unsaid as they are too painful to relate, so I'll leave it to you to read between the lines. I don't have permission to write about everyone who makes this journey real, so I'll change a few names and places along the way to protect the guilty.

I hope that after you read these pages, you judge me not as I was then but as the person I am today, someone who has finally found peace within himself.

Charlie Winger, 2010
Hopefully out enjoying the Mountains

◆◆◆

In the Beginning

Chapter 1 - The Windy City
Life in the Trenches

"Have you ever been convicted of a felony?" the Canadian Border Services Officer inquired. "No," I responded with a straight face and sweaty palms. "Are you sure you've never been convicted of a felony?" he repeated. "Not since 1955," I admitted, guiltily. So began my journey back in time to a place I thought I had forever left behind.

Starting around 2007, the world experienced what experts described as the worst economic downturn since the great depression of the 1930s. Not everyone agreed what caused the recession, but a few things are certain: it was a complex set of circumstances, it didn't just happen overnight, and it was going to take a substantial amount of time to correct the problem.

That scenario could also describe my early life, those years between the time I should have been old enough to know right from wrong and the years that followed when I realized that the path I was taking was leading me down an alleyway with a dead end. I've worked long and hard since then to prove that I have overcome the behavioral problems which led to my incarceration.

The year 1937 saw the end of some things — Amelia Earhart disappeared while attempting to fly around the world — and the beginning of some other things — Jack Nicholson, Dustin Hoffman, and I all came into the world. The year of my birth was a period between the end of the Great Depression and the beginning of World War II. Ten cents would get you a gallon of gasoline (sorry, no unleaded), a new car went for $760 (hard to buy a good set of tires for that amount now), coffee was 38 cents a pound (that sure wasn't Starbucks), and the average income was $1,788 *per year*.

I came into the world in Chicago, Illinois at the hands of my Dad after the hospital sent my mother back home to give me more time to prepare for my arrival. I already had one brother; our sister would be born five years later. Maybe middle children just can't figure things out — my siblings seemed to do just fine.

I don't remember much about those very early years. My Dad was a career military man and we moved back and forth across the country following him to his different assignments. We lived in Chicago during World War II while he was stationed overseas, and we didn't get to see much of him. My Mom worked in a factory in support of the war effort so we were usually looked after by other women who weren't working. There is a big void in my memory of childhood until my little sister was on the scene.

Most commodities like butter, sugar, gasoline, and tires were strictly rationed. We saved our leftover grease, tinfoil, and rubber bands for donation to the war effort. Can you imagine not being able to have your cell phone, iPod, or other conveniences we enjoy today? We mostly listened to radio programs like *Inner Sanctum*, *Amos and Andy*, and *The Shadow*. *Movietone Newsreels* were the TV and Web of those days, reporting on all the latest war news, sports, and fashions.

I can remember sitting out on the stoop of our tenement building in Chicago during many a hot summer night along with

3

the adults listening to Joe Louis, the "Brown Bomber," during many of his fights. I can still vividly picture everyone sitting there drinking beer and cheering like it was yesterday. Even though we were at war, those days seem like they were less complicated than the world we live in today.

When I was six years old, the building we lived in caught on fire. I awoke early before anyone else was up and thought the room was a little hazy until I discovered what I thought was smoke coming out from the bottom of the walls. We had one of those old hand-held bug sprayers that you pumped to kill anything that moved. It was sitting against the wall and when I moved it I realized that something wasn't right. I started screaming about the place being on fire which woke up my Mom. Eventually the fire department arrived and proceeded to evacuate the building. My one-year-old sister was tossed down the stairs into the arms of a waiting fireman (who eventually became my Mom's "special" friend). The building was a total disaster so we had to move. Hopefully, the fire cooked a lot of the undesirable four-legged creatures that roamed the halls of our building.

We moved into a two-room tenement apartment. We would turn on the light in the morning or when we came home at night and the cockroaches would be running for cover by the hundreds. If it wasn't the cockroaches bothering us, it was the bed bugs. Every so often my Mom would buy one of those blue steel DDT canisters and would activate it inside the apartment. It would put out a haze of gas that was designed to kill every living thing in the vicinity. We had to leave the place for the day to keep from getting nuked ourselves. That was inside our apartment; outside the building during the summer the tenants would gather together every so often with garden hoses which would be placed in rat holes to try to flush the vermin out. What followed was a frenzy of people screaming and swinging shovels in an attempt to kill the elusive prey as they raced past in every direction. I found this whole scene very scary.

Tenement living did have its moments. Our apartment was located on the ground floor of the building. It didn't have air conditioning, so we would leave our windows open in the summer due to the heat. One evening, some guy tried to crawl into our apartment through the window. My mother woke up, grabbed a baseball bat, and began striking him on the head. He dove back out the window and hit the ground running. I guess she scored a home run! That was the environment I remember from those early days.

Our neighborhood had a somewhat infamous reputation due to its proximity to the Biograph Theater where the gangster John Dillinger was gunned down by FBI agents in 1934. As kids, we went to the Biograph on Saturdays to see the double feature. After the movie, we would line up outside the theater and be given a free comic book. Those were the days; things seemed so simple. The only thing we had to worry about was whether or not Roy Rogers or Tom Mix would get killed in the next episode of the serial.

Our family grew up without a lot of material things. I don't recall my parents ever owning an automobile, at least not during the years we lived in Chicago. When I say we didn't have a lot of material things, I remember receiving clothes and shoes from the Red Cross so we could go to school. In the years after my parents divorced, things got even leaner. My mother would disappear for short periods of time and we would be alone without much food except for what we would beg from our neighbors or steal.

I soon learned in those early days that if you wanted something, you tried to borrow it. If that didn't work, then begging came next and if all else failed you just stole it. Usually one or the other approaches worked but as time passed I admit I employed the latter tactic most often.

The lack of parental supervision early in my life likely contributed to the events that occurred in the years that followed and allowed me to set a pattern of negative, self-destructive behavior.

Some of my earliest memories are of shining shoes in the bars along Lincoln Avenue in Chicago; this would have been when I was around ten years old. I had my little shoe shine box and several kinds of polish. I would go into bars and tap the patrons on the shoulder asking if they wanted a shine. It really didn't matter to me what color their shoes were, I just used whatever color I had, and it was dark in the bar so they couldn't tell the difference. A shoe shine cost 15 cents, and every once in a while I would get 25 cents, which was enough money to go to the movies and purchase a treat. I guess that set the tone for my being in business for myself later in life.

Other kids had their own shoe shine "routes" and we routinely would get in territorial fights which I don't ever remember winning. A few hard punches and a couple of kicks to strategic parts of the anatomy were usually followed by my wooden shine box being thrown out into the street where it was summarily dismembered by the next passing automobile or streetcar.

In those days, electric refrigerators weren't very common, so everyone in our neighborhood had ice boxes. The ice man would come around in his truck to deliver the ice. They had cards you stuck in the window that read 25/50/75/100 for the pounds of ice you wanted. That was always a big deal to get some shards of ice that came off when the ice man was putting the new ice into the ice box. I still call our refrigerator an ice box, which makes the wife crazy. If you're around my age I'm sure you can remember all of these things.

The late 1940s was about the time my behavior really started on a downward spiral. I was a small kid, so being on the streets had its own perils for me.

One boy who lived in our neighborhood — Jimmy — was bigger than me, as were most kids my age. For some reason which was never clear to me, Jimmy took a permanent disliking to me. Every time he saw me he beat me up — every time! I'm not sure to this day what pissed him off so much. Hopefully the little bastard got run over by a garbage truck.

We didn't have video games or the Web in those days to keep us occupied, so we found other activities. Sometimes we entertained ourselves by stealing baby buggies from the lobbies of apartment buildings. These thefts were usually followed by the race from hell. We would push the buggy down a hill to get it going and then leap into it on the run to see who could go the fastest and farthest before crashing. There wasn't any steering mechanism so it was just hunker down and hold on. I think that's where the slogan "No Fear" probably originated. We knew we were going to get thrown out of the buggy and take a hit when it turned over but no one wanted to be the first to jump out and be branded a "coward." It was better to have road rash to brag about than everyone calling you a sissy. I don't think some of my friends and I were blessed with an abundance of brains. Besides, I've heard it said that suffering builds character.

I wouldn't say we had a "gang" but there were definitely several of us who were in about the same home situation and were constantly getting into trouble. We didn't always get caught, but when we did we were usually sent to the juvenile detention hall.

We were enterprising little snots and there wasn't a scheme we couldn't think up. We observed that a certain grocer stacked his empty pop bottles in a shed behind his store. We would get a cardboard box and load it up with as many empty bottles as we could carry and then return them to the grocer for the deposit. He finally wised up to our game, banned us from his store, and locked up his shed.

Stealing fruit from vendors stalls along the street or shoplifting items from dime stores was a pastime that could be enjoyed any time of the year. Winter coats were especially convenient for concealing stolen items. We learned early on that one kid could bang his head against a counter and fall to the floor screaming to distract the clerk while the other kids loaded up their pockets and fled with everything they could carry. I wonder if all those blows to my head at the Five and Dime stores could have caused my sociopathic behavior.

One very profitable escapade of ours was to take some of the appropriated items, alter the price tag by adding a dollar (a dollar was a lot of money in those days) and present it as a gift to someone's mother or other adult we knew. They would usually say something like, "You shouldn't have spent your money on me!" They would give us back the "purchase" price for being such nice little boys. I'm sure they were on to us, but they probably thought we were in training to be entrepreneurs in later life.

Wanton vandalism seemed to be my way of expressing myself in those days. Another kid and I decided to go into a parking garage where the attendants parked the cars with the keys left in the ignition. We thought it would be fun to take all of the keys we could and throw them into Lake Michigan, so we did. I still shake my head at the stupidity of some of my actions. I hope none of the owners of those cars are reading this today but I can probably still outrun them if necessary.

One of the more risky crimes we committed occurred when we went into an apartment building where people would leave their keys on a pegboard by the doorman's station. We waited until the guy left the area for a few minutes and stole a bunch of keys to the apartments. We knew that no one would be home, so this was like going shopping at a department store. I can't remember what we stole but this is the type of transgression that led to more serious crimes later.

Summertime in Chicago provided some of its own form of entertainment. We had electric streetcars in those days. A long metal connector pole powered the car via a series of wires running along above the tracks. We would wait at the street corner for the streetcar to start moving and then go running along as fast as our little legs would carry us, trying to jump on to the back of the car so we could climb in through a rear-facing window for a free ride. Failure to attach oneself to the rear of the streetcar was known to leave notable road rash on the arms and knees of anyone who tripped or wasn't fast enough to make a successful leap. We routinely got caught and kicked off but it always entertained the other passengers. If we got kicked off, we would reward the motorman for his efforts by running around behind the streetcar and pulling down on the tension cable attached to the connecting pole so that streetcar would lose power and coast to a stop. This required the motorman to get out and reconnect the rod prior to resuming his journey while cursing at us.

Streetcars also provided another unique, if somewhat sick, form of entertainment. Someone came up with the crazy idea of putting unfired .22 caliber bullets on the streetcar track so they would fire off as the wheels rolled over them. Thankfully, to my knowledge, no one was ever injured by one of these missiles. Another odoriferous act involved the throwing of eggs at passengers standing in the open doors of the streetcars as they passed. That usually brought a visit by the CTA (Chicago Transit Authority) police trying to find out which asshole was guilty. I'm sure we would have received a well-deserved beating from passengers had they ever been able to catch us.

We lived in an area of multistory tenement buildings separated by narrow walkways, connecting roofs, and unlit passageways that went down underneath buildings. No one could catch us, as these corridors served to allow us safe passage and instant cover for various and sundry nefarious activities.

Up to this point in my life, the crimes I had committed were crimes against property. No muggings, wielding of weapons, or anything of that nature. I was too small. That was all about to change.

One really stupid trick I pulled was to snatch a purse from a woman walking down the street. The other kids dared me into doing it and I was scared out of my mind. I came up to the woman and asked her what time it was. When she went to look at her watch I grabbed her purse and took off running. A couple of guys took off after me and the chase was on. They didn't stand a chance of catching us in our own neighborhood since we knew all the shortcuts and hideouts. I successfully eluded them but that was too scary. There wasn't much money in the purse. This incident cured me of any future impulse to physically confront anyone to commit a crime.

Streetcars and the Elevated train (the "L") provided cheap transportation for our many adventures. Our destinations included such interesting venues as the Field Museum, Alder Planetarium, Museum of Science and Industry, and Brookfield Zoo. We would spend our days looking at all the neat exhibits. We probably learned as much going to these places as we did in school.

I made plenty of "A"s during my early school years; unfortunately most of them were for being "A"bsent. I always considered these excursions as being "field trips" but school staff viewed things differently. Believe it or not we had Truant Officers in those days who would physically come to where you lived and confront your parents about your absence.

We weren't only interested in things scientific; we also had an affinity toward wildlife. One trip we would take on the streetcar during the summer was to a town out at the end of the line in what would later be termed the suburbs. It was mostly an area of vacant lots with a few scattered houses. We discovered that the area contained a wide variety of snakes — grass snakes, garter snakes, and other relatively harmless species. We would capture a half dozen or so of these reptiles and place them in a jar to take back to town. We realized that the conductor would never allow us to take the snakes on the streetcar, so we would hide them inside our shirts before getting on. When we were close enough to our side of town we would unbutton a couple of buttons on our shirts to allow an errant snake or two the freedom of slithering out and onto an unsuspecting passenger sitting next to us. Their reaction took a page right out of Pavlov's theory of conditioned responses. We always got a *kick* out of this activity; but usually it consisted of being dragged to the front of the streetcar and *kicked* out the door.

Getting home from our outings sometimes had its share of problems. The museums were a long way from where I lived, so if I couldn't sneak on the streetcar or didn't have the 4 cents fare, it was a hell of a long way back home on foot. I would always try to beg money but that didn't always work. I could look pretty pathetic when the need arose.

Chicago during the winter can be a bitterly cold place. The chill resulting from the winds coming off Lake Michigan is especially brutal. Nonetheless, we were able to make the most out of a bad situation by finding activities which didn't cost anything and provided us with plenty of adventure. We would hang around a street corner after a big snow waiting for the cars to start up when the stoplight changed. Then we would run out and grab the car bumper, get into a crouch and let the car drag us along sliding through the snow on our shoes until they got to going too fast or slammed on the brakes. I don't remember anyone ever getting seriously injured with this stunt but we all probably inhaled a substantial amount of exhaust fumes which resulted in our lack of good judgment.

Some of my misadventures had a less than cheerful ending. There was a religious complex near our area which had a large garden within its grounds. I decided one night that it would be fun to run through the garden knocking down corn stalks and pulling up some of the vegetables. All went according to plan until I was apprehended by one of the residents of the complex who beat the crap out of me; at the time I was probably only nine years old. My assailant dragged me up to his office to turn me over to the police. The older and more mature adults in their office were so shocked at the severity of the beating I had received that they threatened to call the police on him instead. They cleaned me up and told me to get out of there immediately and never come back. I just told my mother that I had gotten into a fight. That was one of my first *religious* experiences. My second exposure to religion was a result of going to vacation Bible school during the summer where we were always assured of getting something to eat.

One year the authorities sent me to a summer camp for troubled youths. Unfortunately, the name of the camp was Jolly Boys Camp, a name that would be the cause of several fights over the next few years. I never won many of these fights but I learned how to take a punch and come up swinging. The other kids just got plain tired of thrashing me (and so did I).

One semester I was sent to a Catholic school where the Sisters decided that my penmanship needed improvement. They made me sit next to this guy named Stanley who had impeccable penmanship in the hopes that I might see how "normal" people made their letters. The problem seemed to be that I was left handed and wrote with my hand crooked and upside-down like many lefties do. I guess the training worked as I got good at forging my Mom's name on my grade cards so she wouldn't see them. It also came in handy when we needed a few extra dollars for food. I would write a note — ostensibly signed by our Dad — to our local barber who would give us the money. I'm sure the barber knew the note was false but he gave us money anyway. When my Dad would come back into town and get a haircut, he had to settle up our debts with the barber.

I can only remember one time when my Dad actually got mad at me. He had gathered a nice collection of Indian Head pennies over the years. I succumbed to the siren of the Good Humor man and used the pennies to purchase an ice cream bar. Needless to say my Dad was not in good humor when he found out what happened to his collection. Since then I have always had an affinity for ice cream but I still can remember how angry he was with me.

My list of bad deeds could probably go on ad nauseam but I think I've established the depth of my behavioral problems.

When my parents were both in the same household at the same time things sometimes got ugly. Both were heavy drinkers and my Dad was a real ladies' man. I don't know what started a lot of those brawls but I do remember the cops coming over to break up the fights. Mom hit my Dad over the head with a cast iron skillet during one encounter.

When parents can't get along for whatever reason the outcome is usually not good for anyone. The long absences for active duty overseas and then the fighting finally resulted in my parents getting a divorce. If my mother had problems attempting to control me before, it became an insurmountable task with my Dad permanently out of our lives.

After their divorce, my mother was a frustrated single parent trying to raise "the wild bunch." She worked during the day, came home, made us some dinner, and then usually went out with friends to the bars. Sometimes she would come home afterwards and sometimes not. We pretty much took care of ourselves when she wasn't there. Contrast that with most single-parent mothers today. They're "soccer moms" — they keep their kids occupied by frantically taking them to a variety of sporting events or other organized activities. When the kids aren't doing that, they are watching TV, playing video games, emailing or texting their friends, talking on their cell phone, or taking nude photos of each other to send on their iPhone. We didn't have any of those options. Our recreation was either chasing down streetcars, scrambling over the Lake Michigan breakwater rocks or, in the winter, sliding along behind cars, sledding down "suicide" hill, or just plain being a pain in the ass when we couldn't find anything else to do. You didn't see as many obese kids then as you do now. Go figure.

Little did I know, but my Chicago days were rapidly drawing to a close. Even today this next part is still very painful to recall.

One afternoon my Mom told me she wanted me to take my sister and go to the movies. My brother had previously run away and gone to live with an aunt in Kansas. I was 11 years old and my sister was 6. There was a man visiting who I didn't remember ever having seen before, but that wasn't unusual. Going to the movies was always a treat, so we were overjoyed. After the movie we returned to the apartment, which was dark. This also was not unusual as Mom would frequently go out drinking and return home long after we were in bed.

The next morning, our mother still hadn't returned home, nor did she return the next day or the day after that. We didn't have much to eat in the house, so I went to the apartment next door and borrowed some bread which I used to make fried onion sandwiches for my sister and me. After several days, another of Mom's "friends" showed up asking for her. My sister and I were dirty, crying, and a real mess. He eventually called the police who contacted Social Services. My mother had disappeared without a trace. No note, no phone call, nothing, just vanished. We never saw or heard from her again. She discarded us like a used condom.

Social services worked out a deal with some people living in a nearby apartment to take us in while they were working on some disposition with our case. Finally, it was decided that we would go to Kansas to live with my Dad's aunt and uncle, Gertie and Chet, who were in their 60s. These were the same relatives that my brother had gone to live with. If my great aunt hadn't agreed to let us come to live with her, I was scheduled to be shipped off to reform school since I had been in so much trouble. My little sister probably would have been placed in a foster home.

My Dad had remarried and had two young children of his own, so he was unable to have us come to live with him. I'm not sure what conversations went on between my Dad and our Aunt or what real arrangements were made as my Aunt was not very forthcoming with any of that information. I'm sure Dad made the best arrangements he could, considering the circumstances.

So, on a rainy September morning in 1948, my sister and I left Chicago forever, abandoned, bewildered, and anxious. We were placed on an airplane and flown to Kansas to live with our Great Aunt and Uncle and our older brother.

I find it depressing that most of what I remember from those Chicago days are the appalling things I did.

Kansas • U.S.A.

Chapter 2 - This Land of Oz
Now You See Me, Now You Don't

Out of the frying pan and into the fire effectively describes my transition from street-smart Chicago hooligan to a very confused eleven-year-old boy in a small Kansas town. Going from almost no parental supervision to near total authoritarian supervision was a substantial change for me. I wasn't accustomed to anyone telling me what to do and when to do it, so that proved to be a difficult adjustment for me to make.

Even though my venue had changed, my attitude had not. I was still a very rebellious youth with a smart mouth and a chip on my shoulder. Those first few years in Kansas were very traumatic for me as well as everyone around me.

As the middle of the three children under our great aunt's command, I seemed to be the target of her frustrations. My aunt never had children of her own, so I doubt she had any way of relating to us. My brother was too old and too big for her to boss around and my sister was too young to get into any trouble.

Therefore, this story is about me and my skirmishes with my aunt — a veritable cat and dog fight.

At this point, I should describe my aunt's physical characteristics and general disposition. She was much taller than me (everyone was in those days, and still is today) and weighed around 160 pounds. One of her hands was crippled at the wrist which caused her to carry that arm up close to her side most of the time in a semi-bent position.

Over the years, my aunt had accumulated wedding rings from several of her deceased sisters which she wore on the fingers of the crippled hand. During times of strife, "The Hand" could strike out faster than a speeding bullet and hit me in the head so hard I didn't know what had struck me. If I didn't find myself sprawled on the floor, it was only because it wasn't a direct strike. I would look up and see *The Beast* looming over me with a half-smoked, unfiltered cigarette dangling from the corner of her mouth; the portion by her lips would be wet and dark from saliva. I could always count on her lamenting, "After all I've done for you kids, this is the way you treat me," in response to whatever precipitated the recently-delivered blow to the head.

Now, as I describe some of my acts during my years in Kansas, I would like to reiterate a statement I made earlier:

It is not my intent here to glamorize crime or boast about the criminal deeds I did in those early years, but rather to set the tone of the depths to which I had fallen and how long and difficult the journey to today has been. We can't rewrite history no matter how much we would like to have things come out differently.

School had become a waste of time for me. I was a terrible student and squandered most of my time trying to be a tough guy and behaving badly, which resulted in several expulsions. As I got older, I started taking alcohol to school with me. After imbibing between classes, I was usually wiped out by lunchtime and would just take off from school and wander around town. Drugs weren't as prevalent then as they are today, or I'm sure I would have been heavily into those instead of the booze.

I learned early on that I wasn't big enough to win many fights, so I had to even the odds by using whatever item was handy. I didn't fight to lose, so it was sometimes necessary to do something totally crazy to scare the other guy into realizing that he wasn't going to win. Marginally-controlled behavior enhanced my reputation at school of being somewhat unstable and probably saved me from many a potential beating.

I carried a switch blade knife and set of brass knuckles around with me, just waiting for someone to challenge me to a fight. I must have thought I was Al Capone or some other Chicago thug. Thankfully, I never used either of these during any of my altercations. I would hide them when I went home and retrieve them on my way out to go to school or to roam the streets at night. My aunt finally caught me with them one day during one of her "shakedowns" and threw them away. I replaced the brass knuckles with a steel guitar bar and convinced her I was learning to play the guitar at school. The steel guitar bar made for a wicked punch when held in the hand. Obviously more of that sick Chicago mentality. I probably could have benefited from some of those electric shock treatments they give mentally troubled persons.

There was a kid at school who was always pushing me around and generally making my life a living hell whenever he had some of his friends around to back him up. One afternoon, while riding home on the bus after school, I noticed him walking down the sidewalk carrying some type of musical instrument. I got off at the next corner and waited for him to come past me. I walked up to him and kicked him in the balls, then gave him a couple of good shots to the head and knocked him down. As I started to walk away, I gave his musical instrument a kick just for good measure. I never said anything to him during this whole encounter but I'm sure he knew why he got his ass kicked. He didn't seem so tough without his friends around.

Later that evening, the kid and his dad showed up at my aunt and uncle's house. Uncle Chet answered the door and called me over to answer the man's questions. Of course the dad was pissed. He was whining about his son's testicles being swollen and the bruises on his face. I maintained that the kid called me a dirty name and he got what he deserved. That *really* pissed off the dad and he wanted to have a go at me. My uncle got between us and told the guy that he would "take care of me" and not to worry about me bothering his son again. My uncle was a mellow guy, so I just got a good talking to and was sent to my room for the rest of the evening. The kid stayed away from me at school after that. I thought his buddies might want to jump me but I always tried to act tough even though I was scared of them.

It wasn't long after moving to Wichita that I resumed my old thieving habits. I would wait until everyone was asleep and then sneak out the bedroom window and roam around for hours, breaking into stores and cars. We used to refer to this type of behavior as a "midnight requisition." How many flashlights does one kid need? Mostly, I just took junk or cash when I could find it. There was a certain adrenaline rush associated with breaking into places that was addictive. I would sometimes steal stuff that had no value to me and simply throw it away. Go figure.

One cold December night, a couple of friends and I were walking down the street and saw a car sitting outside a Laundromat with the motor running. We thought it would be a good way to get where we were going and get out of the cold. As usual, I was selected to jump in the car and steal it. I crept up to the driver's side, opened the door, and jumped in behind the wheel, but was startled to find a man sitting in the passenger's seat. I'm not sure who was the most shocked — him or me — but he started shouting and I jumped out and took off running as fast as I could. I outran the guy but in the process ran into a low-hanging clothes line wire which leveled me out. It was a good thing I had already lost the guy chasing me or I would have probably got my ass hauled off to jail. The other guys I was with thought the whole thing was funny.

There was a small grocery store near where we lived which I decided I would burglarize one night. The owner's son was a guy at school that I didn't like, which is probably why I broke into the place. I didn't get anything worth my effort except the satisfaction of doing something indirectly to the kid at school. The cops came to school to question me but they didn't have any evidence. They were sure I committed the burglary but couldn't prove it. That was too, too close to home. I would need to be more selective with my targets in the future.

As I got older — but still in my early teens — I would usually run away from home after some of the altercations I had with my aunt. I'd end up in cities like Galveston, Baton Rouge, New Orleans, or St. Louis. More often than not, these excursions involved various breaking-and-entering events to steal money to support my flight. I hitchhiked all over the country during this period, working in restaurants as a "pearl diver" washing dishes, or helping the cook with his duties. Working in restaurants ensured that I always had something to eat. People would feel sorry for me and allow me to stay at their homes for a week or two, then I would move on in the middle of the night. Usually these jaunts ended up by my getting arrested for something and sent back to my aunt's in Kansas where the same abusive environment awaited me.

It may sound like I was a lazy bum in those days. The opposite was actually true. Hidden beneath my rebellious behavior was a very industrious, self-motivated individual. Even at a very young age, I always had some sort of part-time job. I had a large newspaper route which entailed distributing the papers on foot or bicycle. On one occasion it took me an extra long time to make my deliveries due to a larger volume newspaper. When I returned home, my aunt accused me of not coming home immediately after throwing the papers, which in her mind was a sin of some kind. She broke a switch off of a tree and went after me in a frenzy. I still have some of those scars. If you haven't figured it out yet, my aunt was a hateful and vindictive person, which is why I refer to her as *The Beast*. A truly sick human being. I'm not sure what kind of childhood she had, but I wonder if she was trying to get even with her parents by beating on me all of the time. My uncle, on the other hand, was the nicest guy you could imagine. I never figured out what he saw in her.

Another of my jobs was with a local newspaper company helping to deliver newspapers to the corner newsstands. My partner had an old beater of an automobile with the front doors removed. We would roll up to a corner and fill the newsstand with our papers. We carried bolt cutters in his car which we would sometimes use to cut the locks on the opposition paper's newsstand. We would take all the money out of the stand and throw it into the river. I'm not sure if those acts allowed us to sell more papers, but we got a sense of perverse pleasure out of our actions. The newspaper we were working for was unaware of these illegal acts and would never have sanctioned them — in fact I'm sure we would have been fired and arrested.

Since school was a place where I found out I could act out *my* aggressions, I looked forward to going as it got me away from my aunt. I met a guy at school who seemed to have it worse at home than I did at mine. We'll just call him Bobby. Bobby's father would get drunk and beat the living crap out of him. He would come to school with black eyes and bruises all over his body on a regular basis. The teachers in those days kept their noses out of your home life, so the police were never alerted to these sadistic episodes.

The more our home lives deteriorated, the more we looked for and found ways to get in trouble at school. Bobby, unlike me, had a girlfriend we'll call Maggie who lived with her grandmother. Seems the grandmother ran some type of retail store and kept a large stash of cash at their home in a trunk. Well, Maggie thought we had some type of drug connection, which we didn't dissuade her from thinking. We arranged to sell her some "drugs," which were no more than capsules filled with powdered milk. She, in turn, was ripping off grandma's stash, so we had ourselves a nice little illicit business being run at school.

Maggie decided she would sell some of the "drugs" to other kids at school and the game was over. The principal called us in and threatened to call the police but we denied the whole affair, blaming Maggie for the illegal transactions and disavowing any knowledge of any "drugs." Bobby, Maggie, and I met that night at her grandmother's house where Maggie raided the trunk for all of the cash. The plan was for Bobby and Maggie to split and then I would join them after the heat got off. Well, you can imagine how that story ends. They took off and totally disappeared with the cash. I got busted by the cops and only because I was a convincing liar did I not get arrested for all that had come down.

Bobby and Maggie finally got caught in Kansas City and he got in trouble for the theft as well as having "carnal knowledge" of an underage female. Maggie convinced the cops that it was all Bobby's fault and she didn't get into any serious trouble.

Some of my adventures were more of the risqué variety. In my early teens I didn't have any form of personal transportation, so I took a lot of public buses and hitchhiked around Wichita. One evening I was picked up by a man and woman who were going my way. Shortly after getting in the car they mentioned that they wanted to go out to look at a house in the country they were thinking of buying. I agreed to go along, all the while thinking that something else was up. So, it was no big surprise when he pulled off onto a dark area and started smooching it up with the woman. The guy had his hand under her dress and all over her breasts. All the while I'm just sitting there like a bump on a log. He leans over to me and says something like, "Hey kid, you can join us." So, he's kissing her and I'm doing what most 15-year-old boys would do when an opportunity like this presents itself. After a short time he comes up for air and asks me, "Do you want to get in the back?" I was doing OK in the front seat, but the back sounded like more fun. I got out, followed by the woman, and we climbed into the back seat. This opportunity was like finding a bird nest on the ground. The guy stayed up front while I engaged in working out the mysteries of sex in the back seat with a mature woman. I don't think anyone thought much about safe sex in those days and that certainly wasn't the first thing on my mind. Not sure what the guy did in the front — probably masturbated himself into a frenzy. Afterward, they took me back to town and dropped me off close to where I was going. Luckily, I didn't get VD or some other sexually transmitted disease, but let's face it, I enjoyed the experience. That night fueled my fantasies for many weeks to come, so to speak.

I ran away from home again after one extremely violent encounter with my aunt and met up with one of my friends, who decided we should go to Missouri to stay with his uncle. My friend was driving a late model pickup truck which he apparently had taken from his dad without permission. The next day, we ran out of gas and tried to sell our spare tire. The station owner called the cops, who arrived before we could get away. The officer recognized that we were a couple of runaways and asked us to follow him back to the police station. Shortly after we began driving, my friend turned off on a side street in an attempt to elude the officer. He immediately turned around and started chasing our vehicle with red lights flashing and siren wailing in the air. We fled out of town to the countryside where the officer lost control of his cruiser and crashed into a ditch. We were able to make our escape and continued on our way to Missouri.

Before we got to Missouri, we decided that we needed to get rid of the stolen truck. We went to a used car lot and pretended to look at some of the vehicles they had for sale. When the salesman wasn't looking, we stole the keys to a car we wanted. We returned that night and drove off in the car. The car dealer became aware of the theft the following morning and alerted the police, who put out a wanted notice for the stolen vehicle.

We were eventually stopped by the police while we were traveling through a small Missouri town, and placed under arrest for auto theft. Since we had stolen the vehicle in Kansas and taken it into Missouri, we were charged with a federal crime: the Dyer Act, the transportation of a stolen vehicle across a state line. We were both convicted, but since we were under-age, we were sentenced to a minimum-security, federal correctional institution for a term of one to three years. I was 16 years old at the time.

I may have thought I was a tough guy, but it was a rude awakening when I first walked through the gates of the correctional institution. Most of the inmates there were incarcerated for crimes more serious than just stealing a car. This was to be my first experience at being locked up for an extended period of time and I didn't know what to expect. Before, I was always in jail for a week or so and then would get out on bail or they would just drop the charges. This was the real thing, and I don't think I really comprehended what I had gotten myself into.

Institutional life for me was a big change from the life I had been living on the outside. I was mostly a loner, so being in a group setting without any privacy was very stressful. Their idea was to attempt to teach you a trade and to change your aberrant behavior patterns. Inside, they had rules and regulations and you obeyed them or found yourself doing a stretch in solitary confinement, which I did on occasion.

I've never been to boot camp in the military, but I imagine there is a distinct similarity. We had cellblock inspections where everyone on our tier would have our commissary privileges suspended if just one inmate failed to pass inspection. The guards

21

would come into each cell and make sure our beds were made to regulation and all our clothes and toiletries were placed in proper order, as well as a dozen other nit-picking rules. Any offender responsible for the suspension of privileges would be assured of receiving a visit from the "enforcement" committee. It was unlikely that the infraction would be repeated.

Life in jail was not always regimented boredom. Granted, there was nothing to do but pass time and that passed very slowly. It wasn't unusual for the boredom and frustration to explode into clashes between inmates. I had one such encounter with a particularly aggressive inmate who decided it would be fun to push me around and make a "name" for himself — who knows *why* he took a disliking to me. He initiated an argument, and when I stood up he grabbed my shirt and started slapping me around, backing me into a corner. The years of abuse at my aunt's hands finally erupted into a blind rage as I beat him senseless before the guards intervened. *The Beast* had returned to haunt me.

This thing of getting slapped in the face would resurface to trouble me several times later in life. I seldom came out the winner during these altercations, but my response to being slapped was always the same — a flashback to earlier days at the hands of my aunt followed by uncontrolled anger.

You had to adapt to survive in a place like this, and it wasn't long before I was just another number marking time until I could be eligible for parole or had completed my sentence. I had several work assignments but nothing that I would use later in life.

Little did I know that one of the inmates I met there would play a defining role in my later return to prison.

I was released from the correctional institution after serving eighteen months, and returned to live with my great aunt and uncle. I went back to high school briefly before dropping out again. I would get a job only to be fired for being someone who couldn't keep his mouth shut when appropriate. Anyway, nothing had changed in my relationship with *The Beast*, so it was only a matter of time before I would run away again and get into more trouble.

As before, there were many more unlawful and troubling events that I perpetrated over time. Obviously, it was going to take a cataclysmic event to change my behavior pattern. Getting a slap on the wrist or receiving a good lecture about what would happen to me if I continued getting into trouble wasn't going to solve the problem.

Chapter 3 - Crossbars Hotel
On the Inside Looking Out

My aunt and I were like two speeding freight trains racing through the night on the same track going in opposite directions; a violent collision was unavoidable. There was only so much of her abuse that any human being should endure.

My altercations with *The Beast* had become more violent as time passed. On one occasion she picked up a ping pong paddle and beat me with it until the paddle finally broke into pieces. I can't remember what infraction of her rules I disobeyed, but it never seemed to make any difference. If I held my spoon the wrong way — "The Hand" would send me sprawling on the floor. If I went out with friends and returned too late — or even too early — any nearby object might become a weapon in her grip. These confrontations would usually end up with me running out the door and disappearing for days at a time. Each time this happened, I would end up in jail in some town somewhere.

There seemed to be a recurring pattern to her attempting to "tame" me. The more she tried, the more I resisted, until finally we both reached the flash point in our relationship. I obviously did something that *really* pissed her off and she flew into an uncontrollable rage.

I had always just tried to protect myself from her sustained blows to my face and body by holding my hands up to ward off the strikes. This time, she backed me into a corner and was pummeling me with both hands. Enough was enough. I pushed out at her, attempting to defend myself and bring an end to her violent behavior. I don't clearly remember everything that happened that day but I started punching back at her in an expression of pent up anger and self defense. When this violent encounter was over, *The Beast* lay on the floor, supposedly unconscious. The events that had just transpired scared me not only because I had potentially injured her, but I was also shaken at the level of violence I had just displayed. This time I didn't run out the door and try to hide. I stayed to face whatever punishment would await me. I decided that she would never do this to me again.

My aunt remained on the floor, moaning, for a couple of hours until my uncle came home from work. Then, she miraculously became alert, got up, and went to her bedroom, all the while vociferously berating me. Needless to say, my uncle was very distressed and angry with me for allowing her to elicit such a response to her behavior. He knew what had been happening all those years, so I doubt that the outcome was much of a surprise to him. We had a long talk about my relationship with my aunt, and he merely asked that I not give her reason to become violent toward me again. If she started going over the edge again, I was to simply get out of the house before things escalated to another physical confrontation.

That was the last time *The Beast* ever struck me.

The handwriting was on the wall and I realized that my time living with my aunt and uncle was not a long-term, viable option. I decided that I would have to somehow leave and not return.

It's interesting how a string of unplanned occurrences sometimes creates a life-altering path. Such was to be the case when I received a phone call from a guy named Hal (not his real name) who I had met while incarcerated at the federal correctional institution. When he arrived in Wichita, Hal had already violated his parole by leaving the state where he was living and was on the run. I was also still on parole and things were quickly going to hell in a hand basket for me. Earlier in the year I had forged some stolen checks and was scheduled to go to trial. That was probably going to result in my being locked up again, so it didn't take long for me to decide that this was to be the way out of my present situation. I would quit school and take off with Hal and "get out of Dodge." Hal had a stolen car and we rapidly hatched a plan which included a couple of local burglaries for some cash and then began heading north.

What followed was a string of stolen vehicles and burglaries spanning several states en route to Illinois. We had a plan — but we really didn't have a plan. We were going to Chicago but had no idea what we would do when we got there. There obviously wasn't any rational thought being applied to this process and it showed. With virtually every law enforcement entity in the Midwest now on the lookout for us, it was surprising that we were able to continue our crime spree for as long as we did.

At one point we became lost while driving a stolen vehicle at night on a dark country road. Hal was driving and I was attempting to make heads or tails of the road map under the car's dim overhead light. I guess it was my cursing the map maker that got Hal's attention. I looked up. I found him studying the map as well. You might wonder who was driving the vehicle since we were both studying the map. That question was soon answered as the car violently lurched off the pavement and slammed into a string of rural mail boxes, some of which were attached to steel poles. *Clang! Bang!* Mail boxes came crashing through the windshield and over into the back seat. The car slammed to a stop amid a cloud of dust, glass shards, and flying debris. We both just sat there for a minute in shock, then jumped out of the car running in opposite directions, shaking glass from our clothing and hair. The car sat there among the wreckage of the mailboxes with a crumpled hood, steam rising from the engine, and a solitary, still-burning headlight. Closer examination revealed a large, u-shaped dent smack in the middle of the front end caused by the steel poles.

We had received a few minor scratches but were otherwise unharmed. Once the initial surprise of the accident passed, we had a long fit of laughter followed by concern that someone might have heard the collision. We climbed back into the car, backed up onto the road, and raced off down the highway without worrying about where we were headed. The extent of the damage to the vehicle soon became apparent as we negotiated a curve and our one remaining headlight went out. Another near disaster was narrowly averted as we skidded off the road into some low brush. We finally figured out that as long as we were headed in a straight line, the light would work fine; if we attempted to turn the steering wheel, we didn't have any headlights at all. We turned onto the next side road and pulled off out of sight to await daylight. We were able to "recycle" our damaged vehicle in the next town.

Generally speaking, criminals are not very smart or they wouldn't be criminals; there's no future in crime and we weren't any exception. A store we broke into along the way had a small safe which we managed to manhandle out the door and into the trunk of our stolen car. We decided to take the safe into the country to pry it open. So, there we were, driving down the highway in a stolen car with a stolen safe in the trunk but the trunk lid couldn't close because the safe was too large. The safe was sitting there in the trunk for everyone in the world to see. If that wasn't bad enough, we then had to pass through a small town. Thankfully, it was late at night so no one was out on the street to see how stupid we were.

Not long after leaving town, we pulled off the highway onto a side road and into a field where we unloaded the safe. Several hours and bashed knuckles later, we managed to get the safe open only to find out that it did not contain any money. Guess we'd better not quit our day jobs!

We were always driving hell bent for election at night, so it wasn't too much of a surprise that we had several near collisions. One night I was driving considerably over the speed limit when I rounded a curve and nearly rear-ended a state patrol car on the highway in front of me. They immediately turned on the

27

"bubble gum machine" and I knew we were going to be arrested. Imagine my astonishment when they took off at a high rate of speed in the same direction we were traveling, leaving us sitting there wondering why they hadn't stopped us. They must have received an emergency dispatch concerning something happening on down the road. Perhaps the communication concerned two idiots in a stolen car on the loose in the area!

Our "luck" finally ran out in the middle of the night a few days later as we exited a filling station after stealing a small amount of cash and some hand tools. Just as we were leaving, a police car pulled up behind us and instructed us to get out of the vehicle with our hands up. We started to open the doors of our car as the police officers got out of their cruiser. But before they could react, we quickly peeled out, showering them with gravel and dust as we took off in an attempt to elude them. It didn't take long before they were back in their car and in hot pursuit. You have to be an idiot to run from the police, because they're always going to catch you and then you're going to be in more trouble than you were before you fled, but that's applying rational thought to an irrational situation. So, down the road we went, trying to figure out how to evade the officers who were quickly coming up behind us with red lights blinking and siren wailing away.

We detoured onto every side street we encountered before finally ending up out of control, sliding to a stop among some tombstones in a cemetery! I guess this would have been a fitting place to have ended my life, but thankfully that was not to be.

Hal took off in one direction and I took off in the other. I soon found myself somewhere outside of town in the middle of a cornfield. I forgot to mention that this was in November, so the temperature was near freezing and I didn't have a hat or coat. You don't notice the cold when you're in such a panic mode. My "fight or flight" response kicked into gear and I just kept on running as fast as I could. I heard other police cars responding to the area and could see them cruising up and down the roads attempting to find us, their spotlights trained on the field where I now lay hidden in the dirt. After several hours they gave up the search and I sneaked back into town, keeping off the streets, and hid in a garage until daylight.

Later in the morning I went to the local bus station and purchased a ticket back to — you guessed it — Wichita. Since I had a few hours to kill before the bus departed, I went to a movie where I slept through a double feature. Near the time my bus was scheduled to depart, I strolled over to the bus station. I had tried to clean myself up in the movie theater bathroom but I still looked a little disheveled. I guess I didn't need to worry about that, as I fit in with most of the crowd waiting for the bus. There did seem to be a few people there who seemed out of place. Before I realized what was happening, I was surrounded by several plain-clothes detectives, pushed to the floor, and handcuffed. They search my billfold and found a paper stating that I was still on parole from the federal correctional institution. I was quickly hustled out of the building and into a waiting police car. Apparently, they had been checking the bus and train station for a short, wiry, eighteen-year-old ruffian who looked like he was about sixteen, and were alerted to watch out for me.

I didn't attempt to deny the events of the past evening and they soon had me writing a "confession" which they dictated. I admitted to being one of the people on the crime spree through several states that they were watching out for. Before I even had dinner, I had signed the confession and the wheels of justice were beginning to move toward my being incarcerated. This sequence of events — my signed confession — would not have happened so quickly given the laws that are in place today. Currently, the police must inform the person being arrested that anything they say can and will be used against them in a court of law; this is called giving the accused a Miranda warning. Failure to follow the Miranda procedure can get criminal cases thrown out of court. Nowadays you don't have to answer questions unless you have an attorney present.

That's all well and good, but I did what I did, I was guilty, and I was tired. Tired of the life I had been living and just plain physically tired. I really didn't care anymore — nothing really mattered.

It took only a few short weeks before I found myself with hands chained to my waist and feet shackled together standing in front of a judge in the courthouse while the county prosecutor stated that I was an incorrigible teenager. I was six months past my eighteenth birthday. The court appointed an attorney to explain the charges to me and asked if I wanted to plead guilty. I answered in the affirmative.

Based on my previous Federal conviction and incarceration as well as my obvious disregard for the law by stealing cars and burglarizing establishments in several states, the judge sentenced me to twelve years in the state prison and stipulated that my state-appointed attorney be paid the sum of $20 for his services. This was 1955, so perhaps $20 was reasonable. I doubt that I fully comprehended what had just happened to me, but the judge had ensured that I would have plenty of time to figure it all out.

Incidentally, the total value of the goods and cash I was accused of stealing amounted to a paltry $9.60, less than half of the amount my attorney received as his fee. The usual legal name of my crime is "Petit Larceny" which normally carries a term of 1-5 years. But because there were two people in our vehicle as we left the scene of the crime, that upped the sentencing guidelines to a possible 10-25 years and changed the legal designation to "Automobile Banditry." Automobile banditry brings up visions of something from the Bonnie and Clyde days.

In the movies, the criminal is chased and captured and in the following scene is sentenced to prison as the judge bangs down his gavel. The next thing you see is the criminal walking into prison; there is a loud "clang" as the prison gate is slammed behind him. Then there are a few scenes of prison life before they "fast forward" from there. The inmate gets released to start a new life and everyone lives happily ever after.

Not so fast. What was happening to me wasn't the movies — this was the real deal and it wasn't going to be over before you could finish that box of popcorn. Unless you've been there you probably can't fully grasp the enormity of spending the next twelve years of your life incarcerated, especially when you're a teenager. Let's do the math: that's 4,380 days; 105,120 hours; or 6,307,200 minutes and these numbers can seem like a lifetime. There was a common saying among the inmates, "Don't do the crime if you can't do the time." I should have thought of that before I left Wichita.

It would be extremely difficult for me to succinctly express the range of emotions I was experiencing during those first days in prison. I was frightened about what the unknown years that lay ahead would hold. This wasn't like the correctional institution that I had been in before – this was prison where many of the inmates were doing life terms as habitual criminals or murderers. Those first few nights, I would wake up hoping this was just a dream and I would find myself somewhere else. I am sure I cried, but it was a little late for that.

When you enter prison, you are placed in the "orientation" unit, away from the general prison population for at least a month. You're referred to as a "fish." You are given your prison number, prison clothes, and medical exams, and you're evaluated to see what type of work assignment you're capable of performing as well as where in the general prison population you will reside. I was an anomaly since I was the youngest inmate in the prison by many years. With the exception of those inmates sentenced to a life term, they usually send someone my age to the state reformatory to keep them away from the "hardened" criminals. The judge probably thought I was a lost cause, so he decided to send me to the state prison instead of the reformatory.

The institution where I was incarcerated was classified as a maximum security prison. Prisons with this designation are designed to confine prisoners with the longest sentences or those labeled as "troublemakers." However, some inmates sent to these type of prisons aren't there for violent offenses and are usually classified as "medium" security risks. These types of inmates are often white collar criminals or persons being incarcerated for a variety of other non-violent offenses. The medium security inmates generally were placed in prison jobs outside the main prison walls as gardeners, "house boys" for the warden or deputy warden, or a variety of other positions. Inmates who had nearly completed their sentence or were being paroled could also be considered for medium security jobs.

The prison had its own light industry in the form of clothing and shoe shops to provide for the inmates as well as electrical work, plumbing, and other trades necessary to run the institution. Outside the walls, there was a dairy farm and large vegetable gardens for supplying some of the needs of feeding a large group of inmates.

Most inmates were not locked up twenty-four hours a day as we were required to work in the various prison industries, kitchen, or laundry. We were paid a small daily sum for our work which could be used to purchase various items from the prison commissary. Inmates working in the kitchen preparing and serving food were required to be at work before the general prison population and were allowed to return to their cells between meals to sleep, read, or visit with other inmates who weren't locked up during the day. Inmates working in most other areas were required to remain at their place of work during the entire day and would go to eat lunch from that assignment.

My first few months at the prison were a real learning experience. It didn't take me long to discover that no one is your "friend." Everyone there wanted something from you, be it your personal property or your body or to just make your life a living hell. Potential violence was always waiting around the next corner. I had to be careful of where I was and who was around me at all times. It didn't take long before I realized that you couldn't just go to prison and do your time without someone wanting to make your life difficult. You're literally surrounded by murderers, sex offenders, armed robbers, con men, and various other rejects, and you're one of them. How would you like to have Jeffrey Dahmer (the guy who had seven human skulls in his apartment and a human heart in the freezer) or Charles Manson as your roommate? These are just two miserable examples of the type of inmates you're exposed to while incarcerated. True, you're not there because you were a model citizen either, and the sooner you accept *that* fact the easier it will be to do your time. Adapt or die. The movie, *The Shawshank Redemption,* based on a short story by Steven King, is probably the best portrayal of prison life you'll ever see. After you watch that movie, it is likely you'll never do anything illegal, period.

Once I was released from the orientation unit, I was lucky enough to get an exceptional work assignment — the prison storeroom. In the storeroom we received and stored all of the non-perishable foodstuffs used in the prison. This was a top-notch assignment because we had a small crew and our boss was a very considerate correctional officer. How else can I put that? He was a good guy, he gave me a lot of personal guidance, and made a dramatic impact on my life. Working in the storeroom probably saved my life in more ways than one. That is not to say prison life for me was a walk in the park. It was more akin to a walk through *Central Park* at night, alone.

During the entire time I was in prison, I had just one visitor and was only allowed to correspond with my immediate family a maximum of three times a month. Inmate phone calls were non-existent in those days. After a while you really didn't want to be reminded of life on the "outside" because that wasn't where you were going to be for the next few years.

Earlier I mentioned that newcomers to the *joint* — slang for prison — were called "fish." Given that there were fish in there, then it stands to reason that there were also "fishermen," so to speak. Here's how this works. New inmate, Joe Fish, arrives and is released to the general population after getting out of the orientation unit and is assigned to a cell. Each tier or *Run* of cells in a cellblock has an inmate who is responsible for keeping the Run tidy. He usually also serves as the laundry delivery person, delivering clean sheets, towels, and clothing on a weekly basis. After Joe Fish has been in the cellblock for a couple of weeks, he finds that he is the recipient of clean items more often than once a week, plus perhaps an extra pack of smokes or whatever items he has yet to obtain. Gosh, what a nice guy the Run inmate is to help me out, I'll have to thank him. "No problem," the Run inmate replies. After a couple more weeks of "gifts," Joe Fish is approached by another inmate wanting to collect cash or cigarettes for the deliveries Joe has been receiving. "Huh? I didn't ask for these things so how could I owe for them? I thought you were just trying to help me out." Can you believe he just said that? Joe Fish isn't the sharpest knife in the drawer. Likely poor Joe doesn't have enough loot on hand to pay off his debt but that's no problem as "they" can carry him until commissary day. Commissary day arrives but the debt has ballooned due to "carrying charges" and our man Joe is now in deep waters. If he can't pay up he may have to give up sexual favors to settle the debt or get the crap kicked out of him by the lenders. They can't allow Joe to slip off the hook or else they will look like an easy mark for everyone in the joint. Either way, Joe has been successfully reeled in by the boys. I had seen this "con" being worked on new prisoners when I was in the federal correctional institution, so when my "gifts" arrived, I immediately took them back to the Run boss with some choice words about where he could put them.

Life in a prison is much like life on the "outside." You have all the petty quarrels and gossip that you experience in normal surroundings. Prison has its warden and deputy warden who run the institution. There is a court for prison offenders along with solitary confinement — *the hole* — and a unit named "seclusion" which is something between solitary and being back in the general prison population. Inmates in the seclusion unit are locked up in their cells 24 hours a day. This spartan existence comes along with one shower and one shave per week. An inmate disobeying the rules or getting caught with contraband — things specifically banned — could lose "good time," go to solitary or to seclusion, or all of the above in sequence. "Good time" is given to inmates for good behavior at a specific rate per month of incarceration. Good time is deducted from the total number of years sentenced. My 12 year sentence would have been reduced to 9 years, 6 months if I was never granted a parole and did not get into any trouble resulting in loss of good time. All prisons work differently, so this good time calculation only related to my prison.

I wish I could say that I was a model prisoner, but I retained many of my bad habits from the outside. It wasn't difficult to break the rules and sometimes other inmates would stash contraband in your cell and then rat you out to the "man" (the guards). The guards would "shakedown" (search) your cell and you would end up in prison court denying everything but still going to the hole. If that wasn't enough grief, there was usually a group of inmates who would agitate other inmates by telling them that you were telling lies about them. This always resulted in either a fight or a stabbing or whatever violent act could be perpetrated against you.

During my incarceration, it was my unforgettable experience to make several "visits" to the hole. Life in the hole consisted of reduced food rations and a blanket for a bed, which was removed during the day. There was a single overhead light bulb which remained on 24 hours a day. You were not allowed to talk to the other inmates. One shower per week. Depending on the offense, you could usually count on spending anywhere from ten to thirty days in the hole.

There were no windows in the hole and the door was made of solid steel so the only time you saw anyone was at shift change when the guards would look into the cells to see if anyone had somehow managed to commit suicide during the previous shift. Meals were shoved into the cell by using an opening at the bottom of the door. Sometimes your friends would bribe the inmate from the kitchen detail to slip you something extra to eat. The guards knew the practice was going on but I think they adapted the "live and let live" attitude. Eating utensils weren't necessary as you weren't fed anything which required a knife (wonder why), fork, or spoon, any of which could have been made into a weapon. Sitting on the hard concrete floor for most of the day with nothing to do but think had a way of messing with your mind. I'm here to tell you that that concrete can really eat into your joints. After spending a couple of weeks in the hole, I was always ready to clean up my act. All things considered, it was a good way to lose weight!

While I was in prison, there were several fatal incidents of inmates being stabbed, hacked, or set on fire by other inmates. There were thousands of inmates and a relative handful of guards who were not necessarily the cream of humanity themselves so, as they say, "shit happens." Money talks, and I'm sure there were times when a guard was paid to temporarily look the other way so someone could settle a score with another inmate.

It wasn't only the inmates feuding among themselves that was the problem; the inmates were sometimes attempting to kill the guards. One day, someone loaded a bunch of scrap metal into a pillow case and dropped it from the fifth tier of the cellblock onto the desk where a guard was sitting. The impact destroyed the desk, and I think the guard destroyed his underwear. We never saw him again. It paid dividends for the guards to keep on the good side of the inmates.

Sometimes an inmate just couldn't take the pressure of doing time and ended up overdosing on drugs, slashing his wrists, or taking a "swan dive" from the top tier of the cellblock. Regardless of their motive, the sound of a scream followed by the unmistakable thud of a body impacting the hard concrete floor made you stop in your tracks. No one was ever positive if a jump was voluntary or assisted – maybe someone who couldn't pay up on a debt he owed to another inmate or to society.

The prison hospital was a place you wanted to avoid. The inmates ran the hospital under the direction of a hired doctor. It was rumored that at least one inmate had his IV tampered with while hospitalized, which resulted in an immediate "feet first" discharge. The prison dentist was usually just one of the inmates. He worked under the direction of a local dentist but the level of care left a lot to be desired. I'm currently missing about five teeth from my lower jaw as a result of some overenthusiastic inmate dental work.

I haven't mentioned the communal showers, but they were a place not to be visited without people watching your back. Perhaps I should have said people watching your back who were your friends. You soon discovered that a bar of soap placed in a sock could become a lethal weapon. One game you didn't want to be involved in was playing "drop the soap." It wasn't very reassuring to be taking a shower and turn around to find the man standing next to you smiling while sporting a raging erection. As I mentioned, there was safety in numbers and that was the name of the game.

You've seen it in some of the old prison movies: the inmates in the mess hall banging their cups on the table to object to some prison rule or situation. We would have those every once in a while. These usually resulted in a "lockdown" where no one was allowed out of his cell for an extended period of time.

I was in the mess hall for lunch one day, when an inmate with kitchen duty was serving bean soup from a large metal pot he was carrying. Apparently the server had a problem with one of the other cons, so when it came time to serve him, he decided to dump the entire contents on his head. You can imagine the commotion this caused. Thirty days in the hole and loss of good time! Fighting in the mess hall was a serious incident, as it could quickly spread and cause a riot.

Inmates were taken to the mess hall by cellblock or dormitory one group at a time. Sometimes my cellblock was the first group to be fed. We had to sit at our table until all of the inmates had been fed. If we were unlucky enough to be at the front of the line being fed first, then we would be seated in the front row which faced two wide, double doors. On a rainy or snowy day, it made for a miserable dining experience, since we were exposed to the elements every time more inmates entered the mess hall.

One evening, the inmate standing behind me in the food line was stabbed by the guy behind him because the assailant had been hearing "voices" in his head. Unfortunately, that was just another day in prison life; we never knew what or where trouble would come from.

We had one inmate who had been ratting on a powerful group of inmates. Several of the group distracted the cellblock guard while they systematically searched all of the cells. They finally discovered the culprit hiding under a bed in one of the cells. He never ratted on anyone after that. I suspect that the "stoolie" never ate solid food for the rest of his life, which in fact may not have been all that long. He left the prison the next day in a wheelchair.

I'm not even going to go into some of the stuff I saw while attending church services (which you had to do if you ever wanted to get paroled). We had men inmates and "girl" inmates — also known as "queens" — and church was the preferred place to have a "date." You can figure out the rest of this story. For some reason, church seemed to attract most of the sex offenders. I guess they had a "religious experience."

This isn't stuff I'm pulling out of my ass. These were real events which took place over the years that I was imprisoned. Thankfully, I was never involved in anything that resulted in someone being killed.

A couple of years after I arrived at the prison, another inmate and I concocted a scheme to escape. The plan was for me to remove the grate from an air vent and use the air passage to get down into the main prison vent system where I would be able to make my escape. The other inmate used a bar of soap to make a copy of the cellblock guard's key which he used to get me out of my cell during the night. My co-conspirator was a "trustee," and as such was allowed to take magazines back and forth between the cells. He was to follow me after relocking my cell. I exited my cell and squirmed into the vent system, but was observed by the night guard who alerted prison officials that I was missing. It didn't take them long to determine where I was and apprehend me. That little escapade cost me all my accumulated good time plus 30 days in the hole followed by 90 days in seclusion. Now there's a scenario that will give you plenty of time to think! I'm glad that this effort was a failure, since if I had managed to escape, I would undoubtedly have gotten into a great deal more trouble and served more time than I did. What could I have been thinking? I guess it goes under the guise of, "When in Rome, do as the Romans do." Or act just as stupid as everyone else.

Not everything was doom and gloom during those days; we did have our lighter moments. One of the guards locked himself out of his guard shack. If his superior had found out, the guard would probably have been disciplined or fired for incompetence. Instead, being a resourceful fellow, he did the right thing: find an inmate to pick the lock. That wasn't hard to do, as we used to sit around with a bunch of padlocks to see who could pick the most locks the fastest. If you could have seen some of these guys at work, you probably would never bother to lock your house. Convicts 1, Guards 0, and the guard was safely back in his shack owing a "big one" to the convicts.

Drugs weren't the big problem in prison as they are today but we made do with the next best thing, an alcoholic beverage called "raisin jack." Raisin jack was made by combining yeast with potatoes, fruit, sugar, water, and various other ingredients and then allowing it to ferment for several days. This stuff makes MD 20-20 taste like champagne!

Since we were locked up in our cells for a major portion of the day, it was imperative that we developed a system of communication with other inmates in the cellblock. Talking from cell to cell was prohibited. "Dummy up!" the guard would holler at you if they heard you talking. Trustees could always be counted on to deliver messages, contraband, or whatever to other inmates, but they always expected a few cigarettes in return for their services.

Necessity is the mother of invention, so we improvised when the trustees were locked up at night. The guards frowned on inmates passing anything from cell to cell, so we had to be careful when attempting to facilitate the transfer. The most common method was to hold a small piece of mirror in your hand and stick it out through the bars to see if the "man" was on your tier; this was called "flashing the range." If the coast was clear, you would tie whatever object you wanted to transmit to another cell onto a long piece of string which would be passed through the bars and then flipped in the direction it needed to go. The object would make its way down to the recipient in another cell through the combined efforts of several cells along the path. I know this sounds bizarre, but we were in an atypical environment. The desired object could then be "delivered" to the recipient by pulling on the string.

The prison had all sorts of intramural sports which inmates participated in on evenings and weekends. We had weight lifting, basketball, softball, and boxing, but no cross-country, rock climbing, or pole vaulting! These events took place mainly in the "yard" or gymnasium. Needless to say, when you get a group of violent inmates together in one area, anything could happen, and on some occasions did. The guards were in the guard towers with high powered rifles so everyone knew what the score was. It wasn't uncommon for a group of inmates to surround some deadbeat inmate and do a number on him before the guards caught on.

Any prison story isn't complete without an analogy to a movie plot or two. *The Great Escape* and *The Shawshank Redemption* come to mind. In one, Steve McQueen and company dug a tunnel to escape from a Nazi concentration camp; the other featured Tim Robbins digging his way through the wall of his cell to make his escape while Rita Hayworth's poster was guarding his secret passageway.

Neither Steve, Tim, nor Rita was available, so an enterprising group of inmates got together and concocted a plan to escape. This plan included the construction of a fake wall compartment in a recreation building which was used to house athletic equipment. This fake compartment, along with a false shower floor, provided the entryway from which to dig a tunnel which the inmates hoped would allow them to escape from their keepers. The tunnel, while never completed, ran several hundred feet out toward the prison wall and was equipped with electric lighting, which, when you think of it, was quite innovative. You're probably wondering how the inmates disposed of all the material which was removed from the tunnel. Well, so did the guards. It turns out that permission was requested and received to build a concrete retaining wall around the prison exercise yard. These inmates were well before their time and implemented a successful recycling program which included taking the sandy material from the tunnel and mixing it with prison-supplied concrete to build what was to become known as the "great wall" of the prison.

The always-suspicious guards kept nosing around the recreation building looking for some form of criminal activity being conducted. They were certain that a liquor still was somewhere on the premises, but they were unable to confirm their suspicions.

Alas, the authorities finally discovered the Secrets of the Rue Morgue when the shower floor drain emitted an unnatural glow during a night time shakedown. Needless to say, the tunnel excavation project came to an abrupt halt.

How do I know all these details? Of course, not having first hand information about such a nefarious and far-fetched plot, I can only recount that which was reported in the local newspaper.

Sometimes I had my troubles with other inmates. One unfortunate event occurred when another inmate decided he wanted to be my "special" friend. I guess he just couldn't understand that "No!" was a complete sentence. Next thing I knew, I was sitting on the ground with my two front teeth sticking horizontally back into my mouth instead of in their normal vertical aspect. No one observed the incident and he just walked off without saying anything. I went back to my work assignment in the storeroom and didn't mention anything to anyone. That was the way things went; you took care of your own business. A few hours later this same guy had the audacity to come walking into the storeroom. I guess he wanted to see if I had changed my mind. The storeroom entrance had two sets of double doors, the upper half of each door being glass. As my assailant was reaching for the second set of doors I struck him through the glass with an iron bar. He instantly turned and ran out the door with me just a few steps behind him, screaming curses and the fact that I was going to kill him with the iron bar if I could catch him. It was only a short couple of blocks down to the deputy warden's office and he got there just before I could hit him again. The guards grabbed both of us and we ended up being interrogated by the deputy warden. After I told my story and they saw my mouth, they locked this guy up in protective custody. I ended up at the hospital where our local inmate — "Bones" — placed one hand against my forehead and grabbed my errant teeth with his other hand while he returned them to their original position. Thankfully, I received no disciplinary action for my part of this altercation. I just hope that the guy that punched me in the mouth got someone called Bubba as his next cell mate.

All of these events had a profound effect on me. At first I bought into the whole scene of being a "solid" convict, someone who could be trusted and depended on by the other cons. Later, I began to see that many of the inmates I associated with had become "institutionalized" and this was the only life they knew. These were usually the repeat offenders. I listened as they bragged to each other about their exploits and the different institutions where they had served time. I began to ask myself if this was the life I wanted for myself. It didn't take me long to decide. Of course not! I was merely existing from day to day without any future except what today brought. This was the start of the end of the "old" me and the beginning of what I think of as the "new" me. My transformation in attitude gave me hope.

From that point on, I slowly started to work toward improving myself and began focusing on a life after my time was served, whenever that would be. With the help of my high school accounting teacher in Wichita, Mr. Dye, I was able to resume my education by taking correspondence study classes which I could apply toward obtaining my high school diploma. Within a couple of years, I graduated from high school, in absentia (of course). I knew I was really on to something with my new direction in life. I could feel a positive change in myself. Now, I was driven to excel in my studies and this gave me an achievable goal in life. After completion of the high school curriculum, I began taking college level courses which were made available through the prison education department and the state university. As a result of my ongoing educational endeavors, I earned the Reader's Digest

Award "for the prisoner with the most outstanding achievement record" in the prison system. Was this the same guy who kept getting into all that trouble and attempting to escape?

The road toward the front door wasn't always surrounded by green lights and blue skies and sometimes I stumbled along the way, but I continued to maintain my focus. During one such bump, I ended up in the seclusion unit for 30 days as a result of an altercation with another inmate. My desire to improve myself gave some inmates reason to think I was trying to be better than they were. On this occasion, an inmate came into my cell and started throwing my textbooks onto the floor and kicking them while telling me I wasn't going to amount to "nothing but a common criminal" (which I already was) so not to waste my time. A shoving match and fist fight followed. This event helped me realize how important my education had become to me. The Deputy Warden recognized that I had not started the fight, so I was sentenced to the seclusion unit instead of the hole.

Not wanting to just sit in seclusion and waste my time, I requested and received my school course work. As it turns out, I was working on an accounting course without an adding machine. Ever try to perform journal entries and month end closing without the benefit of an adding machine? You get bleary-eyed looking at all those numbers and mistakes creep into the process. If you don't have an adding machine you do the next best thing: you call on the guy in the next cell to check your math. My cell happened to be adjacent to Death Row. There was a serial killer there who had plenty of time on his hands, so I would pass him my accounting problems to check my math. Not many people around who can lay claim to that scenario, or would want to!

Later on, I was fortunate in being in the wrong place at the right time as computer technology was in its infancy. One of the inmates had previously been the manager of a data processing department before he got into trouble. He started a systems and programming class which I was able to attend. The training I received during that period enabled me find an occupation which I still utilize today. I cannot stress enough the value of the education I received while incarcerated. I had stated during one of my sentence commutation hearings that I was "going to make this time pay for me," and I lived up to those words in the years that followed.

"Nothing is a waste of time if you use the experience wisely."
Auguste Rodin, sculptor ("The Thinker")

The few of us who were in that initial computer class started what was probably the first computer automation system of prison records in the country. One of the participants was hired by the State to oversee the completion of the system after his release.

Even with all I had achieved since being incarcerated, the truth was that I was still an inmate with a sizable chunk of time yet to serve. Unfortunately, the way my sentence was structured, I was never eligible for parole. The Governor would need to commute my sentence to change it from a "flat" twelve years to an indeterminate sentence. That finally happened in November 1960 when my sentence was commuted, five years after I first walked through the doors of the prison. Since I had a shorter sentence, I received a transfer to the state reformatory which was a less forbidding place. Two months later I was granted my parole.

I was taking some giant steps toward turning my life around, but it was due in no small part to the staff and correctional officers of the prison and reformatory. It's strange to say "thanks for locking me up," but *thanks* is in order. I finally realized that I was my own worst enemy.

I will never forget the feeling I had as I sat on a bench at the reformatory watching the bus that would take me to a new life come down the prison driveway. The Warden came out and shook my hand, wishing me good luck. I could easily have said, "I hope I never see you again!" and have meant it. I walked out the door with a crisp $20 bill, wearing a new suit, and I've seldom looked back – until the Canadian border incident.

I can never replace those five years I spent in prison, but I didn't completely waste them either. I've followed through on the promises I made to myself and my life is better for having done so.

Chapter 4 - Free at Last

Return to Oz

As you might imagine, getting released from prison after five years of incarceration was a significant life-changing event for me. All of a sudden I was relatively free to go when and where I wanted even though I was on parole. Just think: I could pick up the phone and call someone —something I hadn't done for five years. Hey, I could even make noise after 10:00 p.m. without getting "written up" by the Man!

The idea of associating with members of the opposite sex was something that was really scary, as was the whole dating thing. I had only had contact with males for the past five years. I could just see myself going up to some young woman and saying, "Hi, I'm Charlie. I'm an ex-convict. Would you like to go out with me?" You don't need to be clairvoyant to guess what her answer to that question would likely be.

The big question for me was how to assimilate the adjustments I would have to make in the "real world" after going from being eighteen years old to twenty-three years old, especially given the changes that had taken place in our culture in the late 50s to early 60s. Still, when all was said and done, life was good again. My freedom was something I didn't intend to misuse!

I immediately noticed that many things on the "outside" were different. Motor vehicles had been drastically redesigned, clothing styles were dramatically different (no one had a number stamped above the pocket on their shirt), even the name of the street near where I used to live had been renamed. Imagine asking a taxi driver to take you to your home on Border Street and he had never heard of it. He calls his dispatcher and finds out that it is now called "Loop Road," or something like that.

One of the surprising things I encountered was a penny I received in change from one of the first purchases I made. Initially, I thought it was a foreign coin. As it turned out, the reverse side of the Lincoln penny no longer depicted the wheat symbols but had been replaced with an image of the Lincoln Memorial. Duh! These things may all seem trivial, but it was almost like going to a foreign country for me. Culture Shock 101.

Even though I had been granted a parole, I was required to have employment and a place to live before I could be released. Once again my high school accounting teacher, Mr. Dye, reached out to help me. Mr. Dye knew the Personnel Manager for the Boeing Company in Wichita and through him enabled me to take a computer aptitude test while at the reformatory, which I aced. Boeing hired me to work in their Data Processing Department on second shift for $2.12 an hour. That wasn't such a bad wage since you could purchase a McDonald's hamburger for fifteen cents in 1961. Not only did I get a job – I was given a confidential security clearance. Go figure. Thank you again, Warden, for allowing me to take all those great computer classes.

I needed a place to live before I could be released so the likely — or unlikely — choice was to return to my aunt's. My aunt and uncle had an apartment which was part of their house which they rented to me. I figured that since I was now twenty-three years old, my aunt wouldn't fall back into her old behavior pattern and attempt to run my life. Well, some things never change, and it wasn't long before I found her snooping though my things and trying to tell me what to do.

Thankfully, I didn't waste any time hanging around where she could poison my life again. I quickly moved out and arranged to share an apartment with a co-worker. I said goodbye to *The Beast* once and for all.

After I had done all of this groundwork just to get out of prison, I was really back to square one, just another human being attempting to eke out a living and find a meaning in life. I had a future again but the hard work was about to begin.

Chapter 5 - Second Chances

Transformation and New Beginnings

Some noteworthy world events happened during the decade after my release from prison.

There will (hopefully) never be another period in our nation's history as tumultuous as what we experienced in the 1960s. Many Americans began to question their values in light of the events that played out during the decade. John F. Kennedy was elected President and subsequently assassinated, Dr. Martin Luther King and Robert Kennedy each were assassinated, and Black Panthers and Students for a Democratic Society (SDS) became household names associated with conflict. East Germany built the Berlin Wall, we had the Cuban Missile Crisis, and a seminal event changed us all forever: the start of America's involvement in Vietnam. Yes, the 1960s were a noteworthy period in our history.

On a lighter note, Neil Armstrong became the first man to walk on the Moon and approximately half a million people slithered through the mud, made love, and sang together at that unforgettable music festival called Woodstock.

Life is full of second chances, but sometimes we allow them to slip through our fingers and then dissipate like the morning fog. I realized just how lucky I was to have this second chance to make something of myself. I was determined to take advantage of every available opportunity to continually improve my data processing and people skills. Luckily, my employer, The Boeing Company, realized the importance of continuing education and offered a multitude of free classes to its employees. I was working the night shift as a computer operator which allowed me to attend some of these classes during the day as well as take some additional college courses. This schedule didn't leave much time for socializing, but since I didn't know anyone it didn't make much difference.

Time passed and my work ethic drew the attention of a supervisor in a Boeing software support group. They had a large project which needed someone with my data processing skills and decided to transfer me into their department. This was a major advancement for me as this was a step up from being a computer "operator" to being a "programmer." It had been a little over a year after having been released from prison and I saw my career path starting to materialize. I recalled the effort I put forth in prison learning computer skills, which resulted in my current opportunities. I was beginning to achieve a measure of success that I would not have dreamed of just a few short years ago.

Two years after being paroled, I was discharged from all supervision. I had paid my debt to society and in the process had found hope and goals that would lead me away from the life I had been living seven years earlier.

Meanwhile, a co-worker who had become a good friend was busy trying to find me a woman (who hopefully wasn't on parole) whom I might enjoy spending some quality time with. His initial efforts were an abject failure due to my complete lack of social skills and my dismal background. The last time I dated anyone was as a sophomore in high school. No one ever accused me of being overly talkative during that stage of my life, and that, combined with my being a bit shy, tended to make date nights relatively short. It usually takes two people to have a conversation. Eventually, I became more at ease with the opposite sex and was introduced to a woman who seemed to be compatible with my personality.

A few months later I got married for the first time. It astounds me to realize that these events happened nearly fifty years ago. They make me feel old, yet some of these things have been burned into my memory as if they were yesterday. Who among us who was alive in 1963 doesn't remember where we were when President John F. Kennedy was assassinated?

I continued taking computer and college courses in an effort to advance up the ranks of the corporate ladder. In the late 1960s, opportunity once again came knocking at my door in the form of a position as Director of Data Processing for an international electronics firm located in Kansas City.

I was hired not because I was the best qualified person for the job, but because I had demonstrated a desire to improve myself by taking numerous computer and management classes in my spare time. This proved to be a quantum leap for my career. Again, I was forced to look back at those bleak prison days and realize that I had indeed made life-changing decisions that were allowing me to reap the rewards of those efforts.

Life — being what it is — throws bumps and curves into your journey which can derail even the best of plans. Unfortunately, my first marriage ended in a divorce. I was growing as a person as well as professionally and found that my life needed to take a different path than when I was first released from prison. After a couple of years, I left the position as Director of Data Processing to become the Manager of Systems & Programming Development at a Kansas computer firm, a job better suited to my talents. The prior director job required me to manage too many aspects of the company that were beyond my abilities at the time.

The next few years, which I spent in management and software development, were personally and professionally rewarding. I had a dedicated group of employees to help create and install client software. The work ethic was all-encompassing, and many of us worked seven days a week, long hours each day, for months on end, but we enjoyed what we were doing.

Our company worked closely with a national accounting firm and shared some of their resources. It was during this time that I met a woman who worked for the accounting firm. We shared a lot of the same long hours and we soon became good friends, and then lovers. We seemed compatible; I proposed to her and she accepted.

This was my second marriage and differed dramatically from my first in that work was the common attribute that we shared. The computer company's information processing division merged with the accounting firm and I soon found myself being hired by them as a consultant in charge of several of their client computer development projects.

Shortly after the merger, the accounting firm moved their national office consulting staff from Wichita, Kansas to Denver, Colorado. My wife and I moved from a relatively small town of 50,000 people to a metropolis of over a million people. In Wichita, you could get across town in thirty minutes. In Denver, that same trip would require an hour and a half during rush hour; that was a big logistical change.

Fortuitously, we decided not to live in Denver proper but opted instead to live in Boulder, Colorado, a decision which would prove to be lifestyle-defining for me. One of my early impressions of Boulder was marveling at people rock climbing at several of the areas just outside the city. My first thought upon seeing that activity was "I'll never do that!" Never say "never." Living in Boulder allowed us to make the short commute to Denver but live in a small college town near a mountain environment.

After the firm moved to Denver, I was assigned the responsibility for a major client in Washington, D.C. which required me to travel back and forth each week, sometimes staying two weeks at a time. This assignment lasted for nearly a year. Needless to say, this was not a recipe for a viable marriage environment and after several years, I crashed and burned on marriage number two.

The 1970s were a time of awakening for me as well as for many people in America. Things were changing at a breakneck pace. I would label this decade a period of disillusionment and discontent for most of us. We saw the final days of the Vietnam war vividly

50

depicted on our televisions, the Watergate scandal, and its subsequent political fallout. Politicians were falling like dominoes. President Richard Nixon resigned, Attorney General John Mitchell and Vice President Spiro Agnew were convicted of various crimes and they resigned as well. Americans began to wonder where the country was headed; the drama was playing out like the rise and fall of the Roman Empire. Radical groups that had formed in the final days of the 1960s were making daily headlines. One of the most deadly of these was the Symbionese Liberation Army (SLA), which kidnapped newspaper heiress Patty Hearst, and committed several murders and bank robberies. Many SLA members died in a mass shoot-out with police in California.

After the failure of my second marriage, I quit my job at the accounting firm. They told me they were going to have to let me go anyway since I wasn't a CPA, even though I had been billing about 100 hours a week! I went from being a short-haired, suit and tie, management consultant to a wannabe hippie with a beard, beads, sandals, and long hair. I bought a 914 Porsche and began a period of personal discovery. I guess everything I had experienced in those prior years finally just came falling down on me and I was looking for ... what, I didn't know. It was just time to let my hair down, so to speak. Those were the days when American mores were rapidly undergoing significant change. We were awakened from having confidence and trust in our government to being more proactive about events, but for me it must just have been time for my mid-life crisis. I spent the remainder of the year hiking and skiing and realized that I finally had found something that I *truly* enjoyed. There's nothing like hiking a mountain trail in the fall amid the scent of decaying leaves with those mild, warm temperatures that are a precursor to the cold, short winter days to come — it soothes the mind and rejuvenates the spirit.

My hiking adventures escalated to the point where just staying on established trails wasn't enough adventure. There were rocks around which did not require those ropes and protective gear to climb (which I said I would never use), so I proceeded to scramble around on them, eventually getting myself into a potentially dangerous situation. I found that I had scrambled up a rock face that was no longer low-angle. I was afraid to go up and afraid to attempt to climb down. Well, if I'm going to fall it made sense that falling while attempting to extricate myself out of a mess required climbing *even higher*. Or did it? The net result of this poor decision occurred as I grabbed onto a large rock which suddenly detached itself from the main rock face. This caused me to lose my balance and immediately begin falling and sliding down the face which I had so recently climbed. The net result was some severe "rock rash" to all of my extremities. I think that I just proved Newton's theory of gravity. It occurred to me that if I wished to remain alive then it would behoove me to seek additional instruction in how man safely ascends (and descends) steeper rock faces. Thus began my lifelong association with a local hiking and climbing group called the Colorado Mountain Club. I subsequently enrolled in many of their outdoor recreation courses including Basic Mountaineering, Rock and Ice Climbing, First Aid, and High Altitude Expeditionary Mountaineering, among others. I eventually volunteered as a senior instructor of all of these courses for a number of years.

Man or woman cannot live on the scent of decaying leaves and warm, mild fall days alone lest they themselves begin to decay. After a few months hiatus from the corporate world and a bank account that resembled the sinking of the Titanic, I realized that I would either need to get a job or start my own business. Getting a job had its own pitfalls: regular work hours (Ugh!) or the specter of having to explain those five missing years in my life (double Ugh!). I sat down and did the math and came to the realization that I only needed to work about half the year to make the same amount of money I was making at the accounting firm as long as I could keep 100% of what I was billing. Deal!

I called up my acquaintances at the accounting firm to see if they had any reservations about my contacting the clients I had previously been working with. They were delighted since they were having difficulty replacing me (serves them right) and I had developed a good rapport with the clients. So, 1973 was the start of my being the boss, the worker, the salesman, and the sanitary engineer.

While I was enjoying my sabbatical, I had occasion to read a book about a couple of brothers who hiked the Continental Divide

Trail from Canada to Mexico, *The Ultimate Journey,* by Eric and Tim Ryback. I never duplicated their journey but this book fired up a passion in me that has stood the test of time.

Being able to work half as many hours for yourself and earning as much as when you worked full time for someone else ... yeah, right. If you've ever had your own business, you know what a fable that is. What followed were several years of balls-to-the-walls effort to establish my business as a viable entity. I worked like a dog (however a dog works). I didn't have many girlfriends during this time. Dates with me involved bringing a pizza to the computer center where I would be working and leave it outside the door where I would finally remember to retrieve it. My sister finally refused to bring me any more pizzas! Friends would ask me when I was going to quit working so hard, but I didn't even have time to answer their question. But, eventually things did begin to stabilize; my client base had gotten established through networking and word of mouth. I had all the work I wanted and decided that bigger wasn't better, so expanding my business wasn't the way to go.

After being able to step back from the abyss of bankruptcy and getting the business on steady footing, I started thinking about finishing my college education which I had started while in prison. I made the commitment to finish and enrolled in night classes which allowed me to take courses as time permitted. I still can't believe that I was that same very mixed-up teenager who got into so much trouble. Life would have been a lot easier if I had just skipped that period of my life.

The years that followed were a mixture of working extreme hours for months at a stretch, interspersed with all the climbing expeditions I could afford. Thankfully, I had developed an understanding client base, so it wasn't unusual for one of them to ask, "Isn't it about time for you to go off somewhere to climb?" I always replied in the affirmative. They'd respond with, "Please don't fall off the mountain!" I'm not sure where people got the idea that the mountain is suddenly going to tilt sideways and you're going to fall off of it to your death, although it would make for an interesting cartoon. I'll have to work on that.

I would return from some of these trips tired, ragged, and sick from everything you could possibly catch in third world countries. It was sometimes difficult to just jump back into the middle of all the computer problems my clients had accumulated after I had been literally miles from anything or anybody for several weeks. Some of my clients joked that I had imbedded secret code in their programs to make them crash about the time I returned so I would have work to do. I would just smile; I know that made them wonder if their joke was in fact not really a joke.

Back home in Colorado, I enjoyed the fruits of my labor by going hiking and climbing in my free time. Enter wife-to-be number three. After having been single for a number of years, I decided I wanted a relationship that would last more than two weeks as had been the case while I was working non-stop in the corporate rat-race world.

One weekend, I went on an easy hike with a group of Colorado Mountain Club members and struck up a conversation with a very attractive young woman. For me it was "lust at first sight" or something like that. Here was someone who was intelligent, attractive, *and* liked to do the things I most enjoyed: hiking and climbing. Plus, she owned a truck. I've always had this thing for women who own trucks. Problem was, some other guy on the outing had attached himself to her like glue. How to get her to notice me and get rid of him? Hmmm. Why not send an "emissary" down the line to infiltrate the ranks and emphasize my numerous good traits? The plan worked like Vaseline on the bedroom doorknob when you have kids you want to keep out. We spent the remainder of the trip visiting while I extolled all of my virtues and complimented her on what a strong hiker she was. She obviously was very intelligent or very gullible as we started dating the following week.

You know how these things go and it wasn't long before we were living together. One thing led to another and we eventually decided to sell the house we were living in and build a home up in the mountains. There was just one problem. In those days financial institutions weren't likely to recognize a non-married couple living together for the purpose of purchasing property. Getting married made the financial arrangements easier to negotiate. So, get married we did. Am I really doing this a third time?

Everything was finally coming together for me; I was on the verge of having all my dreams come true. I had economic security with my business, a wife who shared my interests, and a home in the mountains. What more could a person want?

Unfortunately, we both probably rushed into the relationship and it *was* too good to be true. We weren't quite ready in life to "take the plunge," so to speak. When the reality of being married and living in the mountains sunk in, I think we both started asking ourselves, "Is this all there is?" There isn't an answer to that question — you need to have confidence in your relationship and the desire to nurture it through the doubts that arise after reality sets in. We weren't able to overcome some personal obstacles and the relationship slowly came apart, ending in divorce after a couple of short years. I can truthfully say that I thoroughly enjoyed those years and was sorry that things didn't work out for us. Looking back, I can see the fallacy in my thinking that nirvana was just over the horizon. As I have come to realize, a successful relationship of any kind takes plenty of give and take as well as being truthful with yourself about what you desire. Scratch marriage number three.

After my third divorce I began hiking and climbing a great deal of the time. I started out by hiking a few of Colorado's fourteen-thousand-foot mountains and then got the bug to climb all fifty-four of them. That achievement whetted my appetite for more adventure, so I enrolled in a rock climbing course and pursued that activity as well. Rock climbing led to ice climbing — described by some as "a sport for lunatics." I ended up climbing high and low points all over America including the highest point in each of the 50 states. Yes, every state *does* have a highpoint (Florida's highpoint logs in at 345 feet above sea level).

I hadn't totally abandoned my business venture as it served as the basis of financial support for my climbing endeavors. Luckily, I had a group of very understanding clients who didn't mind my going off to Nepal, Russia, or South America for several weeks at a time.

During one period when I wasn't out climbing, I attended a business conference where I noticed an attractive young woman (there's a trend here) standing next to a guy who was enthusiastically "bending her ear." I tried not to stare at her but something about her demeanor kept me looking back that way. Perhaps it was the "deer in the headlights" look in her eyes as she listened attentively to her companion. More than likely it was her petite figure and long, silky, dark brown hair (you know where this is going, don't you?). I stayed in close proximity to her as she courteously listened to what appeared to be a long, drawn out story. I edged closer and did a little eavesdropping and realized that her companion was describing every line of computer code he had ever written in great detail. Her eyes darted over to me, looking for a respite from his boring dissertation.

Good things come to those who have patience and I waited until the guy talking to her paused for a breath before I stepped closer and introduced myself. He departed in search of another victim. Her first words were, "I hope you're not another computer programmer!" I laughed and sheepishly admitted that indeed I was, except that I represented myself as a "software engineer." "What's the difference between a programmer and a software engineer?" she queried. "Twenty dollars an hour," I replied. This comment elicited a big smile from her. "In that case, I'm not going to call myself a programmer any more. Hi, I'm a software engineer, too!" she declared.

She confirmed what I had overheard, a "memory dump" of computerese from that guy's lips to her ears. I asked her name and we engaged in the normal "small talk" that people do when they're attempting to see if they have a common interest.

We spent the remainder of the evening talking about everything and nothing. It was one of those chance meetings where you feel you've known the other person forever. We exchanged telephone numbers and agreed to stay in contact for a later lunch or dinner date.

If someone would have told me when I was in high school that I would get married four times, I would have scoffed. I always wonder how we get from being in lust with someone where you can't keep your hands off of each other to find yourself in the divorce courts. I think a mandatory precursor for marriage should be that you must sit in divorce court for at least a week listening to the tales of woe. That sad experience might keep some of us from making a costly mistake. Someone once said, "Marriage is like a cafeteria: take what looks good to you now and pay for it later." Sadly, this is too often true.

I sincerely can't say that my three divorces were the fault of the other person in the marriage. Basically, they were three different women whom I married at different stages of my life. Looking back, I have no regrets, for the person I was marrying fit well into my life at that time. I learned a great deal from each of my failures and was able to bring that knowledge to the table for my fourth and current marriage to Diane, which has lasted for eighteen wonderful years. She stayed the course for thirteen long years after that initial encounter before I finally "saw the light" and asked her to marry me. I figured that our relationship didn't hold any more surprises after all that time. I may be slow but I'm not totally brain dead!

I've always been interested in how and where people met or where they proposed, so I'd like to share my marriage proposal story with you.

Lucky thirteen. After thirteen on again, off again years during my relationship with Diane, I decided it was indeed time to "tie the knot" before someone else caught her fancy. "Tie the knot" sounds like some of that kinky bondage stuff I fantasize about. I needed to make a level of commitment to our relationship that Diane had long since abandoned any hope of achieving from me. Finally the hour had arrived. What more could a woman want: we were in Hawaii on a beautiful summer evening, sitting in an upscale restaurant, and she had me as her companion. Okay, two out of three isn't bad.

I rehearsed my proposal speech in my mind several times, then waited for the right moment, that time between finishing our salad and the arrival of the main course. We were enjoying a view of one of those fabulous Hawaiian sunsets that all lovers come to adore. It was now or never. Oh, oh, here comes our waiter, followed by a young couple with a very young baby. There was no one else in the restaurant, but lo and behold he seated them at the table next to ours. The baby immediately started screaming to high heaven. Ah, ha, this is a signal from God *not* to propose. Said waiter soon returned with our main course and I miraculously avoided taking the plunge. "Relieved" is too kind a word to describe my feeling about not having gotten into the middle of my proposal just as the baby arrived.

We hurried through our dinner and departed the restaurant as soon as possible to enjoy the serenity of walking hand-in-hand along the palm tree lined walkway. We both laughed about the "romantic" dinner we had just finished. Hmmm, she took that really well, perhaps she's a "keeper" after all. Time to rethink the marriage proposal thing. The setting was again right, evening was descending on the island, light breezes caressed the palm trees, and I had butterflies in my stomach. After spending the better part of thirteen years together, why should asking Diane to marry me be so hard?

What the hell, here goes. "Diane, I think we need to make a change in our relationship," I declared as I held both of her hands in mine while staring into her eyes. I did the hands thing so she wouldn't take a swing at me. She likely figured this "change" was going to be another transition into the "off again" mode of our long-term relationship. The look on her face reminded me of someone who had just found out that their 401K had become a 101K. You just get that gut-wrenching feeling. Giving credit to her, she didn't spit on me or attempt to knee me in the crotch. In fact, she just stood there silently, looking forlorn. I felt like a complete jackass, which I was, so I decided to give her "the rest of the story."

"I think we should get married," I said. Her forlorn look changed to one of rapture and the waterworks turned on. "Are you kidding?" she asked. I definitely would have taken a crotch shot had I replied "Yes." Her reply of "Yes" to my proposal was the start of a life filled with adventure and happiness. The evening ended up perfect and I'm still with the ideal partner to complement my life.

Yes, I've had "second chances" — life has looked favorably upon me. Over the years I've built a successful software consulting business, earned a college degree, and travelled all over the world hiking and climbing. Diane and I have collaborated on writing three hiking and climbing guide books; *Highpoint Adventures, The Essential Guide to the Great Sand Dunes National Park and Preserve,* and *The Trad Guide to Joshua Tree.*

I have seldom looked back at those dark days of half a century ago. So, it was with trepidation that I answered "No" to the Canadian Border Services Officer when he asked me if I had ever been convicted of a felony. I thought "No" was a white lie since I had been to Canada several times and it felt like my conviction occurred during a previous lifetime. "Are you sure?" he reiterated, as he obviously knew the true answer. "Yes," I finally said, realizing that my past had caught up with me. "But that was fifty years ago," I added.

So, there I was at the Canadian border in 2007 with my climbing partners Randy and Dan, heading up to the Canmore area to spend a week or so climbing some of their frozen waterfalls, but the Canadians won't allow me to enter their country. Rats!

Up until that embarrassing moment, I had told very few people about my past. Sure, in those first few years out of prison I informed my employers and closest friends, but as the decades slipped past, this number dwindled down to a very few individuals. Randy was one of these individuals while Dan was not. Dan thought I was kidding as I walked back from the Border Services desk and explained that I was going to have to return back to the US. "I don't think I've ever known anyone who was kicked out of a foreign country," he said with a smile.

To say I was pissed off is an understatement. The Border Services Officer gave me a piece of paper explaining the procedure which needed to be followed to allow me to be "rehabilitated" in the eyes of the Canadians. For lesser sentences than mine it would cost around $500 for processing the request; for my particular sentence it would cost me over $1,000, without any guarantee that my application for rehabilitation would be granted. It wasn't only the money that went against the grain. I would need to be photographed, fingerprinted, and produce copies of all the legal documents associated with my conviction. The good ol' USA was looking better every minute.

But, I've jumped far ahead of myself. How did I go from hiking up peaks in the western US to traveling around the world on expeditions and climbing adventures?

My experiences and deep friendships with other climbers are a big part of who I am today. I've been asked what motivates me on expeditions to get out of a warm sleeping bag in the middle of a cold dark night, get dressed, and start out climbing. That's a good, intelligent question – one that really doesn't speak well of my intelligence. The answer, my friends, is *passion*, pure and simple. It doesn't matter if I'm part of a team or doing a solo climb, it's passion which drives me to go out and see what adventure lies ahead, what stunning vista might lie just over that next rise, or what lies around the next bend in the trail.

Remember when you met that "special someone" in your life and you could hardly wait until the next time you got together? Remember the excitement and the anticipation of your next encounter? Well, that's the same emotion I experience when climbing. Sometimes that special someone rejected me and sometimes she allowed me to explore all of her secrets. It's the same with mountains. It's all about passion, the unlocking of the secrets. Passion – the mind rules the body.

Mountaineering for me is not simply a hobby, it's a lifestyle.

Climbing Adventures

Ginni, Gary, Dave C, Randy, Diane, and Charlie   *Tom and Dave R*

Chapter 6 - Special Relationships

Climbing Partners

The type of relationship that develops between hiking partners and climbing partners are very different from each other. Hiking partners are people you enjoy sharing non-life threatening experiences with, whereas climbing partners are people who you depend on to keep you safe and alive. The bond between climbing partners can easily surpass any relationship you may have with a spouse or sibling. Technical climbing can involve potential life and death decisions on a daily basis.

That said, I have to share with you a story about a special climbing partner who has joined me on many, many adventures. This is a person who I have hit with falling objects and nearly knocked unconscious on three occasions, taken to the emergency room after an ice climbing accident, and who has helped me realize so very many of my goals. He has helped me put on my crampons when my hands were too cold to manage the straps and helped me zip up my jacket when my frostbitten fingers were too sensitive to grasp my zipper. I arrived on the summits of many mountains simply because he was there to give me that nudge (or was it a kick in the seat of the pants?) that helped me succeed when otherwise I would have failed. We've become lifelong friends and best climbing partners since the first day we met. I would and do trust my life with him each and every time we tie into a rope together. His name is Randy Murphy.

It was my fortune to meet Randy in 1983. We were holding practice qualifications for a Colorado Mountain Club rock climbing class which I had volunteered to help teach. The next would-be climber to take our qualification test was Randy, a somewhat nondescript guy who stepped forward, tied into the rope, and put on his helmet – backwards! I knew immediately that this joker was going to be one of my students. Anyone who was so confused he didn't know the front of the helmet from the back was someone I was sure I could help. Once we got Randy pointed in the right direction, he aced the qualification. Later, I discovered that he had never worn a helmet before, so front and back all seemed the same to him. Randy later became my assistant instructor in both our rock climbing and basic mountaineering schools.

Some things never change and through the years the forgetful Randy has locked his keys in various vehicles several times, changed clothes and left his pants containing keys alongside the trail, descended from the summits of peaks sans pack which required him to re-climb same, and appeared on climbs without essential equipment. Have you ever heard of someone climbing steep snow with crampons attached to worn-out tennis shoes? I had a hard time explaining *that* setup to our Basic Mountaineering students.

Before you get the impression that Randy is unreliable, I need to clarify something. When the situation gets critical, he's always the guy we look to for guidance and to finish what we started, and there's no one better to have at the other end of your rope, anywhere, anytime. I look forward to many more climbing adventures together.

He's the original "No brain, No pain" guy; why else would he still be calling me his climbing partner after all these years? I've surely given him plenty of pain. With the passage of time and through many adventures, Randy has acquired the nickname "Dip Nut," but then, that's another story.

To all of my other hiking and climbing partners, I didn't mention each of you individually because extolling all of your virtues would fill another book. You are all very important friends to me and at one time or another have helped me become a better, safer climber. Many thanks to all of you!

Climb safely.

(Photo courtesy of the United State Geological Society, November 1999)

Chapter 7 - Ecuador
Climbs in the Andes
Cotopaxi, Chimborazo & Tungurahua

Not all mountain climbing adventures are rife with hair-raising, death-defying tales of avalanches, crevasse falls, collapsing seracs, and the like, although I have certainly encountered all of the above at one time or another. However, my first foreign climbing trip (excluding Nebraska) turned out to be an enjoyable mountaineering vacation; no one got killed or injured. This trip has significance for me because I met two other climbers who would become life-long friends, and it set the stage for events that would end up shaping my climbing life for many years to come.

After having made a successful ascent of Mt. Rainier via the Kautz Glacier in 1981, I felt I was ready to undertake a more ambitious adventure the following year, namely, climbing a few volcanoes in Ecuador. I signed up with Rainier Mountaineering,

Inc. to go on a guided climb of Cotopaxi (19,348 feet), Chimborazo (20,702 feet), and Tungurahua (16,480 feet).

Previously, the highest I had ever been (controlled substances notwithstanding) was the summit of Mt. Whitney (14,505 feet). I realized that to get to the summit of any of these lofty peaks I would need to significantly ratchet up my training regimen; that meant cutting down on deluxe ice cream, beer drinking, and TV time. Sacrifices had to be made, so getting up early in the morning to run became my regular routine.

After months of training, it was finally time to pack everything up and head to Stapleton Field, our Denver airport at that time. I checked my bags with the air carrier and proceeded to the gate area to await the departure of my afternoon flight to Miami. The Miami flight would subsequently connect with a midnight flight to Quito, Ecuador. While sitting at the gate, I noticed another individual who had the "look" of a climber (whatever that is). I strolled over and introduced myself and inquired as to his destination. He told me his name was Dave Reeder. He was also going to Ecuador to climb, albeit with a different guiding company. We started to talk about various climbs we had done and then went on to talk about some of the people we each knew. During the conversation the name of Randy Murphy came up. I knew Randy from our Colorado Mountain Club basic mountaineering and rock climbing classes. It turned out that Dave and Randy had been friends since high school. Small world.

After arriving in Miami, Dave went off to find his group and I wandered around the airport while waiting for my midnight flight to Quito, which is located just south of the Equator. Shortly after heading over to my departure gate, a couple of guys came to the area with back packs and started pulling out the type of stuff climbers usually keep with them while traveling. We started exchanging glances so, finally, I walked over and introduced myself and asked them if they were climbers. They were, and both of them were on the Ecuador trip with Rainier Mountaineering — and that is how I met lifelong climbing partners Burt Falk and Jim Scott, along with Dave Reeder. Burt and Jim had been friends since kindergarten. Just think, in one 24 hour period I met three people with whom I would share climbs all over the world for decades to come. I wonder what the odds are of that happening again?

We all arrived at Quito bleary-eyed and tired from not having gotten much sleep during the flight. I cleared customs and went over to claim my baggage, along with a hoard of other equally-sleepy passengers. The carousel went around and around and everyone got all of their luggage, except me. I spent the better part of the next day attempting to locate one of my bags containing climbing equipment which had apparently gotten lost. The following day it was going to be necessary to leave Quito and start the expedition, bag or no bag. The missing bag did not appear, but I was able to supplement the climbing clothes I did have with those borrowed from other climbers on the trip.

On our way out of Quito, we stopped at a rustic little restaurant in the countryside for dinner. I ordered a bowl of potato soup whereupon the waiter asked, "Would you like that with blood?" I thought that I had mistaken what he had said, but no. It seemed that the local custom is to have goat's blood mixed in with your soup. I wonder if blood soup would fall under the category of "blood doping" which seems to be so prevalent in competitive sport activities? My answer to the blood question was a resounding "No!"

The climb of our first peak, Cotopaxi, started from a hut located at the base of the peak. Cotopaxi is located approximately 50 miles south of Quito.

I set a personal best for altitude achievement and a personal worst for wearing the correct clothing for the cold and wind that we experienced near the summit. Who would have thought it could get *really* cold so close to the Equator? I envisioned palm trees and other tropical vegetation when I was at home in Denver imagining the climb. I have seen palm trees up high but only after smoking the aforementioned controlled substances.

The climbing on the peak was very straightforward, so we made it up to the summit and back to the hut in good time. As we arrived back at our vehicles later in the day, Burt discovered that someone had been able to get into our vehicle and steal a very expensive camera lens. This had been accomplished without any visible sign of forced entry — makes you wonder if it was an "inside" job.

We departed Cotopaxi for the town of Ambato where we spent a night resting and preparing our equipment for the Chimborazo climb. Due to being higher and covered with steep snow and crevasses, Chimborazo was to be a more serious undertaking than our previous climb on Cotopaxi had been.

Leaving Ambato, we drove over to the Reserva de Produccion Faunistica Chimborazo which forms a protected ecosystem. From there we hiked up to the Whymper hut at 16,000 feet where we would spend a cold but short night before starting our climb shortly after midnight. Upon leaving the hut, we did an ascending traverse through most of the really dangerous sections of the climb as we were unable to see them in the dark.

As the sun rose, we slowly became enveloped in fog and low clouds making it difficult to see the person in front of you on the rope. Sometime during this period, the middle climber on our rope lost his footing and started sliding out of control down the slope. Luckily, our snow travel training on the prior peak proved invaluable as we were able to sense rather than see what was happening and immediately got into a self-arrest position, stopping his fall. If we had not stopped the fall, we all could have been stripped off the mountain and fallen to our deaths — a rather sobering thought. This was a bit more challenging than my childhood days of grabbing car bumpers for a sledding ride on a snowy Chicago street. After that excitement, the remaining climb to the summit went without event.

After a short stay on the summit, we departed for the long descent back to the hut, mindful of the threat of rockfall caused by the sun warming the mountain above us and melting out rocks. The "whizzing" sound the rocks made bounding down from the slope above kept us alert to this new danger. Thankfully, no one had a "bulls eye" on their helmet and we all arrived safe and sound back at the hut.

From Chimborazo we headed down to Baños, located in the Amazon rainforest at the base of Tungurahua, the largest and most active volcano in Ecuador. Tungurahua was to be our final climbing objective. Baños is noted for its hot mineral baths which derive their heat from the volcano. It didn't take a rocket scientist to figure that out.

Tungurahua, the "Black Giant," is a very interesting peak as the trail up to the climber's hut (refugio) travels through several diverse ecological zones as it climbs out of the tropical rainforest to arrive at a (previously) snow-capped summit. A volcanic eruption in 1999 melted all of the snow and ice from the summit and caused the town of Baños to be evacuated. It's still occasionally spewing out ash and golf ball sized rocks.

From the climber's hut, we trudged steadily up the slopes to snowline where we donned our crampons for the climb to another very cold summit. Even though the summit was snow-covered, we were treated to a stunning display of smoking fumaroles. I thought they were a little more than scary but a couple of members of our group decided it would be exciting to go over and pee into their opening. I wondered if these guys slipped into the gene pool when the life guard was away. Third degree burns on the Johnson did not particularly appeal to me.

From the summit of Tungurahua, we could clearly see our previous mountain, Chimborazo, the highest peak in Ecuador.

Climbing is not always the most challenging part of any climbing trip and after having successfully reached the summit of our three peaks our real adventure was about to begin. We returned to Quito where we were to catch our flight back to Miami. The good news was that my missing bag had been found and all the contents seemed safe and secure. The bad news was yet to come.

We waited for our flight to be called...and we waited, and we waited. As the hours slowly passed, our excitement about returning home began to turn to abject despair. Finally, someone from Braniff Airlines, our carrier, came over to tell us that the flight had been "unexpectedly delayed." We were taken to a local motel where there were beds to relax on. No mention was ever made about something to eat. Several more hours passed before someone appeared to return us to the airport. Once there, we were told that we were going to Guayaquil, Ecuador, where a different flight would take us on to Miami. While waiting for the Guayaquil flight, we encountered a passenger coming from Bogota where our flight was to have originated. He informed us that our plane was sitting on the tarmac with one of the engines completely dismantled for repairs. Not a very comforting thought. The

Guayaquil flight arrived and soon we were airborne.

We arrived at Guayaquil around 8:00 p.m. still without having been given anything to eat. By now we had been joined by numerous other passengers also heading to Miami who were probably about as hungry as we were. After milling around for about an hour, everyone headed out of the secure waiting area to the main terminal where the Braniff ticket counter was located. This transition required us to surrender our passports to a guard at the security gate.

No sooner had I walked into the main terminal when I noticed a large group of people shouting and screaming in Spanish. Walking in the direction of the disturbance, I noticed several people *standing* on top of the Braniff ticket counter, obviously having a heated confrontation with airline personnel. The gist of the matter was we were all starving and wanted Braniff to do something about feeding us. After making several hurried telephone calls, the airline official announced that we would all be given "vouchers" for food at the restaurant located elsewhere in the terminal building. Cheers went up and vouchers were indeed passed out. Being fleet of foot, I was one of the first passengers to grab a voucher and race toward the designated eatery.

As well as being fast, I can also be very loud when hungry, so it didn't take long before one of the restaurant waiters approached to see why I was being so obnoxious. I handed him my voucher and proceeded to order a hamburger with papas fritas (French fries). The waiter gave me his best "did your mother have any children that lived?" look and proclaimed, *"We don't accept those vouchers here."* I in turn gave him my best "is it true you had a sexual relationship with your mother?" look and tried to explain about the Braniff connection, whereupon he summarily turned around and walked back over to where he had been visiting with some of the other waiters, totally ignoring me and everyone else.

News of my denial of service spread like wildfire through the crowd of about fifty very angry passengers which was quickly becoming a mob. They turned like a swarm of angry bees and headed back toward the Braniff ticket counter. Braniff personnel, observing the approaching angry passengers and sensing that their lives might be in danger, headed toward their office followed closely by cursing and screaming passengers, some jumping on and over the counter in hot pursuit. It appeared that a riot was about to ensue, so I headed in the opposite direction back through the secure waiting area where I retrieved my passport (which luckily happened to be on top of the passport pile) under the not-so-watchful eye of the puzzled guard. Hardly had I reentered the waiting area when the outside terminal doors burst open and a dozen armed soldiers ran toward the Braniff ticket area. Better to be a coward than be mixed up in a melee with a bunch of hunger-crazed Ecuadorians. I didn't hear any gunshots so I guess the situation must have somehow been peacefully resolved. A couple of hours later an aircraft arrived and we joyfully departed for the US, landing safe but hungry back in Miami. I was so happy to be back in the US. I was ready to kiss the ground in the terminal. Nebraska was looking better every minute.

Burt later told me that before he could get on his flight back to Los Angeles, they made him pull up his pant legs because they thought he had drugs taped to his legs (he just has large calves). They also X-rayed his large balsa toucan souvenirs, ostensibly looking for drugs which might be hidden inside of them. Go figure.

Your first expedition is usually the most exciting because you don't really know what to expect. Subsequent expeditions can also have their share of excitement because you *do* know what to expect. I guess it follows that expeditions are fun?

Camp at 16,000 feet on the West Rib

Chapter 8 - Denali - The Great One
West Rib & West Buttress

Denali: "The Great One," also known as Mount McKinley. The highest peak in North America, soaring to a breathtaking 20,320 feet above sea level. A glaciated, crevasse-ridden monster of a peak and a magnet for mountain climbers from all over the world.

In recent years, the mountain has seen an influx in the number of climbers attempting the peak to the tune of 1,000 to 1,200 climbers a year, even though the success rate on Denali is historically in the 40% to 60% range. Why do so few climbers make it to the summit? The primary contributing factor is the weather. Denali is located in the extreme northern latitudes where, because of the shape of the earth, the air is thinner and the temperatures colder and the storms fiercer. In 2003 a Japanese weather station located at 19,000 feet recorded temperatures of -75°F with wind chill readings of -118°F. That redefines the definition of cold! Obviously there are other factors such as lack of experience, overconfidence, stupidity, and, last but not least, just bad luck. Denali is not a "walk in the park" by any of its routes.

Denali 1983

In May 1983 I got the wild idea to attempt to climb Denali's West Rib route as part of a guided group of eight climbers. Michael Covington, a well-respected world-class climber, was to be our guide. The West Rib is considered technically challenging; it's definitely not what some call the "tourist" route up the mountain, if there is such a thing.

The climb up the West Rib traverses through an intimidating feature aptly termed the *Valley of Death*; a deep valley guarded by ominous hanging glaciers which can break loose without warning, launching boxcar-sized chunks of ice that sweep away or bury everything in their path. Beyond the Valley of Death lies a 9,000 foot ridge with steep, sixty degree ice and snow leading to the summit. All of this is climbed while carrying a series of heavy loads up the mountain in your backpack. To further exacerbate the situation, the atmospheric pressure at the top of Denali is relative to being at 23,000 feet in the Himalaya. This effect is due to the thinning of the troposphere near the poles of the earth. That's the technical description, but the bottom line is that there just isn't as much oxygen there as you'll find on the beach in Hawaii. That's my description.

Getting to the summit on the West Rib is only half the climb; getting back down can be another story. The descent usually follows a feature called the *Orient Express*. The Orient Express earned its name due to an inordinate number of Asians who have fallen to their deaths descending this steep, dangerous slope.

For non-climbers, I should explain that traditional expedition climbing on big mountains involves a theory of "climb high and sleep low." Using this technique, we put the gear we'll be using up higher on the mountain into our packs, haul it up a thousand feet or so to an elevation where we plan to make our next camp, and stash it there. After leaving our haul, we return to our lower camp to sleep and/or take a rest day. The next climbing day, the remainder of our camp is carried up to where we left our

73

equipment on the prior carry. This sequence becomes important later in the story.

My plane arrived in Anchorage, Alaska on a blustery May morning along with my skis, ice axe, crampons, and various other mountain climbing equipment. After retrieving this mess from the baggage area, I hailed a taxi and proceeded over to the Alaska Railway train station where I was to meet the remaining members of the expedition. I hauled all my gear into the station, piled it against the wall, and began the task of trying to determine who might be a climber from my expedition. I must have looked totally lost, for it wasn't long before a couple of people walked over to me and asked, "Are you on the Denali West Rib expedition?" A quick exchange of names revealed that these were my tent partners for the climb, Jim Shafer and Claudia Berryman. We immediately took a liking to one another and I could tell the climb was going to be fun.

Soon we drew a small crowd in the form of the remainder of our group. As we were all getting acquainted, I noticed a person walking past wearing a neck brace. I joked about him being one of our other expedition members. It turned out he was a climber, but on another expedition.

We gathered up our gear and began dragging it across the lobby to the train platform where a special Denali climbers' baggage car was located. There we met several other groups also heading to Talkeetna, a small, normally sleepy village located about 120 miles north of Anchorage, and the drop off point for all Denali climbing expeditions. Finally, all the baggage was loaded, the train whistle blew, and we boarded for the three hour ride up north.

Time flew past and, before we knew it, we were at our destination and helping unload the baggage car. Spirits were high with a lot of joking and bragging going on. A truck arrived to transport our climbing equipment to the airstrip where we would catch a "commuter flight" on to the mountain.

Flights from Talkeetna to Kahiltna Base Camp, at an elevation of 7,200 feet on Denali, go on an unscheduled basis due to weather conditions on the mountain. Luckily, our flights departed early the next morning, May 1st. I say flights – plural – as it usually takes multiple trips in the specially-equipped, single engine aircraft to transport the climbers and gear to base camp. The planes are equipped with retractable skis which are lowered when landing on the snow.

The established route from Talkeetna to Kahiltna base camp flies through a feature called *One Shot Pass*. You feel as if you can reach out and touch the sheer walls of the peaks on either side as the pilot expertly guides his craft through the pass to your destination.

Thirty minutes later, our plane skidded to a stop on the snow. The pilot opened the door, jumped out, and immediately began to unload the plane. Everything was literally thrown out of the plane into big piles on the snow. A few short minutes after it landed, the plane turned around, engine revving to a high pitch, and was taxiing for take-off for the return trip back to Talkeetna. Speed is of the essence here as the weather can "sock in" within minutes, making flying impossible. Pilots will only fly when they can see where they're going. I like that plan!

We all turned and looked at each other, the enormous pile of equipment, and the departing plane, and realized that it was going to be a long, long time before we saw anything green again. The temperature was below freezing but the sun radiating off the snow made it seem like 50 degrees Fahrenheit. When the sun goes down, so does the temperature. Funny how that works. And boy, does it go down. We hurried to set up our tents and started the laborious process of sorting gear and getting everything ready for the next day's start of the expedition.

The next few days just kind of drifted past in a mental fog. We all had a lot to learn about climbing a mountain as big as Denali. I would look ahead at some feature and think that we should get there later in the day. Several days later it didn't look any closer; this is a *very* big mountain.

Claudia, Jim, and I worked well as a team, cooking and carrying loads up the mountain. This was my first true "expedition" and as it turned out, I had a few things to learn. First, in a cold environment like Denali, everything left out at night will freeze. My toothpaste, sun screen, water, and other small items which I had absentmindedly left outside of my sleeping bag that first night, were frozen solid the next morning! OK, lesson learned...in the future I'll sleep with all those goodies. Now, it's time to make that first carry up to a higher camp. Hmmm, this pack seems a little too heavy so I'll just take out a few things. Ah, that's better. Nothing to this climb high, sleep low routine.

May 9ᵗʰ – 13,000 feet – Happy birthday to me. A few shots of Schnapps at elevation and I'm sick. I'm being held by my feet, throwing up into a crevasse. Guess you don't get smarter as you get older. Just ask me this again next year!

The following day I've recovered from my drinking binge. We're preparing to move everything remaining in camp up to the prior day's high point. Oh, oh — I have all this gear that has to go up today and the pack is already full. It's so heavy I can hardly lift it off the ground! Everything that can't fit inside the pack will just have to be lashed on the outside somehow. Remarkably, I manage to find a place for everything which was left. Why don't they make wheels for these things? Everyone jokes that I look like an old time traveling salesman with all this stuff hanging off my pack. If my legs weren't bowed before, they will be after carrying this load. Lesson two learned: split your loads up evenly! Thankfully, lesson three was easy: don't violate lessons one and two! Do I really need all this stuff?

We managed to safely negotiate the scary traverse through the Valley of Death, a valley where a large climbing group disappeared after being caught in an avalanche just a few years ago, to establish a camp at 14,700 feet. Everyone was in high spirits and feeling good. It looked like we had a good chance at reaching the summit in another few days.

Another series of carries saw us establish our "high camp" at 16,500 feet. Everything was going as planned as we readied our gear for a summit attempt.

May 14ᵗʰ – Finally, summit day! We start up the final reaches of the West Rib and reach an elevation of 19,200 feet. The climbing is steep here and the air is thin at this elevation. We're not moving as fast as we should be for the distance we need to cover. Michael, being the experienced guide that he is, decides that we don't have sufficient time to reach the summit. A return to camp makes sense so we wisely abort our attempt. We arrive back in camp at 10 p.m. Time to rest and regroup! Everyone is exhausted; we've been climbing hard for fourteen straight days.

May 15-19th – Wind, snow, cold, blizzard conditions – just the norm for Denali weather but I'm really getting tired of sitting in this stinking tent — it's depressing. Each day the time passes more slowly than the day before.

We can hear the wind howling like crazy. It's like lying on the railroad tracks and having several trains pass over us. I wonder if the tent will survive the night?

We didn't know it at the time, but the jet stream had descended down onto the mountain and we were in a fight for our lives. Are we having fun yet?

May 20th - We're still alive, but the intensity of the storm has dramatically increased. Snow is starting to blast into the tent through rips which have developed due to the severity of the wind. Time passes in a cacophony of extreme sound and mind-numbing cold. The tent is becoming a real mess as we aren't able to move from our sitting positions, backs against the tent wall.

Jim, Claudia, and I sat in the tent with our arms linked together and hands braced against our knees as the roof of the tent literally molded itself to our bodies. Suddenly, the tent would explode to the point where we could see through openings, the threads barely holding the tent together at the seams. *Bang!* Just as suddenly, the tent would implode and tilt upward at a crazy angle as it strained to rip itself off the ground and hurl us thousands of feet down the side of the mountain. The sensation was like being on a small ship that is violently rocking back and forth while you're holding on to the mast.

Eating, drinking, and talking were impossible. My thoughts were mostly confined to listening to the noise, which was deafening, and anticipating the next major gust of wind.

After hours of being battered by the wind and cold, fatigue began to set in. It became apparent that we were all experiencing the beginning stages of hypothermia. We needed help and we needed it soon. But help would have to come from one of the other tents of our group who were camped a short distance uphill. The question was how to let them know of our plight and were they possibly in worse shape than we were?

Our four-season mountaineering tent had given us all it had and slowly started to rip apart at the triple-sewn seams. I screamed to Jim and Claudia that I would try to go up to one of the other tents for help. I didn't know it, but by then, the wind speed was estimated to be well in excess of 100 mph. Releasing my arm lock from whoever was next to me, I rolled over on hands and knees to crawl through a rip in the tent. Visibility was near zero from clouds and blowing snow. The wind literally sucked the air out of my lungs. I gasped and rolled backwards, clawing my way back in to the tent, struggling to catch my breath. It took a few minutes for me to regain my composure and breathe normally again. The looks on Jim and Claudia's faces told me how scared we all were. The situation was getting desperate and the tent was losing more of its structural integrity.

I gathered several hiking poles which were lying in the tent and we jammed them solidly upright into the floor, creating a temporary support for the tent roof. Looking back at Jim and Claudia again, I took several deep breaths and steeled myself for another trip out into the storm. Going back out into a life-threatening situation is not one of those things you give a lot of thought to or you probably wouldn't do it.

Kneeling by the now ripped and wildly-flapping tent opening, I grabbed an ice axe and launched myself head first out of the tent, ending up lying face down on the snow, ice axe and feet firmly dug in. I lay there for several minutes trying to gather my wits and get up the nerve to leave the relative safety of the tent. Finally, I pulled the ice axe loose and, reaching up, drove it securely in the snow ahead of me, dragging myself up inch by inch, digging my feet in to the snow to keep from being stripped off the mountain. The effects of the temperature and wind noise were mentally debilitating. I don't know how long it took for me to cover those few yards, inches at a time, but it seemed an eternity.

Upon reaching the side of one of the other tents, I beat against it with my arm in an effort to alert someone of our plight. *Oh, no, they can't hear me with all the noise the wind is making.* I beat savagely against the tent again and again until I finally realized that they knew someone was outside. The door unzipped and a hand reached out and I was pulled into the safety of the tent. By this time I was shivering uncontrollably and hyperventilating such that I could hardly speak. They said they didn't think anyone would be outside and thought the sound of my beating against the tent wall was caused by blocks of snow striking the tent. Finally, I was able to control my emotions to the point where I was able to describe the situation down in our tent. The response was silence. No one, including me, wanted to venture back out into the raging storm. Michael decided that we should get into our sleeping bags and stay in our tent until the wind subsided.

After a brief rest, I left Michael's tent to go back out into the storm. The wind seemed even stronger as I crawled downhill.

When I reached our tent, Claudia disclosed that she had no feeling in her feet. The situation was deteriorating rapidly. I found a little unfrozen water in a bottle and some candy bars. We shared a few quick sips and the candy bars, our first food and drink in almost two days. Jim dropped one of the candy bars as I handed it to him. He was beginning to exhibit signs of hypothermia.

In the meantime, Michael directed one of the assistant guides to go down to our tent and bring Jim and Claudia up to his tent using a rope as a safety line. With our guide's help, Jim and Claudia were able to crawl up to the "rescue" tent. I was able to follow them up to the tent where the remainder of our group stayed. There was so much going on that we didn't have time to be scared; that would come later.

So here we were, a pile of bodies all askew in the tent, one piled on top of the other, unable to figure out just whose arm or leg or knee was jabbing who, and here we stayed for some untold number of hours.

Suddenly, without warning, complete silence descended upon the camp. Everyone looked at each other in astonishment. Michael quickly unzipped the tent to look out upon a scene of devastation: blown-away ice walls and climbing gear scattered every which way. "Let's get the hell out of here *now*!" he commanded. It took only a short while for everyone to untangle themselves and retrieve what equipment we could to prepare for an emergency descent down to the 14,200 foot camp on the West Buttress, the mid-point camp on the "standard" climbing route. Our completely destroyed tent was left where it was to be retrieved later.

May 21st – 2 a.m. It's still light out. Arriving at the 14,200 foot camp, we were all traumatized, hungry, and thirsty. Several of the climbing groups camped there got together and fixed us hot drinks and food. We soon discovered that Claudia had experienced frostbite to both feet and would not be able to hike back to the base camp at 7,200 feet. I subsequently realized that I had worn my cold, wet gloves for the last 24 or so hours; my fingers and thumbs had turned a deep purple.

We had barely started to relax after our ordeal when some sadistic asshole grabbed the side of our tent and began violently shaking it while hollering, "Wind storm!" We all totally lost it and a near fight broke out before calmer observers removed the offender from the area.

The camp at 14,200 feet had a very proficient and well-equipped medical staff. They immediately started hydrotherapy on Claudia's feet to mitigate any potential damage. The next day she was evacuated by helicopter to be taken to Talkeetna.

You would think Claudia's adventure ended there, but no. The helicopter had experienced a difficult time reaching the 14,200 foot camp and used more fuel than they had planned. After picking up Claudia and flying for a short time, they were able to be clear of the mountains and drop through the clouds to look for an emergency landing spot due to the low fuel situation. The pilot found a highway pullout and landed the helicopter with just a few minutes of fuel to spare. He called for emergency fuel which was delivered via an aircraft that also landed on the highway. The helicopter refueled and proceeded to its destination in Talkeetna. After being dropped off in Talkeetna, Claudia was airlifted on to Anchorage. Once in Anchorage, she hired a cab to take her to the hospital but insisted that the driver stop at her favorite hamburger joint before proceeding on to the hospital. What a gal!

Climbers owe a big thanks to the helicopter pilots for the risky rescues they make flying in challenging conditions on Denali.

May 24th - Looking at the peaks as I fly out to Talkeetna from Denali, I know that someday I will have to return to finish what I started.

Claudia fully recovered from her frostbitten feet and ran in a 100 mile marathon in Colorado the next spring. She and Jim married and moved to Nevada where they both taught school and pursued various outdoor activities. Sadly, Claudia died from breast cancer in 2005.

When the going gets tough, the tough get going ...

"When I [Claudia] got home [from my Oncologist] I checked for the dates of races and picked a challenge a month. During chemo I completed a 50k mtn. bike race, a 50k trail run, two International distance triathlons, I climbed Mt. Rainier and went on a 4 day backpack trip with my husband. Six months after my last chemo to the day, I summited Aconcagua — at 22,820 ft it is the highest peak in the western hemisphere ...."

Now that's tough! Claudia was a truly outstanding woman, a good friend, and should be an inspiration to us all.

Our guide, Michael Covington, said that this was the worst storm he had ever experienced. He estimated that the wind was blowing at 150 - 200 mph during the height of the storm! He later stated that he was suffering from hypothermia during the storm and thought we would have fatalities.

As for me, thankfully the frostbite to my fingers was superficial. The bandages came off on July 5th, and I was able to rock climb again, albeit with some rather colorful-looking thumbs. I returned from the mountain fifteen pounds lighter, a tough way to lose weight!

As my friend Randy always says, "If you can't take a joke, you shouldn't climb!"

Denali Redux 1984

Not long after my return from the abortive 1983 Denali trip, I was hiking up Pikes Peak in Colorado with Randy. "How would you like to go to Denali with me next May?" I asked. Randy looked at me and then at my still bandaged-up fingers and replied, "Why not?" and the trip was on.

This was to be my second Denali expedition in as many years. Last year we attempted the more difficult West Rib route; this year it'll be the easier West Buttress route. Easier than what?

Having been turned back in May 1983 by bad weather just short of the summit, I was determined to mount another attempt on the mountain during May 1984. Last year I joined Michael Covington in a guided attempt on the West Rib route; this year I wanted to organize and lead the expedition myself. The first problem facing me was finding a strong enough team to launch a successful summit bid. We would probably spend a minimum of three weeks on the mountain carrying everything we needed to climb, wear, and eat during that time. I wanted a minimum of four dedicated climbers for this effort.

One of the things I found out on earlier expeditions was that the best climbers do not always make the best tent partners. That's an important consideration when you're going to spend several weeks eating, drinking, sleeping, and peeing in close quarters in a small tent. The stress of actual climbing activities combined with various personality conflicts can result in some volatile confrontations.

Since I had been a member and senior volunteer instructor in the Colorado Mountain Club (CMC) for many years, I had a good climber pool from which to select potential team members. It didn't take long for me to find seven CMC members who were enthusiastic about joining me on a Denali expedition. The climbers I selected all had extensive winter camping and snow climbing experience and were personally known to me. We got together at my house as a group of friends and left that evening as a team. We decided on *Fourteen Twenty* as our team name. Our team consisted of Randy Murphy, Cort Weaver, Susan Schwartz, Dave Reeder, Tom Maceyka, Judy King, Steve Dodson, and myself.

Over the following winter we worked out the logistics of climbing together as a team. Tent partners and rope teams were selected and everyone was assigned an expedition task. We would need to select and purchase all of our food for the expedition and package it up according to where we would be on the mountain each day. The resulting mountain of food was a staggering sight. Each member would carry a large pack and be tethered to a "drag bag" which would contain all those items too voluminous or heavy to fit in their pack.

The months seemed to fly past and before we knew it we were on the plane winging our way to Anchorage, Alaska where we would catch a train for the starting point for most Denali expeditions, Talkeetna. From there we took a ski plane which deposited us at Denali base camp on the Southeast Fork of the Kahiltna Glacier at 7,200 feet.

We had decided to attempt to eat well on the lower part of the mountain so Susan, our food manager, went to a local grocery store and returned with five packages of bacon, three bottles of syrup, several boxes of pancake mix, and three pounds of butter. I can still remember how scrumptious those pancakes smelled and tasted as we ate breakfast while lounging around in our warm tent. Climbers returning from summit attempts were willing to trade anything they had for just a single pancake! We later heard that only seven climbers had made the summit so far this season due to temperatures of -40°F and winds of 50 - 60 mph.

Climbing on a big mountain like Denali usually breaks down into very monotonous days with repetitive tasks. We had 18 - 20 hours of daylight, so it wasn't necessary to get everything done before it got dark. We would arise when it got too hot to be in the tent and go to bed when it got too cold to be outside. Our most time-consuming chore was melting snow for water, followed immediately by cooking. By the time we had enough water, it usually took three hours for breakfast or dinner.

When we weren't melting snow or cooking we were making carries up to our next camp or just taking a rest day. Sound exciting? You just get into a routine and one day merges into the next day without anything significant taking place. Well, sometimes we had ripples in our day-to-day existence. Tom went into a crevasse up to his crotch, while at our 17,200 foot camp, Judy became very sick from altitude; other team members got blisters, sunburn, toothaches, and headaches. The altitude, temperatures, and remoteness made some of these trivial maladies more serious than they would be back in civilization.

May 9th rolled around and I found myself on the mountain again with the same symptoms as last year on this date, being ill from too much birthday celebration. Throwing up into a crevasse isn't a good way to spend your birthday. Forget that comment about being a little slow, you have to be an idiot to think you can imbibe at altitude and remain sane.

On May 10th an unexpected tragedy struck the group while we were camped at 11,200 feet. K2 Aviation flew past our camp and revved up their plane engines while circling — a sign to make radio contact with the plane. Unrelated personal tragedies had occurred back home affecting not just one but two members of our expedition. Both skied back down to Kahiltna Base where they were picked up by plane and transported to Talkeetna. A very sad day for everyone on our team.

We were always looking up at the summit, attempting to evaluate the weather conditions for the coming day. We could see the lenticular clouds capping the summit indicating extremely high winds, but temperatures were impossible to judge. We knew the higher we climbed, the colder it was going to be, but just how cold?

The *real* climbing begins after you leave "Basin Camp" at 14,200 feet. The dominant feature above this camp is a 2,000 foot, fifty-five degree headwall which ends on a ridge at 16,200 feet. This may well be the most strenuous portion of the climb. Once on the ridge you have the option of caching your load or climbing on up to the high camp at 17,200 feet. Either way, most parties will descend back to Basin Camp for a rest day.

By the time we had reached the ridge at 16,200 feet, the wind was screaming down the mountain. We encountered some Japanese climbers who were on the mountain looking for the missing adventurer Naomi Uemura who had disappeared while making a solo winter summit attempt; his body has never been found. The Japanese climbers told us, "You go up, maybe you die."

We may be a little slow, but we're not stupid. We cached most of our load and descended back to a bergschrund at 15,500 feet where we set up tents for a cold night.

Eventually, both of our rope teams made the transition from Basin Camp up to the high camp at 17,200 feet. We took a rest day while planning for our summit attempt. What followed were two days of bad weather, sick climbers, and bad tempers, including mine. This is the point at which you begin to wonder if you've lost your mind. It would be easier to just turn around and quit. You're cold, the wind is driving you crazy, food doesn't sound good, you have trouble sleeping, and your tent partners are totally inconsiderate. Oh, and going outside to go to the bathroom when it's -20°F is hazardous to the extremities. We needed a summit day.

Sunday, May 20ᵗʰ, 1984, 3:30 a.m. – I come fully awake from a restless sleep — something is wrong. I reach out from the comfort of my sleeping bag and unzip the tent door. I'm greeted by a clear sky, no wind but the cold is intense; our tent walls are frozen like cardboard. "Summit day!" I yell over to the other tents. From the responses I receive, it appears that most people are already awake.

It took us three hours to get ready to go for the summit. Breakfast was followed by putting on climbing gear and attaching crampons to our plastic boots. My previously frostbitten fingers were aching from the cold and had become wooden again. Randy, great climbing partner that he is, helped me attach my crampons after he observed me fumbling with the crampon straps.

We started climbing toward the summit some 3,120 feet and 2.5 miles higher. *My feet feel like I am wearing lead boots, my breath is freezing on the outside of the face mask that is covering my mouth and nose. It's just step, step, step, and stop to catch my breath and then repeat the process over again and again.*

Higher up on the mountain we found some "fixed" climbing ropes which we used to attach our ascenders for safety. Due to numb hands, I found that I couldn't make the transition from one anchored rope to another without using my ice axe to jam open the ascender and then move it on to the next rope using my palms. I decided there wasn't any use in turning around at this point, as any additional frostbite damage I might have incurred was already done. Randy came to my rescue again by sitting me down and giving me a Snickers candy bar, hot drink, and the use of his armpits to warm my hands. A *real* friend would have allowed me to put my hands on his bare stomach, but then beggars can't be choosers.

Climbing on pure adrenaline, we approached the summit. The pace of our steps became slower, our breathing faster, endorphins masking the pain of those final few brutal steps. At last we had reached the highest point in North America, 20,320 feet! It was 2:34 p.m., temperature 0°F with light winds. All but one of our remaining members had been able to summit. Judy was on the summit ridge when she turned back, but she had given a monumental effort after having been sick earlier.

Even with all the excitement and congratulatory "high fives," we realized that our summit effort was only half done; we still needed to get safely back to camp. Going down is always a dangerous time, as climbers are tired and start to lose their focus instead of thinking about getting off the mountain.

Charlie celebrating a successful climb atop Mt. McKinley

Our descent back to Kahiltna Base went mostly without incident. There was a rumor that someone traded a quantity of surplus expedition food for some of those funny unfiltered cigarettes that were illegal everywhere except in Alaska, but I wouldn't know anything about that. However, some of the group seemed very mellow while waiting for the ski plane to take us back to Talkeetna. Good thing we had buried some beer and Mexican food at Base Camp.

Another year older and deeper in debt.

Chapter 9 - Argentina - Chile

Aconcagua

I don't remember when or where the idea to climb Aconcagua (22,841 feet) — the highest peak in the western hemisphere — was conceptualized, but my best guess is that it came from my old friend and climbing partner, Burt Falk. Burt wasn't as old then as he is now but then neither am I — this trip took place about twenty-five years ago in 1985.

I owe a big "thanks" to team member Dick Norgaard for keeping such a detailed journal of our Aconcagua trip. His clear-cut notes have helped me refresh details which I had long ago forgotten.

We hooked up with Rainier Mountaineering, Inc. for a January climb of the peak. Since this was in South America, inside Argentina within a few miles of its border with Chile, the seasons were reversed; January occurs during their summer. Also, since we were in South America, we got to see the Southern Cross, not visible in the night skies of the northern hemisphere. Way cool. Even a non-astronomer like myself was able to pick it out among the galaxies with relative ease.

To keep this narrative from getting too confusing I'll only mention the names of friends I have since climbed with. All in all, there were eleven climbers signed up for the expedition. Our climbing team included Dave Reeder, Steve Dodson, and myself from Colorado; Burt Falk and Jim Scott from California; and Dick Norgaard from Connecticut. The other team members were people we didn't know before the trip nor have we seen them since.

Our journey took us from Miami through Panama and into Santiago, Chile. After a few days, we departed Santiago in a heavily-loaded van heading to Mendoza, Argentina, our official starting location for the expedition. Shortly after leaving Santiago, the road climbed steeply up 7,300 feet, making thirty switchbacks before arriving at the Chilean-Argentine border. Believe me, this was a terrifying road with breathtaking drop-offs and no guard rails. No one wanted to look out the window at the scenery. In fact, everyone who was Catholic was on their knees saying their "Hail Marys" and everyone who wasn't Catholic was lying in the fetal position on the floor sucking their thumb crying for their mother. The only hope we had was that the driver had more courage than our intrepid bunch of mountain climbers.

The transition from Chile into Argentina proceeded without incident although this was not too long after Britain had invaded the Falkland Islands. We wondered if the Argentineans would still be pissed, especially since we had a guy named *Falk* along.

I think we arrived in the beautiful metropolis of Mendoza in mid-afternoon. I say "think" because at that time they had thousands of those diesel put-puts and buses that emitted pollutants on a scale that was far worse than ever seen in Mexico City. Friends who have been in Mendoza more recently say that they have totally done away with the polluters and you no longer actually *see* the air you're breathing.

We needed to go to Mendoza to get our Aconcagua climbing permits which were required by the Argentine government. Part of the process at that time included producing a doctor's statement that you had a good heart and had taken a physical examination. We obtained some of these forms along with a goodly supply of beer and everyone got to play "doctor" signing each other's name as the examining MD. Before you get your hopes up — no, we didn't do physical examinations on each other and, sad to say, we didn't have any female team members. I hate it when that happens.

In Mendoza, all business activity stops from noon until 4 p.m., then reopens for the evening. They call this *Siesta* time down south — that sure sounds like a good way of doing business to me. During one of the days while we were in Mendoza, we decided to go out to eat at an expensive restaurant; a "last supper" if you will. I really don't remember much about the food but I do remember that as we left the restaurant I asked if everyone still had their passport. Greg, our fearless leader, slapped his pocket and exclaimed that he had left his pouch containing his passport, travelers checks, papers, and about $1,000 in cash on our table. Oops! Everyone immediately ran back into the restaurant, but the missing pouch was nowhere to be seen. A frantic search ensued which finally located the missing pouch on a roof located just off the men's bathroom. The pouch had only been missing for a few, brief minutes, but of course it was already empty. Greg quizzed all of the waiters and patrons sitting near us but to no avail. The police didn't seem interested in investigating the theft unless we could identify the perpetrator. That sure was a large tip Greg left for someone.

From Mendoza, we drove over to Punta del Inca where we spent the night at a hostel while preparing our equipment for transportation up the mountain by mules. The following morning we caught a ride to the start of our climb at Punta de Vacas. This is where the expedition *really* started to get interesting.

We had too much climbing equipment to accommodate everyone in the vehicle at once, so the journey from the hostel to the trailhead was going to require several trips. Dave and I went with the first load. While we were waiting for the rest of the group to arrive, Dave suggested that we occupy ourselves with a game. He found a rather large rock which weighed about ten pounds and we decided to see who could throw it the farthest, sort of like doing the shot put. I don't remember who won, but Dave is a far better athlete than I, so I am sure he smoked me big time.

After the remaining expedition members arrived at the

trailhead, we started hiking slowly up a very steep hill to a plateau where we planned to eat our lunches. For some reason, I had the lunches for the whole group in my pack and the weight was really dragging me down. I could hardly wait until lunchtime when I could get rid of my burden. After several hot, sweaty hours we finally reached our lunch spot. I quickly threw down my pack to get those stinking lunches out and off my back, forever. Reaching down into my pack as I was removing the lunches, I was surprised to discover a hard, round object residing below where the lunches had been. I set the lunches aside and pulled out the unknown object which was no less than the large rock Dave and I had been tossing about when we were back at the trailhead. "Reeder, you asshole!" I roared. He sheepishly admitted putting the rock in my pack but claimed he thought I had taken it out before hiking up that long hill. Yeah — if you believe his story then I have some prime swamp land in Arizona to sell you. Trust me.

The climbing route we had selected was called the Polish Glacier, a semi-technical snow and ice climb. We would need to make three climbing camps on our way up to establishing our highest camp at 19,000 feet. From our high camp we would need to gain 3,841 feet of elevation before reaching the summit at 22,841 feet. Getting to these camping areas would initially take us through the Vacas and Relinchos valleys. Hiking up these valleys was like being in an oven — it was extremely hot. I woke up one night with the heat from the day's sun radiating out of my sunburned body like I was in a dry sauna. After that experience, I wore long pants, a shirt with long sleeves, light gloves, and a sun hat. I'll probably die from some internal melanoma after all that radiation.

Following are some excerpts from Dick's journal which give a little insight into the spirit of the approach:

"... the group had come to a block, in which Charlie took the lead of going up. This proved impassible and Charlie then went it alone on a higher reach to ostensibly find another path rather than ford the river. I doubt that many of the group had the experience to follow the path Charlie was on even assuming he could have made it."

And,

"Jim brought along a video camera — total weight probably 8 pounds."

Compare the weight of Jim's camera to current models which weigh about 10 ounces and you *know* that this trip took place a quarter of a century ago.

Another observation by Dick:

"Jim was almost never without diarrhea and vomiting."

I remember once when Jim dashed past our tent at a dead run, unbuttoning his pants while hollering that he was in dire need of toilet paper. I grabbed a roll and threw it through the air — he made a perfect catch and never missed a step.

A final remark from Dick:

"...the avocation of climbing is not conductive to a stable marriage."

Well, we always tell our significant others that if they wanted stability, they are with the wrong person (and some have not-so-silently departed).

As we ascended to the higher camps, we traveled through a wide variety of geological features. One area we encountered had a long stretch of snow features called *nieves penitentes* (snow pinnacles).

Some of these pinnacles were four feet tall separated by deep, sun-cupped, snow trenches. Penitentes are formed by strong mountain winds and large diurnal temperature ranges. Climbing through these features is a very time-consuming and risky business. The cupped areas can be filled with water and the spires themselves can collapse on you as you climb through them. Bad juju.

After negotiating the penitentes, we were faced with the most dreaded feature on the mountain: the scree slope from hell. It was two steps up and then one step down for several thousand feet. We would have fun coming down but it was a bitch going up, straining under heavy loads of gear.

Our base camp was located at 13,500 feet. From there we established Camp 1 at 16,500 feet and finally our high camp at 19,000 feet. During this progression, we followed the traditional high altitude regimen of climbing high and sleeping low as a means of acclimatizing. We took rest days in between moves to each camp. Aconcagua has a very large cemetery as a testament to those climbers who, unfortunately, didn't take the time to properly acclimatize.

While I was climbing the peak, Diane was at home where she heard a radio report that a climber from our Denver suburb had died while climbing Aconcagua. The radio did not give a name or tell where on the mountain the climber had died. Needless to say (I would hope) this created a great deal of anxiety until she contacted the radio station and found out the dead climber was not a member of our group. Remember: this was long before cell phones, email, and instant messaging.

Finally, all of our group and climbing equipment arrived at our high camp. We would take a rest day and then make a summit attempt. Temperatures at high camp ranged from 20°F in the day to below zero at night.

Dave, Steve, and I decided to wander out onto the glacier for a short walk during our rest day. We didn't plan on going very far out, so we didn't bother to rope up, although we did wear our crampons. While we were wandering around, I found a very tiny, oblong opening in the snow. I took my ice axe and started probing the hole and yelled, "Crevasse!" to the other guys as a joke. As they approached, I continued to punch my ice axe down into the ever-widening seam. Without warning, it grew larger and pieces started caving in and cascading down into the bottom of the expanded hole. Finally, what had started as a little seam revealed itself as a full-blown crevasse about sixty feet deep and twenty feet wide! To say we were startled would be a gross understatement. We hastily retreated to the edge of the glacier and back onto solid rock, more appreciative of the known dangers of glacier travel. What an idiot!

We were still restless, but further glacier exploration was temporarily out of the question. We had to find something else to occupy our time. Rumor had it that there was a dead body "buried" not far from camp. It didn't take us long to find the frozen corpse of a fallen climber. We curiously examined the pile of rocks covering the body. I wanted to see if he had died with his boots on, but the other guys thought that would have been in bad taste. Besides, with all the rocks, it was difficult to see any features. The body would remain where it was until the Army could come up and retrieve it, as no one else was allowed to remove cadavers. That could eventually lead to a virtual graveyard of bodies on the mountain, since the Army wasn't particularly predisposed to perform the removal task in a timely manner.

Finally, summit day — if you can call midnight "day." We were up shortly after midnight and made our last-minute equipment preparations, ate breakfast, and then had time remaining to wonder what lay ahead. We roped up and started climbing around 3:30 a.m. The ambient temperature was minus 10°F. It didn't take long before mind-numbing cold penetrated through our clothing to chill us to the bone. I never get used to the alpine starts when it gets this cold. I just try to think of something else and put one foot in front of the other.

The climb up the glacier was long but mostly uneventful with the exception of Jim falling into a crevasse up to his waist (which made it *very* eventful for Jim, who was already suffering from bouts of diarrhea). For most of us, the most exciting part was when the sun rose enough to warm us up and feeling returned to our nearly-frozen extremities followed by the "screaming barfies," a dose of burning, paralyzing pain, which can cause tears to come to your eyes (that's the "screaming" part, and the "barfy" part is pretty self-explanatory). We crested the ridge in front of us and finally stepped on to the summit.

We returned to high camp totally exhausted, sixteen long hours after we departed. Jim was so tired that he didn't even eat or drink anything — he immediately crawled into his sleeping bag and went to sleep. I remember being almost too tired to eat or drink, but everyone in our tent kept each other awake long enough to make hot drinks and a quick meal.

Dave had been experiencing a hacking cough most of the way up the mountain. The morning after the climb, he informed Steve and me (his tent partners) that he thought he had pulmonary edema.

High Altitude Pulmonary Edema (HAPE) is a condition that usually occurs at high altitude wherein the lungs begin to retain fluid and the victim essentially drowns. The only sure cure for this affliction is to descend as rapidly as possible. HAPE can be the result of attempting to ascend too fast without proper acclimatization. Many of the graves at the bottom of the mountain are the result of HAPE.

Being the considerate tent partners that we were, Steve and I proceeded to gather up Dave's climbing equipment into two separate piles. The semi-conscious sufferer asked what we were doing with his stuff. We replied that, since he was about to die, we were just splitting up his equipment between us. Dave didn't think that was very funny and gave us a good cussing. Turned out he didn't have pulmonary edema and we had to give him back all his gear. Sometimes you win and sometimes you lose.

During the next couple of days, we moved our camp back down to base camp at 13,500 feet where it was relatively warmer and there actually was air to breath. And yes, that scree slope was much easier to descend than it was to ascend.

While we were in base camp waiting for the mules to return and take our gear back to town, I would get up early in the morning and walk up the dry stream bed near camp until I would finally meet the oncoming water as it started to make its daily flow down the mountain from the glacier. The flow would stop each night as temperatures plummeted, to be renewed in the morning as the sun warmed the glacier, releasing its life-sustaining flow. I looked forward to these short hikes, anticipating around which bend I would hear and then see the water as it came rushing toward me. Each morning was a joyous new beginning.

After a couple of days in base camp, the mules arrived and we began the long hike back out to the trailhead to Punta del Inca, this time without any rocks in my pack.

We departed Punta del Inca, and headed back toward Mendoza in a decrepit van, again overloaded with eleven people and our mountain of gear. As we started up a particularly steep hill, the van suddenly started sputtering and finally convulsed to a dead stop. The driver applied the brakes and everyone quickly evacuated the van and ran over to the side of the road to gather up

95

a few large rocks to put under the wheels to keep it from rolling backward down the hill. We had run out of gas. In the meantime, someone noticed smoke beginning to come from under the hood. A quick inspection of the motor compartment revealed that the wiring was starting to catch fire. The smoldering wiring was pulled loose and the smoke began to dissipate. At least there wouldn't have been a major blaze, as there wasn't enough gas in the tank to feed the fire if the wiring had continued to ignite.

Our next task was to push the van so it faced downhill and could coast back to a petrol station we had passed earlier. As soon as we got the van turned around, everyone leaped in for a terrifying ride back down the hill while the driver furiously kept applying the brakes in an attempt to slow our nearly-uncontrolled descent. By the time we arrived at the gas station, the brakes were smoking. If we had had much further to go, we'd have needed to jump out of the van to pee on the brakes to cool them down. That would have made an interesting picture for our trip slide show. After all that excitement, I had to rush into *el baño* to change my underwear! Another third world adventure was safely concluded.

Repairs to the wiring were made, petrol was purchased, and the brakes no longer had a red glow, so we all piled back into the van secure in the knowledge that we were likely to die before making it back to Santiago.

Upon reaching Santiago, everyone except Dave and I decided to head directly to the airport to see if they could fly out that same day. Dave and I stayed in Santiago a couple of extra days to play tourist.

The following evening, we returned to a restaurant where we had eaten before with our climbing group. During our earlier visit, the atmosphere was very festive and cordial; this time things were definitely more restrained. The manager would announce the home country where the individual tables were from and then everyone would applaud, until they got to Dave and me. They proclaimed that we were from the United States — dead silence. So much for that south of the border hospitality.

However, all was not lost as the manager came over and asked in Spanish if we could read the menu. The looks on our faces convinced him that we were just a couple of dumb gringos, so he proceeded to order for us. I could see this was going to cost us an arm and a leg. Thankfully we had four of each. Surprisingly, we had one of the best meals I have ever eaten anywhere, complete with a killer bottle of Chilean wine. The waiters rushed over to our table to applaud after Dave ate an entire jalapeño pepper. Obviously, the pepper-eating event had been preceded by more than a few glasses of the wonderful wine. I think the total cost of everything came to about $20. Amazing.

Our time in Chile drew too quickly to an end. We spent our last morning there sampling the local shops. We purchased a couple of bottles of the local liquor called Pisco Sour to take back to the States. One of the last places we stopped was a bakery with delicious-looking pastries to die for. Dave selected a yummy-looking éclair for himself, but I was too big a coward to try anything.

Later, we grabbed a taxi and arrived at the airport in plenty of time to catch our flight. My main focus in the terminal was on what time the local ice cream parlor would open for business, but for Dave it was the chills, fever, and the diarrhea he was experiencing, probably as a result of the éclair he had enjoyed earlier. I don't think ice cream was high on his list of priorities.

I kept looking at my watch to see how soon the ice cream place opened and suddenly realized that we had to leave *before* it opened. In fact, we had to leave *now* as our plane was scheduled to depart in about fifteen minutes! Off we ran down the concourse, one ice cream-deprived, short, white guy and a near-death companion with a complexion turned a shade of gray, carrying our two bottles of booze. Not a pretty sight.

We arrived at the gate and announced that we were ready to board the aircraft, which we could see was still at the gate. The airline official informed us that the aircraft had departed. I replied, "No it hasn't. I can see it sitting there." The response was the same, "The aircraft has departed." Read my lips, forget it, you're not getting on the plane, you've missed your flight. My ashen-faced companion had now turned that yellowish color you usually only see on cadavers in the mortuary. Dave was definitely not a happy camper. I was chagrined — my bad. I offered to purchase him a ticket at my expense to see that he got back home as quickly as possible, but thankfully we were able to get another airline to accept our tickets for their flight departing within the hour. Try getting the airlines today to do anything that benefits the passengers!

The only excitement on the flight home occurred when I looked over at Dave and decided that he had indeed passed on to the promised land of éclair eaters. There he sat with mouth open, eyeballs appearing to have rolled back into his head, skin the color of death warmed over, and totally unmoving. I shook him a couple of times just to reassure myself he was still alive. My reward was a string of curse words that would have made a sailor blush. I'm lucky he didn't throw up on me. Guess he was still alive. I can still remember those famous last words:

¡Viva Chile! ¡Viva Argentina! ¡Viva los éclairs!

Chapter 10 - Africa
Mt. Kilimanjaro & Mt. Kenya

I remember the many fascinating hours I spent reading spellbinding books about Africa like *No Picnic on Mt. Kenya* by Felice Benuzzi and *I Married Adventure* by Osa Johnson. As a young boy, I would be the first kid in line to see the latest Johnny Weissmuller Tarzan movie

The snows of Kilimanjaro may disappear, the names of the countries may change, but the magnetism of deepest, darkest Africa will forever remain the same. It's the stuff dreams are made of.

And dreamers we were. The music was loud and the beer was cold. What better surroundings could you want for cooking up such an exciting adventure? Thankfully, no one remembers how much alcohol was consumed before I and four of my long time friends, Alan Mosiman, Tom Maceyka, Steve Dodson, and Steve Holonitch hatched up a scheme to go to Africa over the 1986 - 1987 holidays and climb Mt. Kenya (17,058 feet) and

Mt. Kilimanjaro (19,340 feet).

Mt. Kilimanjaro is the highest point on the African continent, thus being one of seven coveted continental summits. Mountain climbers enthusiastically pursue these seven summits as a prized list of peaks to conquer. While not as high as Mt. Kilimanjaro, Mt. Kenya has three peaks which comprise its central massif. The summits of two of these peaks, Batian (the highest) and Nelion, can only be reached via technical mountaineering routes; the third peak, Pt. Lenana (the lowest) can be easily reached by trekkers in good physical condition.

Most climbing trips begin and end with an adventure of some type and this trip was no exception. After a seventeen hour, mind-numbing plane ride from Denver to Nairobi, the capital of Kenya, we were herded off the aircraft, through security, and thrown to the mercy of literally hundreds of yelling, screaming, and tugging vendors. *Overwhelming* seems like too kind a term for that melee. This scene resembled something out of the Christians being thrown to the lions in ancient times; guess which ones we were. Perhaps some of these vendors were lions in a past life? The trick was to separate you from the rest of your group and your luggage, then someone would pile your luggage onto a cart and race off across the terminal to load it onto a friend's waiting van. What, you don't speak Swahili? *Kila la kheri!* You get the picture – *good luck.*

We lived through our initial arrival madness and spent the next several days preparing ourselves for our climb of Mt. Kenya, located just south of the equator.

Mt. Kenya

What better way to spend Christmas and New Year's than to make an ascent of Africa's Mt. Kenya? Okay, I *can* think of better ways, but we can't discuss them here.

Our climbing route up Mt. Kenya was to be a technical rock climb named McKinder's Chimney which goes up the south side of the peak. McKinder's Chimney is rated 5.7 on the Yosemite Decimal System (YDS) of climbing, which places it in the low- to mid-range of rock climbing difficulty. This rating is exacerbated by the fact that the climbing takes place at over 16,000 feet elevation and you have a fairly hefty pack on your back. I know it got my attention.

Climbing McKinder's Chimney

We departed Nairobi and soon arrived at the luxurious Naro Moru River Lodge, an oasis located at the base of Mt. Kenya. We would fondly remember the Lodge later in the trip when we were staying at a place called the Jet Club in Dar es Salaam, Tanzania. We spent a few decadent days enjoying the comforts of the good life and consuming a significant quantity of Safari Lager beer. We felt it was important to get totally hydrated and to carbo-load before attempting to climb the peak — at least that was what one member of the team had suggested. They say the road to hell is paved with good intentions and I'm sure we added more than a few bricks to *that* road in our pathetic attempt to prepare for our adventure.

While sitting at the trailhead enjoying an early lunch, we were entertained by people arriving by vehicle for day hikes. We had witnessed some earlier events where people had left their car doors open with food on the seats while they went to examine the trailhead kiosk. Unbeknownst to the unsuspecting hikers was the fact that a large group of rogue monkeys hung out at the trailhead for the express purpose of stealing food from hikers' vehicles. The monkeys would mount a screaming attack on the vehicles, stealing everything in sight, including a watermelon on one occasion. The hikers would respond with resounding screams followed immediately by a string of curses directed at the monkeys. This scenario was repeated time and again much to our amusement until the predictable occurred. One of the more aggressive monkeys decided that the energy bar one of *our* group members was eating was fair game. The monkey made a lunge for the bar just as Steve Dodson was about to take a bite. That summarily ended our amusement with those accursed monkeys.

The approach to the upper reaches of Mt. Kenya takes you through a feature affectionately called the "vertical bog."

Charlie toting his typically huge "death-pack"

The vertical bog is a somewhat steep, slimy quagmire of wet moorland predominately inhabited by tussock grass. As you might imagine, the footing here can be rather mucky and is downright treacherous, especially when carrying an unwieldy climbing pack. We agreed that the first one to slip and fall on his ass had to buy everyone else a Safari Lager back in Nairobi. I don't remember who won that contest, but I do remember buying beer for everyone back in Nairobi. Go figure. We were all relieved when we finally had that section of the trek behind us.

As we crested the ridge above the bog, we were treated to a stunning view of the beautiful Teleki Valley. Our route made a long traverse through the valley to eventually arrive at McKinder's Camp, elevation 14,100 feet, our destination for the night. By the time we got to McKinder's we were hungry, tired, and some of us (guess who) had very muddy rear ends.

The next morning we sorted out the gear we wanted to take higher on the mountain and departed for our next stop, the Austrian Hut, elevation 15,715 feet. We would stay overnight at the Austrian Hut and make our summit attempt early the following morning. Sleeping higher would give our bodies more time to acclimatize.

On summit days, morning comes long before the sun even thinks of rising. I'm usually the first one up, so I feel it's my duty to make sure that everyone else gets up. I've found that if I holler, "Daylight come and I wanna' go climb!" in my best hog-calling voice, that frequently does the trick. My call to arms is usually followed by sexually explicit comments regarding my character from those souls unlucky enough to have been within earshot of my voice.

After an early breakfast, or midnight snack as the case might be, we headed out from the hut and crossed the Lewis Glacier on our way to our climbing route on Nelion at the base of Mt. Kenya.

The route-finding and climbing up the side of Nelion ended up being very convoluted and somewhat challenging. It seemed like there were a thousand different ways to go, and I think we ended up trying at least 999 of them. As the day wore on, we passed features with esoteric names like the Rabbit Hole, McKinder's Chimney, One O'clock Gully, Baillies Bivy and McKinder's Gendarme.

Steve H at McKinder's Gendarme

Our group of five had been reduced to four as one member felt ill and decided to go back and wait at the base of the climb. The climbing went slowly and it wasn't until the sun was about to set that our lead climber, Tom, shouted, "I see the hut!" By the time everyone arrived at the Lobonar bivy hut it was completely dark. It had been a long, strenuous day but we had reached the summit of Nelion, elevation 17,057 feet.

Lobonar bivy hut

We had carried up our sleeping pads and bags as well as cooking equipment, so it wasn't long until we were melting snow for water and preparing to cook our evening meal.

Our lodging for the evening barely allowed us to sit up, much less stand. It was quite cramped with all four climbers inside, so those not near the door suffered from fewer bathroom breaks and even less fresh air. I ended up getting sick from the stove fumes and as a result kept us from attempting Batian the next day.

After a miserable and cramped night in the "bivy box" we hastily prepared for the day's work, rappelling back down the face of the peak to the Lewis Glacier. Weather is always an issue on Mt. Kenya and we had no desire to get caught in one of the sudden snowstorms that sometimes blast the peak.

It took most of the day for all of the rappels, as it was a time-consuming process to find a safe anchor, set up the rappel rope, and then have four climbers rappel, pull the rope down, and repeat the process a total of eighteen times. It was late afternoon before we found ourselves happily trudging across the Lewis Glacier back to the Austrian Hut.

At one point during the climb, I was making a particularly dicey traverse rock move as my watch started to come undone from my wrist. I could either let go with one hand and possibly plummet down the face of the mountain to my death or just "watch" the strap slip open and see the timepiece take its journey to the bottom of the abyss. I chose option B. As I was walking out from the peak the next day, I passed a couple on the trail who had heard about the watch incident, and they remarked, "Your watch was found, but it was in three pieces." I'd rather not guess how many pieces I would have been in had I tried to save my watch.

Upon leaving Mt. Kenya, we decided that it would work better to have just a couple of us go to Nairobi with all the luggage and get the group checked in to the hotel. That would make traveling easier for the remainder of the group. That sounded like a good plan to me, so Alan and I elected to take the luggage and make the arduous trip to Nairobi.

We secured a cab, loaded everyone's baggage, and headed for Nairobi. As you might imagine, our cab ride had a few adventures in store for us. The first event was a flat tire which our driver had to repair using a crowbar and hammer to free the tire from the rim. These were very old, mostly bald tires with tubes inside like you used to have on your bicycle. The guy produced a patch kit from his glove compartment and made the necessary repairs. No sooner had we started back along the highway when we headed up a steep hill with a warning sign about not attempting to pass. They had recorded twenty-seven fatalities on this particular hill in the last year due to drivers trying to pass! Well, of course our driver and several others were passing each other in the no passing zone, requiring three vehicles to occupy a space designed for two. Thankfully, we were surrounded by baggage in the back seat so I thought there was a remote possibility we might survive a head-on collision.

Alan and I arrived unscathed at our hotel and were able to get everyone checked in to their respective rooms. The two of us headed to the hotel dining room for a well-deserved, celebratory dinner. We ordered steaks and a fine bottle of wine. We had just started to eat when the rest of the team arrived, all in a twit. It seems as though they had a nasty time with their transportation. One guy described having to sit on the floor in the back of a pickup truck staring at the crotch of the stranger sitting on the bench seat across from him during the entire trip. To add insult to injury, their transportation dropped them off on the far side of Nairobi and they had to walk across town in the dark to get to the hotel. We described how great the steak and wine were but they didn't seem interested. Guess they couldn't take a joke.

Mt. Kilimanjaro

We arrived at the Nairobi airport and boarded our aircraft with great anticipation and trepidation, thinking about the adventure which awaited us in Tanzania, our destination. We sat and we sat and finally the Captain announced that we were waiting for a soccer team from one of the neighboring countries to arrive. A while later another announcement informed us that some of the soccer team didn't have the necessary inoculation papers to allow them to get into Tanzania and there would be a further delay. After what seemed like hours sitting on the plane in uncomfortable seats in the heat and humidity, we departed amidst quickly-fading daylight.

Arusha, Tanzania isn't a long distance from Nairobi — only about 150 air miles — so it shouldn't have taken an inordinate amount of time to make the journey. We knew we were in trouble when one of our group who had been to Kilimanjaro before stated, "We're not going to land at Kilimanjaro International Airport." Indeed, we were still gaining elevation when we should have been descending. Perhaps there is another "Arusha" and we're heading toward Cape Town or some other ungodly place? Another announcement by the Captain: "We don't have the proper equipment to safely land in the dark at Kilimanjaro airport so we will proceed to Dar es Salaam instead." Everyone received another bag of peanuts to tide them over until we landed.

To make a short story long, we landed at Dar es Salaam around midnight. There we were in the middle of who-knows-where trying to find out where we could spend what was left of our night. We hailed one of the few cabs in sight and everyone piled in. The discussion which followed is to this day still not known by any human being, least of all the passengers — us. Basically, the cab driver attempted to engage us in a conversation which simply came out as "Kilimanjaro." "Oh, yes, Kilimanjaro," he acknowledged. We ended up at the Kilimanjaro Hotel, a very opulent-looking place. We were impressed — until we entered the lobby and found people sleeping on every available space. I could see the "You're not sleeping here, mate!" looks in their eyes as we surveyed the depressing scene. A hurried conversation between the cab driver and the hotel clerk determined that we were indeed in the wrong location; we should have been taken to the "Jet Club."

The Jet Club is the location where airline personnel lay over between flights. Great, that should be a comfortable place to grab a few badly needed zzzz's. Well, "comfortable" is a subjective term. The concrete walls around the Jet Club compound were about ten feet high and topped with several strands of barbed wire. We passed through several gates guarded by soldiers with guns who looked like they would shoot first and ask questions later. I wonder if they have a problem with the locals here? Our "rooms" each had one bed, one sink, no toilet. The toilet was located across the compound which looked like something out of the movie *Stalag 17*. The dim light in the room was furnished by a single naked bulb dangling from the ceiling by a long, black, frayed electrical cord. The rooms were so tiny that it was necessary to open the door from the inside out.

We arrived at the Jet Club around 2:30 a.m. We were told that our flight back to Moshi was to depart at 8:30 a.m. and to be sure to be ready to leave. Short night. We were all up and ready to leave by 8:00 a.m. Well, 8:30 then 9:00 comes around and no one has given us any information about food *or* departure time. In fact do they *really* know that we are still here? Finally, 10:00 a.m. and someone comes to take us back to the airport.

Another surprise awaited us at the airport. Passengers were lying around all over the floors and sleeping in chairs. Most looked as if they were permanent residents. One passenger we talked with said that he had been stuck at the airport for three days. "Good luck" was his only statement to us when we inquired about the next flight out. That seemed like a prophetic statement to me.

We finally complained to airline personnel about not having been given anything to eat, so they instructed us to go upstairs to the dining area, which we did. We sat at the tables for about forty-five minutes when a "waitress" finally asked us if we wanted to eat. Duh! We replied, "Yes," whereupon she immediately disappeared, never to be seen again. In the meantime, someone from the airline appeared, "Why are you sitting here? You should be on the plane!" We grabbed our belongings and made a mad dash for the boarding gate, arriving totally out of breath. "What are you doing here? The plane will not be departing for some time," the attendant declared. We attempted to explain the sequence of events, but he wasn't interested. We traipsed back up to the eating area and resigned ourselves to being hungry.

After about an hour someone else appeared and asked if we were on the flight to Kilimanjaro which was in the final boarding stage. Huh? We rushed back to the departure gate again and, yes, the plane was indeed loading for an immediate departure. Hurray! After the usual dissertation on aircraft safety procedures we pushed back from the gate and shortly were again airborne. Life was good.

We had hardly taken off before an announcement came over the speaker from the Captain: "May I have your attention. We have insufficient fuel to make the trip to Kilimanjaro Airport so we will be returning to Dar es Salaam." You've got to be kidding! Read my lips, return we did. Back we went into the airport lobby now understanding the meaning of the words "Good Luck" from the earlier stranded passenger. The motto of this saga is "Don't count your airline miles until you land at your destination!" If all this sounds convoluted, it unquestionably was.

They apparently located enough jet fuel to satisfy the pilot that we weren't going to need to make a crash landing at Kilimanjaro Airport. We were finally allowed to re-board our flight and arrived at Kilimanjaro Airport mid-afternoon with fuel to spare. And, we didn't need any stinkin' parachutes to get there. Yeah!

Food, we wanted food. Food was important, but our most immediate concern was transportation from the airport to Moshi. Other passengers were boarding busses and a few got into cabs. The busses were apparently some sort of organized tour and not available to our group. Before we knew it, we were the only passengers left at the airport; not a good sign. We soon found out that the airport is only open on Wednesdays (today) and Sundays and they close it down as soon as the plane departs. No food.

There was a single cab left sitting by the curb with its motor running and what we took to be African music blasting from obviously-damaged speakers. We casually eyed the driver as he sat lackadaisically behind the wheel smoking a cigarette, pretending we didn't exist. One of our group finally went over to discuss the remote possibility of securing transportation to Moshi. Upon his return, he indicated that the driver wanted $50 USD to take us to Moshi. That would come out to $10 apiece which didn't seem too exorbitant. "No," he said "That's $50 *each!*" Holy crap, that's highway robbery, no way José, was our reply. We gave the driver the "finger" and he responded with the all too familiar "I slit your throat" gesture before he roared off to find some other suckers to fleece.

"This place is totally deserted," I mentioned to my companions while lounging atop our very large pile of climbing baggage. We looked around and then at each other wondering how it might be possible to solve our current dilemma. Before anyone could come up with a viable suggestion, another cab pulled up to the curb. The driver got out and approached us. "You need cab?" he inquired. This guy was obviously not the sharpest knife in the drawer. Hell no, we're just sitting here waiting for the monsoon rains to begin. After some spirited negotiation, we finally agreed on $30 USD each and by that time were quite happy to pay it.

Everyone jumped in the cab and off we went, but not to Moshi. "Houston, we have a problem," came to my mind when it was apparent that we were headed off to the sticks. We asked the driver where we were headed and he replied, "We need to go to my father's house to purchase some black market fuel." It seems that Tanzania, one of the world's poorest countries, was having a recession of sorts and most commodities were only available on the black market. How you can have a recession when you don't have any goods and services to begin with is beyond me.

We arrived at the father's house which was in the Middle of Nowhere, Tanzania. Just a nondescript, stucco, one-story shack surrounded by bare dirt with chickens and goats wandering the premises. That scenario doesn't give you a lot of confidence. This place looked like a scene from *The Grapes of Wrath* during the dust bowl days. Perhaps we should hide some money in our underwear or socks so we'll have some cash if we're dumped off in a ditch somewhere along the road.

The driver disappeared into the house, ostensibly to secure the required fuel. The whole thing sounded suspicious to us. We all sat silently in the cab with thoughts of being murdered and never being seen or heard from again. Suddenly, a man exited the house and came over to the cab. Now this guy looked like one of those characters from *Raiders of the Lost Ark*. He was very rotund (a kind term if there ever was one) and was wearing one of those Fez-type hats. He stuck his head into the cab and said, "That is my son, your driver, treat him with respect." We replied that we had been treating him with respect to the tune of $150 USD. "Do you want to exchange some US dollars for shillings?" he asked. "I can give you a good rate," he said with a smile (I hate it when people in

110

third world countries smile at you; you know something sinister is about to happen). "Yes, yes," we quickly replied, whereupon the Rotund One disappeared back into the house.

We had a quick conversation among ourselves regarding our safety and decided that we were screwed no matter what so why not go for broke. Each of us ponied up $50 and gave it to our friend who drew the short straw to take into the house.

Before long, our guy returned to the cab, smiling (I also hate it when non-third world people smile when it doesn't seem appropriate). "You're not going to believe this," he said. "That guy was sitting there watching *Rambo* on the best VCR setup I've ever seen!" "How about the money?" we asked. "We got 250 shillings to the US dollar," he said. "The official exchange rate is 16 shillings to the dollar." Do the math: 250 times the $250 that we gave him came to 62,500 shillings! There we were in a strange land with more currency than any of us had ever seen in one place at one time. The question was what to do with it all? Before long, we were sticking shillings in our pockets, inside our shirts, and into our backpacks. I didn't put any into my underwear as I didn't want to resemble the Rotund One. A truly amazing volume of bills. The last time I looked the exchange rate was something like 1 USD = 1,316 shillings. We would have needed a trunk to haul that much money around with us. As it turned out, inflation would quickly eat up our windfall, requiring additional "black market" financial transactions.

Our driver returned, smiling, and drove us to the Marangu Hotel in Moshi without further incident. Sometimes just getting to the mountain can be the most exciting part of an adventure.

While in Africa, one of our preferred meals was a dish called Ugali Stew, made with either beef, chicken, or mystery meat. It turns out that this delicacy was a local rural favorite as well. Nothing better than a hot steaming bowl of Ugali Stew followed by an icy cold bottle of Safari Lager to make you want to go climb something, the sooner the better.

At one eating establishment in Moshi we all ordered bottles of a not-to-be-mentioned-in-prime-time beer only to notice that every bottle seemed to be filled to a different level. One of our party detected the scent of gasoline in his bottle. We all gave it the smell test and agreed that the octane level was too high and it was better not to drink it. You sure wouldn't want to light up a cigarette after drinking one of those.

From Moshi, we took a cab to the Marangu Gate at Kilimanjaro National Park where we were required to sign in at the Park office and get our assigned porters. Porters are a required way of life for anyone wanting to climb Mt. Kilimanjaro. Being a porter provides a steady source of revenue for the locals who have been trained to accompany hikers up the mountain. It's a win-win deal.

Our actual climb of Mt. Kilimanjaro was fairly uneventful. We had earlier decided to split up into two groups with Tom and both Steves doing a more difficult route, the Machame, while Alan and I would do the "standard" tourist route, the Marangu.

The Marangu route climbs through a lush, exotic rainforest teeming with chirping birds and unseen animals of many types. We could hear large groups of monkeys screeching at one other as we passed. This definitely wasn't Kansas, unless it was on a Saturday night.

After a few days of hiking and staying at pre-established camps, we arrived at one of the upper camps on the mountain. Alan was feeling a little crook, so the next day my porter and I finished hiking up to the final camp at 15,500 feet to the Kibo hut. Upon my arrival at the camp, my porter declared, "I want your shoes." I explained that they were quite small for a man and were in fact totally soaked from having walked many miles in the rain. He replied, "No problem," and disappeared. I was the only occupant at the hut so things were very quiet.

Around 1:00 a.m. my porter returned and we donned warm clothes, left the hut, and began our long trek up to the summit. The idea was to climb the notorious scree slope leading to the summit while it was still frozen. The night sky was opaque but billions of luminescent stars, like brilliant diamonds, pierced the void.

We reached the summit, Uhuru (Freedom) Peak, just as the sun made its radiant appearance on the eastern horizon. We were treated to breathtaking views of the surrounding countryside; this was the highest point in all of Africa. I had been advised by my porter not to leave my billfold behind in the hut as it may not have been safe. I took the hint and rewarded him for his efforts when we reached the summit. Oh, well, I had to get rid of some of those shillings somewhere.

Top of Kilimanjaro (Uhuru Peak)

The other part of our group also had their share of adventure in the form of a dead body (a seemingly normal occurrence in Tanzania) found along the trail. Their porter told them, "Someone here," and pointed over to a dead person lying in the weeds. We never did find anything more out about this incident. Welcome to Africa.

We all returned safely to our hotel in Moshi, having reached the summit and experienced the snows of Kilimanjaro, which soon may only be found in old photographs and older fading memories. So sad a thought.

What would a trip to Africa be without going on safari? After returning to Nairobi, we decided a quick trip to visit the Masai Mara Game Reserve was in order. There, we were treated to great photo ops of a wide variety of the local wildlife including the majestic King of the Jungle (and yes, Katanga, they really were *flies*).

Lion eating its prey

As we checked in at the Nairobi airport for our flight home we were told that we were grossly overweight and would be charged $1,023. Imagine our mortification upon hearing this news. We attempted to convince the airline person to waive the charges since the plane wouldn't be very full, hence they had not exceeded their flight weight limit. He reluctantly agreed and we boarded the red eye flight to London.

It seems like the excitement never ends on these trips. About six hours before our plane was to depart London for New York, I decided to go over to the airport in order to avoid any last minute hassles. Everyone grumbled that that was simply too early to leave. I insisted and we all arrived at the airport and proceeded to the check-in counter. I noticed that they had a sign posted for our flight and no one was in line so I approached the counter. I asked the woman behind the counter if we could check in now. "Yes," she replied. We completed the check-in process and she stated that we should hurry to the gate as our flight was in its final boarding process! Unknown to us, the airline had changed our departure time by five hours. We narrowly made our connection back to New York.

View of Peak Lenin

Chapter 11 - USSR - Russia

Climbs in the Pamirs

Peak Communism & Mt. Elbrus

"You must have really freaked out when you heard Charlie almost died!" *(Offhand comment made to Diane while awaiting the arrival of our flight from the USSR)*

Remember 1987 when regular gasoline cost 87 cents a gallon, shares of Microsoft were going for $21 (And I didn't buy any! *Sigh.*), we didn't know what a "cell phone" was, "blackberries" were something you put on your cereal, and we associated the "web" with spiders? How were we even able to survive back then? That was the year I celebrated my 50th birthday and I've had *at least* twenty-three more since then, but who's counting? It's likely some of you reading this weren't even alive back then, and *that's* even scarier than how fast technology has progressed.

In many ways, 1987 was a big year for me. My friends got

together to help me celebrate a half-century of (non)progress by throwing a great birthday party, complete with a hired stripper (the wife wouldn't do it). Everyone told me that I had a good time and they presented me with photos to prove it! Mysteriously — or not — one of those stripper photos found its way into someone's passport. Luckily, the recipient of said photo (OK, it was Randy) discovered it just prior to handing his passport over to Boris ("we have ways to make you show your papers"), the Soviet Customs official.

I surely must have been "under the influence" at the party, as that was when we (Randy Murphy, Steve Holonitch, Steve Kaye, and myself) hatched the plan to climb a very high mountain in the Pamirs named Communism Peak (24,580 feet). That's the only excuse I can think of for such an insane adventure. The four of us were friends who had shared many campfires throughout the years in diverse places like Kilimanjaro in Africa and on Denali in Alaska. Now we proposed to venture to a remote area in what was then the USSR, and is now known as Tajikistan.

The year 1987 also saw the end of another adventure which started during the 1950s while I was still in prison — I received a degree, and this time it wasn't the third degree. I finally graduated from college with a Bachelor of Science degree, summa cum laude no less. Sorry, I needed to give myself an "atta boy" for *that* achievement. I had come a long way from that hoodlum, high school dropout of my misspent youth. Enough chest beating, let's get on to the climbing stuff.

Getting to the USSR required one of the longest airplane rides I think I have ever endured. Communism Peak is literally half-way around the world from Denver. You pass through ten time zones in fifteen hours of flying and arrive in Moscow in full jet lag mode not knowing whether it is today, yesterday, or tomorrow. *I just want to sleep!*

It was mid-morning when we arrived, and of course we needed to get out and be tourists. Bad choice. We were already suffering from extreme sleep deprivation and were acting like glassy-eyed zombies. I still don't remember much from that first day except the brightly colored domes of St. Basil's Cathedral.

Our aircraft was scheduled to depart for Osh, Kyrgyzstan at

midnight the day we arrived, but "Murphy's" Law intervened. One unnamed member of our team had lost his boarding pass which created a delay which was then further exacerbated when that same unnamed person became locked in the toilet from hell on the aircraft. It wasn't until 2:30 the next morning that our plane, a TU-150 throwback from the Boeing 727, finally departed Moscow for Osh.

We arrived at Osh at 8:00 a.m. — after 2,200 miles of travel and two additional time zones — still not having gotten much sleep. What followed was one of the worst four-wheel drive rides I have ever experienced. We traveled in a school bus for eight hours, covering 273 miles along the Marco Polo Silk Road (or was that the "Sick Road"?) to our base camp destination, Achik-Tash. The road was so bad that passengers in the back were literally bouncing up and hitting the ceiling of the bus when a bad section of road was encountered. As you might imagine, the bus ride was not conducive to catching up on our sleep either. How many days, nights, hours had we been awake?

Achik-Tash is a climbing camp located on the border between Kyrgyzstan and Tajikistan. It sits in a beautiful, grass-filled valley under the watchful eye of what was then called Lenin Peak. Expeditions arrive at Achik-Tash base camp and subsequently travel to what is called Moskvina (Advanced) Base Camp (ABC) at 13,300 feet. The 45 minute trip to ABC is made via a very scary and decrepit looking Aeroflot helicopter. I kept expecting to see bullet holes in the fuselage from the Soviet War in Afghanistan, but thankfully there were none. The morning after our arrival at Achik-Tash we were awakened by what sounded like someone beating on a drum. In reality it was the local helicopter pilot standing on the aircraft and beating the ice off the rotors with a hammer. That's "de-icing" — Soviet style!

The next morning the helicopter returned with passengers from ABC. As we waited patiently for them to open the door, a group of Russians appeared and rushed over to the helicopter. The door finally opened and they unloaded a woman who was clearly exhibiting the symptoms of severe cerebral edema. We all looked at each other wondering if we really wanted to go to the higher camp. Before we could even make up our minds, more Russians appeared carrying several hind quarters of what they explained was beef for ABC, but I thought the hoofs looked more like horse hoofs. The meat was thrown onto the kerosene-soaked floor of the helicopter. How to "marinate" your meat — Soviet style.

Camp life at ABC had its entertaining moments, usually in the form of watching avalanches cascading down the sides of the surrounding peaks. The avalanches threatened most of the standard climbing routes on Communism Peak and, before we left, were responsible for at least eleven climbing deaths.

If the avalanches weren't entertainment enough, the sight of the camp doctor's dog rabidly attempting to snipe at the heels of anyone who wasn't speedy enough to evade his snarling jaws was. And, last but not least, there was always the anticipation of just what comprised the evening's "mystery meat." Too bad it wasn't the dog.

ABC was primarily a camp from which you could ascend some of the lower surrounding peaks as a method of acclimatization. For our acclimatization climb, we selected White Rock Peak (16,730 feet), which had a twenty-five foot, YDS class 3, white rock tower adorning its summit, as being a worthy adversary.

Early one morning, we set off across the fragmented glacier and began our ascent up the mellow, snow-covered slopes of the peak beneath a sky emblazoned by brilliant sunshine. I was feeling strong as we climbed higher up the peak. As the morning drifted gradually into afternoon, our group became spread out with me bringing up the rear.

At some point I began to feel slightly weaker than when we had started. The harder I tried to keep up, the slower I became until I decided I had to sit down and rest for a few minutes. After resting, I began climbing again, but realized that I wasn't going to be able to catch up with my three climbing partners.

Following are the events which were related to me by Steve Holonitch and Randy Murphy, since I can't remember much about what happened next.

From the journal of Steve Holonitch:

I decided to return to find Chas. About 50 yards from the edge of the snow field I spotted Charlie waving to me about 100 yards below me. When I got to him he said he had stopped because he felt he had some pinched nerves in his shoulder and he was exhausted from carrying the typical Winger "death pack."

When I reached Charlie he was sitting on a rock; he had made several stops to rest. He said he was tired but felt that he could continue on if he rested often. He wanted to go for the summit. We decided that I would make double carries of our packs while Charlie carried the tent under his arm. We did this for two sections and onto a snow field where I lost sight of Chas.

When I came back to find Charlie sitting in the snow, he said that he had totally run out of gas. He wanted to rest for a while and keep on going for the top. We talked and decided that I would try to catch Randy and Steve [Kaye] and get their assistance in getting him up to where we would camp. Charlie was going to wait at this point for us to return and help him up to the summit. I stamped out a platform in the snow for Charlie to sit on and put down his pad and took the tent out and wrapped it around him to stay warm. I tied his pack to him and secured them both with an ice axe anchor. Charlie had me ask him some questions and we decided that he was alert, warm, and feeling fine except for being extremely tired. We said goodbye and I told him I would be back in an hour or two with some help and he was good with that and he would stay put. I grabbed my pack and headed up trying to push it as fast as I could to catch the others and looked back often to check on Chas. When I could see him he looked all right and had not moved except for one time I thought I saw him wave.

I began slowing down and was out of breath. I could not see the other guys anywhere but kept on going up and slowing down. I am sure the first hour had already passed and was getting anxious hoping that Charlie was OK and that I did the right thing in leaving him alone in the snow. I continued up the snowfield and finally reached the lip between the lower and upper snowfields and I could see the White rock at the summit. I saw two people climbing to the top of it. As I continued up another 60 steps or so I could see someone on the summit waving — to me? I motioned several times for that person to come down but suddenly the person disappeared. I hastened my pace and in another 2000 steps or so I neared the summit and Randy walked down to greet me. I told Randy that we needed to all go down and get Charlie and bring him up that he was having trouble carrying his pack and was very tired. Randy grabbed his ice axe and started down immediately. I walked up further and in another 5 minutes made it to the summit and found Steve Kaye stomping out a platform for the tents.

They had been on the summit at least an hour before I arrived and I guessed that I had left Charlie about 2 hours ago. I told Steve about Charlie and he too grabbed his ice axe and headed down to assist Randy. We decided that I would set up the tent and get some snow melting for hot drinks and soup. I was tired and it sounded like a good idea to stay at the top. When Steve headed down from the summit it was close to 8 p.m. I set up the tent and put all of the packs inside and started melting snow. Working at 16,700 feet is tiring and it all took a lot longer than I thought that it should. By 10:30 I had two quarts of water melted and was in my bag. I could not reach anyone on the radio. I drank and ate a little and decided that I would wait until 11:00 for them to get up to camp. If I did not see them by then I reasoned that they decided to go down or bivy. Steve and Randy didn't have any gear with them that I knew of, their packs sitting there in the tent with me. I went outside to see if I could see any headlamps or any sign of them but it was starting to snow and the visibility was getting low. I tried the radio again and with no response I turned it off. I was finally all warmed up and sleepy and I hoped that they had all gone down and that they were all right. There was nothing that I could do and I felt a little helpless and hoped that I had done the right thing. I reasoned that I could get in trouble myself if I left out in a snow storm. I am not sure what time I finally fell asleep.

7/15/87, Wednesday. I awoke around 5 a.m. when I heard people outside. There were some Czech climbers who had camped in a permanent tent set up below the white rock. Steve, Randy and Charlie were not in camp and the Czechs were heading down to base camp. There was about 8" of new snow and the visibility was crummy. I decided to sleep a little longer until the described *time to make radio contact to base camp. At 7 a.m. it was still lightly snowing but no wind. I cooked up a drink and breakfast and started radioing base camp at 7:30. I tried several times to make contact until around 8:15 and then decided to pack up and head down. I still had that knot in my stomach about how things happened yesterday. I packed up my gear and took down the tent and started down by about 9:30. I started by carrying my pack and dragging Randy's and then going back for Steve's pack. Once on the snowfield I was able to clip both of their packs together and haul them behind me on the snow. The packs always wanted to roll and twist and pulled at me many times.*

The clouds moved back in to the mountain again and it became difficult to find my way. All of yesterday's tracks had been filled in overnite. I could not see the sun at all for a while and decided to wait it out at one point when things didn't feel right. When some visibility returned I headed S.E. but had gone down too far? I got into a small couloir that did not look familiar. It was full of big rocks and made carrying the packs difficult and then I lost grip of Kaye's pack and it tumbled down 60 feet or more before it stopped. When I got to the pack I noticed that the tent pole bag was missing. I could not locate the poles in the snow and rocks and finally gave up and continued down, falling and dropping the packs a few more times. I finally got near the bottom of the cloud layer and could start to make out the tents at base camp. I managed my way to the bottom of the couloir and left Steve and Randy's packs there and bee-lined for camp.

I was relieved to see Randy and Steve and heard all about their ordeal in getting Charlie down to camp and into the medical tent. They said that he had nearly died last night, almost overcome by hypothermia, and surely would have if they had not come to his rescue. I felt terrible about leaving Charlie there all alone but felt so relieved when I got to see him in the medical tent. Apparently some other rescuers helped carry Charlie down. He was weak and dehydrated but showing improvement. We were all there in the hospital with Charlie, talking about what happened and Oleg assured me as did the others that the correct actions were taken by all. [Oleg was the Camp Climbing Director. He had achieved the *Honored Master of Sport* for his climbing achievements under the USSR Sports Classification System].

Charlie told me that he felt peaceful sitting there in the snow on the mountain and he said to himself that he might die there and he said that it felt all right. And then he thought how funny that was but it was OK. After spending a couple of hours with Charlie, we went to pick up the packs left at the bottom of the couloir and then had dinner in the mess hall. Charlie was going to be in the medical tent for at least another day to rest up and rehydrate. We were all alive and almost all right.

After I was brought down to ABC, the camp doctor shot me up with all sort of drugs. I'm not sure if I got altitude sickness or food poisoning from one of those mystery meat meals à la kerosene marinade, but sick I was. It took me three days to sufficiently recover to be able to eat any food. When I finally was able to return to the camp mess hall to eat, everyone there stood up and applauded my recovery – very moving. That was the good news. The bad news was that I had not acclimatized and would not be able to attempt Communism Peak with the team.

Several days later, I had finally regained my strength but the team was already up on Communism Peak. I decided to make a solo attempt on my nemesis, White Rock Peak. The next morning I set out, determined to attempt to redeem my self-esteem (OK, my ego). I was able to successfully climb the peak in good time and felt healthy on the summit. Who knows what the problem was before, but this achievement made me feel better about myself. As a footnote, the team reached an elevation around 21,000 feet on Communism Peak where they experienced nearly three meters of new snow during a snowstorm. Their downclimb back to ABC was quite an epic in itself.

A few days prior to our departure from ABC, we experienced one of those once-in-a-lifetime events. Around mid-morning, we were startled out of our regular routine of hanging out sleeping bags and clothes to dry after their overnight use by a loud, thundering, roaring sound. All eyes turned in the direction of the "launching pad," a large cleavage in the mountain which routinely disgorged small avalanches. A massive avalanche – far larger than any we had previously witnessed – was cascading down from the upper reaches of the 24,580 foot crest of Communism Peak.

Avalanche thundering down the "launching pad"

After observing this phenomenon for several minutes, it occurred to everyone in the area that this avalanche had the speed and power to overrun the camp. We hurriedly retrieved sleeping bags and everything which was within reach, throwing them into our tents before they could get blown away.

Wind-blast cloud from the avalanche overtaking the camp

Within minutes the main avalanche portion of the avalanche had reached the Fortembek Glacier, depositing tons of ice and snow as it encountered the steep wall below our camp. Rapidly, an immense, snow-laden, wind-blast cloud lashed up and out from the glacier. Within seconds, this monster had grown to several thousand feet in height and was approaching our camp with unbelievable speed. I snapped a few quick photos, then hurriedly leaped inside my tent, zipping up the door against the fury which was about to overtake the camp. The tent began shaking back and forth violently as the maelstrom outside vented its energy as it roared past. The view which awaited me when I unzipped my tent door was mind-boggling. Where a few seconds before there had been dry ground, there were now several inches of snow which had been deposited by the passing wind blast. The outside walls of my tent were plastered with snow as if someone had attempted to stucco the surface. Anyone who would have remained outside would surely have been blown away.

We returned to Moscow and prepared to wind up our stay in the USSR. While there, we were told that we would have the "privilege" of viewing the old guy himself, Vladimir Lenin, safely entombed in a mausoleum located in Red Square. Our guide took us to the mausoleum area where we were astounded to see a line of people waiting to get in that stretched around the building and out of sight. I didn't think there was enough time left in the day for us to wait in that line. Well, rank does have its privileges and, as it turned out, we outranked all of the locals. Our guide summarily marched us up to the front of the line waiting to view Lenin's body and informed the guard who was stationed there that "we" had just returned from climbing "*His*" peak (a boldfaced lie) and wanted to make our trip a resounding success by being able to view "*Him.*" The guard clicked his heels together, stood up straighter, and importantly stepped in front of the next person who was waiting in line. We were given the royal treatment. So, we found the old guy resting peacefully in a hermetically-sealed glass case kept in a spotless room with purified air, guarded by several really tough-looking Russian soldiers. "No backpacks allowed, keep moving, keep your hands in plain sight at all times, and no talking," they directed. No to kissing, no farting, just swallow your saliva if you think you have to spit, and, I would have added, no "tagging." The big guy was looking a little sallow, but then he had been dead for over sixty years.

We returned back to Denver without our Communism Peak summit but still friends and still alive, so that was the most important thing. Guess we wouldn't have made good communists.

One of the team members had called his wife from Russia and described my ordeal. His wife was to call Diane to tell her that I was okay. Diane arrived at the gate (that's when you could still go out to the gate to greet arriving passengers) with a pint of gourmet ice cream for me (what a gal!). While waiting for our flight to arrive, another spouse made the aforementioned observation, "You must have really freaked out when you heard Charlie almost died!" You can imagine the shock that statement must have caused. Diane didn't know if I would be coming off the plane in a wheelchair, on a stretcher, or what. We had a good laugh about the incident later, but it did create some hard feelings about not being informed about what had happened.

In 1999, I returned to the USSR – now just called Russia – for a successful ascent of Mount Elbrus (18,510 feet). Mt. Elbrus is the highest mountain in Russia as well as the highest mountain in Europe; it is therefore one of the seven continental summits which climbers covet. On that trip we were "detained" by Russian border guards as we approached the Georgian border, but then that's another story for another time.

Climbing in the Himalaya of northern India

Chapter 12 - India

Trisul

Once upon a time, not so long ago, in a land far, far away where we outsourced our Help Desk functions, a group of Colorado climbers decided to attempt a climb of a remote and mysterious mountain. Seventeen mind-numbing, muscle-cramping, sleep-deprived airplane hours later we arrived at our final destination: New Delhi, India, a multi-cultural city that never seems to sleep. Have you ever wondered just how many of those mysterious airline meals you can consume during 7,727 miles of flying? Many more than I should have, as these meals now lay solidly entombed somewhere within the depths of my bloated stomach, like a 5,000 year old Egyptian mummy.

We worked our way through customs, an always enjoyable experience after a long flight when you can't even remember your name or what day it is. We arrived at the baggage claim area where we encountered a scene of total confusion. There was a crushing mass of humanity — passengers frantically shoving and pushing each other in a mad scramble to retrieve their luggage. Surprisingly enough, no one seemed to get too upset about the situation. Welcome to India.

Finally, after retrieving our luggage, we carefully negotiated our way through the airport terminal while attempting to avoid running over people sleeping on the floors and walkways. Don't any of these people have a home?

Arriving outside the terminal, we were greeted by an ear-splitting clap of thunder followed immediately by a sudden, torrential downpour. Ah yes, they're still in the monsoon season here.

The scene was even more chaotic than inside with the usual collection of beggars and vendors descending upon us like a swarm of locusts attacking a Kansas wheat field, trying to sell us everything from monkey idols to "genuine" Rolex watches. The level of noise was deafening; sing-song voices of people pointing this way and that, grabbing your sleeve while hollering, "Please Sir — taxi, Sir, taxi!" I pointed across the street to a microbus where we saw a man in a turban holding up a sign with the name of our group. We started over to the vehicle when — *screech*! The first thing we needed to learn was they don't drive on the right side of the street in India. OK, look both ways before attempting to cross the street. We definitely weren't in Kansas now.

The rain stopped as quickly as it began, replaced by sweltering heat and an oppressive level of humidity. *Wow, I think my underwear might have gotten steam cleaned. Maybe we are in Kansas after all. I'll have to be careful not to let my family jewels get some sort of jungle rot from all this humidity!*

Our ragtag group continued across the street, pulling an outrageous mound of baggage behind us. We were a collection of five climbers and hopefully would have enough equipment for a month-long attempt on the southwest ridge of a peak called Trisul I (23,360 feet). Trisul I is located approximately 150 miles northeast of Delhi in the Garhwal Himalaya of India. "Trisul" stands for the three-pointed trident of the Goddess Nanda, and no, she was not my third wife. Actually, the first three wives would probably like to see me skewered on the points of the trident! Dream on, ladies.

"Namaste, Sirs," our driver said as he stood staring wide-eyed, probably wondering how he was going to be able to fit all our equipment into and on top of the tiny microbus and still have room for us. In the blink of an eye we were suddenly engulfed by a horde of other drivers screaming for a fare while other people attempted to pick up our baggage and load it onto the microbus. Our shouts of "No, no!" fell on deaf ears. It was time for our leader to step forward and sort things out, which he did.

The microbus thing didn't work out, so we hired three taxicabs and somehow managed to push, cram, and lash all the equipment onto the vehicles. We piled in and drove off to our five star hotel amid more arm-waving, shouting, and a black cloud of automobile exhaust. Do you know of any climbers who stay at five star hotels? Well, neither do I. Maybe in my befuddled state of mind I became confused and someone said, "The five of us are off to the hotel." Go figure.

I wish I could say that the rest of our first day in India went as smooth as silk, but that was not to be. It was more like burlap.

Let's face it, I'm not a good foreign traveler when it comes to food. My stomach doesn't do well with exotic or unusual foods. It likes the three main food groups: burgers, fries, and ice cream. Be that as it may, when in Rome – or in this case New Delhi – you eat what is available even if you can't read the menu or pronounce what you're reading.

After checking into our hotel and unpacking, we gathered together again in the lobby to decide on a dinner plan. While food didn't sound all that inviting after the airline fare, we did need to get out and try to start overcoming our jet lag. So, off we went to one of the local eateries.

Indian cuisine is decidedly different from that which you might find in somewhere like Mobile, Alabama, but I apparently lucked out and ordered an interesting meal, or so I thought. "Very good, Sir," the waiter replied when I pointed to the item on the menu I had selected. "Not sure what I just ordered," I whispered to the person next to me. Time passed and just when I was about to fall asleep, our meals arrived. I wasn't sure what was on my plate but it didn't look that bad. The person next to me had something which resembled the legendary "mystery meat," a morsel that is sure to strike fear into the hearts of foreign travelers. I've found that it's always a good idea to inspect your meat in some foreign countries to see if any jewelry is still attached to the bones. Another criteria to use when selecting an eating location is to count the number of cats and dogs in the immediate vicinity.

I managed to consume all the food on my plate and made a mental note to try to order the same thing next time. When asked once by a waiter at a restaurant I frequented why I always ordered the same thing, I replied, "Like women, when you find one you like, you don't keep trying new ones." Well, to make a long story short, the waiter returned and exclaimed that the person next to me had received the meal I ordered and I had received his. So much for my theory about ordering the same thing every time. I found out the next day that the guy who got my meal became deathly ill during the night from the dish I had ordered. Whew — dodged a bullet there!

We spent several frustrating days in Delhi going back and forth between the Indian Mountaineering Federation (IMF) and various other governmental organizations in an attempt to secure the permit for climbing the mountain. Finally the IMF got their act together and issued the permit and introduced us to the Liaison Officer (LO) who would be assigned to supervise and report on our expedition. We discovered that we were required to outfit the LO with all of the equipment he would need for the expedition. This equipment had to be of the same "standard" as the other climbers on the expedition, even if the LO doesn't climb! A couple hundred more US dollars just went bye-bye.

Finally, we departed Delhi and began our long journey by bus to the trailhead. There we would meet up with the porters who would transport our equipment up to base camp.

September 14, 1990 — we arrived at base camp, elevation 14,000 feet, after five rain-soaked days of traveling on slimy, leech-infested trails through dense rainforest. Throw in forging across a couple of freezing rivers running at near flood stage and everything we had was totally soaked, including ourselves. The monsoon season had unleashed its full force on us with a vengeance. I was beginning to resemble a prune from constantly being wet. We took a couple of days off to sort and dry out our sopping-wet gear. It was nice to be in one place for more than a day without the need to pack and unpack everything, especially while it was wet.

During the following days, our group ferried ropes, tents, food, and climbing equipment up a very nasty, steep rock gully to establish Camp 1 at 16,000 feet at the foot of the glacier.

Our next task was to push the climbing route on up the mountain to 18,000 feet where we hoped to establish Camp 2. This part of the expedition involved climbing across and around crevasses and up steeper snow slopes. We travelled in rope teams of two or three climbers to protect against the possibility of falling into a crevasse. During one carry, we rounded a corner and were shocked to see debris from a recent, three-foot deep, slab avalanche. This had a sobering effect, since we realized it's the danger from above which we can't always see that could easily kill us.

After establishing Camp 2, the process of moving additional climbing gear and food up through Camp 1 occupied our days. We planned to use Camp 2 as our primary staging area for the push through to Camps 3 and 4 from which we hoped to make our summit attempt. The climbing from Camp 2 and above appeared to be quite a bit steeper than what we had experienced below. The pace of placing ropes up the steep snow slopes above us would become slower, more tedious, and more dangerous. Each three-hundred foot section of rope would be connected to the section below by using either snow stakes or ice screws depending on the snow conditions at that spot.

One night, while sleeping at Camp 2, I was awakened by a very loud rumbling noise followed by a giant blast of wind, the result of a nearby avalanche. Again, it's what you can't always see that can kill you and that thought was probably paramount in everyone's mind for the rest of the night. It's doubtful that many of our group went right back to sleep. Any little noise brought me to an upright, attentive position.

The combination of cold, wind, and being at 18,000 feet while working hard climbing up and down steep slopes began to take its toll on everyone.

Tent life at elevation during inclement weather can be difficult due to the stress of being in close quarters for hours on end with other people. After a while, even the best-organized person can become a complete slob. Getting in or out of the tent would allow the freezing wind to blast a layer of spindrift snow over everything while the door was unzipped. We would try to time our tent entry and exits to coincide with the wind gusts but usually failed miserably. Whoever was responsible for the "snow storm" inside the tent was usually roundly cussed. How many ways can you say "asshole"? Hey, when nature calls, you just gotta go, snow or no snow!

We began pushing the route up to Camp 3 at 19,000 feet. The climbing had become very steep and the pace slowed accordingly. It took 8½ hours to fix one six-hundred foot section of rope. One group of climbers returned to camp relating a hair-raising tale about a scary climbing traverse they had to make. No one was looking forward to following that section after listening to their story. To exacerbate the situation, everyone had been complaining about the second rope section being strung too tight. A tight rope makes it a nightmare when you're trying to place your rappel device on the rope while descending.

The ascent up the ropes with gear to supply Camp 3 turned into a struggle against the elements. Snow had been falling at an alarming rate and was being blown up the mountain by the now-raging wind. The steps of another climber just a few feet ahead were filled in with snow almost as quickly as their boot left an impression. Small spindrift avalanches were continually coming down on my face.

The steepness of the slope and the horrible weather conditions conspired to cause everyone to begin climbing slower, creating a veritable traffic jam on the ropes. After climbing 600 feet and standing around waiting to climb higher, I decided that it was futile for me to continue. Sometimes it's better to be part of the solution than part of the problem; I rappelled back down to Camp 2 for some much-needed rest.

During the night at Camp 2, a major storm moved in. Blasts of snow were blowing against the tent walls, creating a feeling of being inside a punching bag. Between the wind noise and tent flapping it made for a long, sleepless night. We spent the next day digging out the tents and finding buried equipment that had accidentally been left outside overnight. The slopes above Camp 2 were now too unstable with new snow to allow any progress for pushing up the route, so no progress was made that day. There were only five more days scheduled for us to finish putting up the route and going for the summit. We needed a break in the existing weather pattern of daily snow and wind.

I now faced a dilemma. An injury caused by a bamboo shoot that jabbed me between my fingers during the approach to the mountain had become infected. I woke up in the middle of the night with shooting pains halfway up my left arm. By morning, I considered going back down to Base Camp where there is more oxygen in the atmosphere. It's a known fact that injuries don't heal at high elevation due to the lack of oxygen to make red blood cells for healing. We did not have a radio or helicopter support for evacuation and it would take several days to get back to the trailhead if my infection got worse.

I felt like I would be letting everyone down if I went back to Base Camp now. I desperately wanted to summit with the group after all the effort we had expended. I think I had what is termed "summit fever," a phenomena where you sometimes don't use good sense to make a logical decision about continuing to climb or turning around.

If I could just get past this day perhaps everything would be okay. So, against my better judgment, I decided to give it one more try. I loaded up my pack with equipment and slowly ascended two rope lengths. The pain had now progressed up to my armpit. I stopped, removed my glove, and began squeezing blood and pus from my injury. This was crazy — I needed to go down.

I felt lousy — the infection and being at altitude were wearing me down. I carefully descended down toward our cache. A fall here would have meant going over a 200 - 300 foot cliff. One small slip and I wouldn't have to worry about a dinky hand infection.

I'm really beat. I've made it back to Camp 2 where there is a tent but no stove. Damn! I need to melt some snow for drinking water before I go back down to Base Camp. It's 2,000 feet back to Camp 1 at 16,000 feet and another 2,000 feet down to Base Camp before I'll have a stove available so I can have something to drink. I'm the only one at Camp 2. It's still snowing along with poor visibility. The slopes below me are loaded with wind slab snow – prime avalanche conditions. I'll wait an hour to see if things improve, but I've got to go down relatively soon or risk getting caught out in the dark and having to bivy.

I started hiking down but it was difficult to find the path due to the amount of new snow which had fallen. Finally, I spotted a wand placed near a small crevasse. The footing here was treacherous but seemed doable. Perhaps I should have put on my crampons. Suddenly, I slipped on the steep snow slope and immediately began to slide out of control. The weight of my pack made it difficult to self-arrest. I grasped the head of my ice axe, rolled over on my stomach, and frantically drove the pick into the snow. Finally, I slid to a stop, arms extended, literally hanging from my ice axe with a death grip.

I'm scared out of my wits. The toes of my boots won't penetrate the hard snow surface to give me purchase and I'm not wearing my crampons. Crap!

That big avalanche field we noticed earlier was about ten feet off to my left. That was my only hope to keep from plummeting out of control down the slope and into a large, ominous crevasse below. The avalanche debris had settled into large blocks of snow which had formed platforms which I hoped I could use for climbing down the slope.

I slowly pulled myself up to a semi-kneeling position, leaned forward and quickly jerked my ice axe out of the snow. Lunging to my left, I plunged the point of the axe securely back into the snow as I slid several more nerve-racking feet down the slope. I repeated the maneuver several more times before I was able to reach the relative safety of the debris field. Finally, I made it over to a safe spot in the avalanche debris; it took me a few minutes to catch my breath and regain my composure.

I started cautiously climbing down through the debris field and eventually was able to follow the wands through deep snow back toward Camp 1.

Damn! The clouds are returning, visibility is dropping to zero.

133

I'm so tired. Must hurry. I'm finally down off the steep section but now I need to negotiate through this crevasse field. No visibility. I've lost my way. This is dangerous – if I go into a crevasse I'm S.O.L. No one knows where I am. This is not good.

I attempted to keep a positive mental attitude by talking to myself. *This is stupid, you need to stop.* I needed to stay where I was until I could see where I was going. I kept hearing the "whumpf, whumpf" of snow settling around me. Not a good sign: avalanche warning. I was in this all by myself, so I needed to keep it together.

The clouds thinned slightly. I was up on my feet and moving as fast as I safely could through the crevasses. More clouds. I couldn't see but I was feeling better about my position so I sat down to wait again. If it didn't clear soon, I'd need to do a bivy near a big rock slightly downhill and wait until morning. I was near the edge of the cliff band so this wasn't the place to be foolish after what I had just experienced.

The clouds briefly cleared again. I located the wands just off to my right. I breathed a measured sigh of relief. After a few minutes, my muscles began to relax; I felt the tension start to flow out of my body. I realized that I was going to make it safely down to Camp 1 before dark. Talking to myself had really helped me keep under control.

I saw the tent! Finally, I was there. This was the kind of experience that gives you a whole new outlook on life. It's the little things that are important, like being alive. I found a half-liter of unfrozen water at camp so I could make it until morning without having a stove to melt snow for water.

The next day was very cold and windy. My pack was heavy, I was tired and the scree slope I needed to descend was a frozen, snow-covered mess. Again, I wasn't sure where the trail was supposed to go as we had earlier removed all the wands to use higher up on the mountain. *I need to be careful here not to slip as falling could still be extremely dangerous. Ouch! Damn!* Spontaneous rock fall caught me in the back of the leg and nearly knocked me to the ground. *I'm glad I'm wearing my helmet! I must keep moving.* After what seemed like days, I reached base camp and looked at my watch. It had been a long four hours from Camp 1, but it seemed much, much longer.

If, after reading this story, you're thinking, "What an idiot!" I would tend to agree with you. In my defense, I would plead extreme fatigue, altitude, and illness as contributing factors to some of my very questionable decisions. Sometimes you just have to "cowboy up" and do what has to be done.

At some point while we were higher up on the mountain, marmots ate a hole in the Camp 1 tent and consumed a large quantity of freeze-dried eggs and two kilos of Yak Cheese. Their plundering made for short rations for the rest of us during the remainder of the trip. I wonder if those marmots were planning to climb the peak?

Amidst a heavy, wet snow, the porters began to arrive at Base Camp to transport our climbing equipment back to the trailhead. They were wearing loafers without socks, thin trousers, and a blanket wrapped around their shoulders. Most of them were soaked from the wet snow. I would have been hypothermic but they all seemed to be in good spirits. At that time porters got paid about fifty rupees a day – around $3 US – plus a package of cigarettes.

The remaining team members returned to base camp after an unsuccessful summit attempt, looking haggard and very exhausted. High winds and cold temperatures at 21,000 feet had forced them to retreat.

Finally, everyone was back down and we broke down the camp to start heading back to Goht. Those raging rivers we crossed on the way in were now just quiet little streams, easily waded across without the use of the rope. The lower altitude and warmer temperatures made for a restful night of sleep after the frigid conditions higher on the mountain. Lower altitude and less stress had also allowed my hand to begin the healing process. Made me wonder what all the fuss was about.

Everyone experienced sore feet and stiff muscles from days of hauling loads up the mountain with an inadequate amount of rest from the wind and cold. Several of the climbers who reached the highest camp had a bit of frost nip on their toes. Of the four climbers at High Camp, one person slept outside the last two nights as they only had one three-person tent. Now that's being tough!

Back at the trailhead, we were treated to a plethora of fresh, hard boiled eggs and chapatti bread. I probably ate a half dozen eggs myself. Later, we boarded our bus to begin the two day journey back to Delhi. I can't count the number of near head-on collisions we had, but judging by the amount of beer that was consumed by all to sooth our nerves it was a significant number.

We arrived at the Coconut Grove Hotel, our lodging in Delhi. Something about the name "Coconut Grove" had a bad ring to it. Hmmm – in 1942, a Boston nightclub fire at the Coconut Grove killed 492 people. Well, there wasn't much that could burn in this building. The rooms were constructed out of poured concrete with a single naked light bulb hanging suspended from the ceiling. Each room had a mattress lying on a raised concrete platform, no phone, no TV, no hot water, but yes, they did have TP, a modern western convenience. Did I forget to mention the lovely concrete toilet and sink? Don't forget to put up the lid when you're peeing. How charming. Perhaps the interior decorator had previously worked at the "Hanoi Hilton" in Vietnam. The cleaning staff used a fire hose to clean the rooms between residents; very rustic.

Checking out all the emergency exits seemed like a worthwhile idea since we were staying on one of the hotel's upper floors. A walk down the hall revealed an elevator. Hmmm, again. They forgot to install the elevator, so all that was there was the shaft with an opening where the door would have been. It's doubtful that the little 1" X 2" board across the opening would stop anyone from "getting the shaft" should they accidentally fall against the opening. That would, however, be the quickest way to the bottom floor in case of an emergency. But then, the fire department always warned against using the elevator in case of fire. Sounds like an intelligent idea to me. Where was OSHA when we needed them?

Our trip ended with a final disappointment. We were unable to go to Agra to visit the Taj Mahal due to a transportation strike. So, I leave you with these words written by Emperor Shah Jahan himself, describing the Taj.

Should guilty seek asylum here,
Like one pardoned, he becomes free from sin.
Should a sinner make his way to this mansion,
All his past sins are to be washed away.
The sight of this mansion creates sorrowing sighs;
And the sun and the moon shed tears from their eyes.
In this world this edifice has been made;
To display thereby the creator's glory.

By this time in my life, I was beginning to believe that all my past sins *had* been washed away.

Strikes seemed to be a way of life in India, so it came as no surprise to us that our last couple of days in India would be filled with grim tales of self-immolation and violent demonstrations due to some unexplained situation. With the specter of a looming "general strike" we opted to go early to the airport for our return flights to the United States. Security at the airport was extremely tight. Our bags were X-rayed twice and then subjected to a hand search. The three week old underwear at the top of the bags has always served to separate the diligent security personnel from those just passing the time of day.

So ends another adventure in a land far, far away.

Burt, Jim, and Charlie, 1983

Chapter 13 — Nepal

Climbs in the Himalaya

Annapurna Sanctuary, Fluted Peak, Gokyo Ri

Twenty-five years elapsed between my first and last trip to the Kingdom of Nepal. My first trip occurred in 1983, followed by a 1999 trip, and then my final trip in 2002. Each visit allowed me to experience different areas of Nepal and have exciting third-world travel adventures.

Nepal has gone from being a quiet, peasant farming country to one torn apart by armed political conflict. In the early 1980s, trekkers flocked to Nepal attracted by the laid-back attitude of the populace and beautiful scenery. By the late 1990s, all this had changed for the worse. A near insurrection by the Communist Party of Nepal, the Maoists, threatened to tear the country apart. Many Nepalese were killed in the ensuing violence which lasted for nearly ten years. The number of foreign trekkers drastically declined as a result of this upheaval.

In the 1980s, I saw beautiful, rolling, verdant hillsides and valleys flourishing with successful agricultural endeavors. By 2002, some of these same hillsides exhibited the scars of armed conflict, trenches dotted with machine gun emplacements, and buildings surrounded by heavy coils of razor wire. People on the street no longer greeted strangers with the usual "Namaste" — they averted their eyes as they silently passed. The attitude of the people had changed from one of peace and tranquility to an atmosphere of suspicion and fear. The streets outside the Royal Palace in Kathmandu were decorated not with beautiful flowers and trees but with pill boxes manned by heavily-armed soldiers.

In 2006 the conflict between the government and the Maoists was finally resolved when peace was declared between the warring factions and elections were held to accommodate the ideology of both parties.

Let's turn the clock back 25 years and take a closer look at events that helped shape my first trip to Nepal. I've found that my first trip to any country often sets the mood for future visits. Nepal is a country where time seems to have stood still. In the early 1980s, there were only a few roads outside Kathmandu; electricity and telephone service was available in just a couple of bigger cities. You could walk out of the city and feel like you had been transported into the fifteenth century in the blink of an eye.

1st trip – 1983

As I mentioned, the early 1980s presented the traveler/trekker with an atmosphere of time standing still. No television, few telephones, and for the most part no electricity outside of the major cities. There was no reason to get in a hurry as there wasn't anywhere to go that couldn't wait until tomorrow. Cows are considered sacred in Nepal, so it wasn't unusual to be walking or driving down a busy street and see a cow sitting in the middle of the road nonchalantly chewing its cud while the traffic drove around it.

Outside Kathmandu, commerce was mainly transported on the backs of porters, primarily Nepalese men and women who substituted as the "big rigs" of the western world. If something went from Kathmandu to the far mountain reaches of the Kingdom, it went on foot by porter, zopkio (a cow-like animal — very dangerous as they are very dumb) or yak (also dangerous because they are dumb *and* mean). The zopkio has horns that point more or less forward while the yak has horns that point up and slightly backward. Horn orientation can be an important factor when one of the hairy beasts has you in his sights!

Zopkios are used in the lower elevations while yaks are used at higher elevations. When you stop at one of the villages with your animal and say, "Fill it up!" you mean, "Throw out hay and water for my beast of burden." Small stores or tea houses were located conveniently along the main trails. These were akin to our 7-11 type stores. You could usually purchase cookies or a Coke to assist you on your up and down journey to your next camp. Thinking about it, I don't believe I've been anywhere in the world where I couldn't purchase a Coke.

It wasn't unusual to see some slightly-built man or woman carrying a load that approached 100 pounds up and down the hills of the countryside. Many porters were even smaller and thinner than I am! These porters used a handmade walking stick with a flattened top for balance. When they stopped to take a break, they didn't put their load on the ground western style, they supported it on the top of their walking stick which had been placed behind them so they wouldn't have to lean over to pick their load up from the ground when they started walking again. When they were walking, their load was mainly supported by a "trump line" in the form of a wide strap that went around their forehead and was attached to their load. It's no wonder that these folks generally had zero body fat. Many of the porters walked without shoes or used the basic "flip flops" commonly seen in third world countries. Our lazy western asses wouldn't last a day putting in the amount of effort they did. I doubt anyone in the Nepalese culture during those days had Attention Deficit Disorder (ADD) or told someone they "needed their space." Theirs was a subsistence lifestyle, one that they had been practicing for centuries.

Most Nepal trips usually begin and end in Kathmandu, the capital city. As you arrive at the International airport, you are immediately overwhelmed by the typical third world country culture, which can be a shock if you've never experienced it before. The Nepalese have a different view of customs than we do in the west. Pushing, shoving, and shouting — which we might consider rude — are no more than normal, everyday activities. If you don't make your presence known, you will likely be ignored. I guess it goes back to the old adage "make dust or eat dust." They are accustomed to being packed in together in smaller spaces than we are.

As we made our way out of the airport customs area, a man approached us and said *Namaste*. "What did he just call me?" I asked my traveling companion. "Charlie, *Namaste* is a form of greeting which loosely translates into 'I bow to you, we are all equal'," he explained with a smile. It probably means different things to different people but it's better to not get too involved in the semantics. We quickly adopted the *Namaste* form of greeting and felt like we were seasoned travelers. The locals probably wrote us off as just another bunch of ignorant Americans.

We made our way through exhaust-laden streets to our hotel and, after checking into our rooms, set off for some sightseeing. We needed all the exposure to sunlight we could get to help mitigate the effects of jet lag.

Kathmandu has its own forms of what can pass as "entertainment." People-watching can be quite rewarding, sometimes. I must have looked like a "mark" because this unkempt-looking guy dressed in long colorful robes sans shoes came up to me on the street, stuck his face about an inch from mine, and asked if I wanted to purchase some hashish. "No," I replied, as I staggered backward to escape his foul-smelling breath and the view of yellow jagged remnants of what probably once passed as teeth. "Bad sport!" he replied, and walked off to confront the next unsuspecting tourist. It's unlikely the guy was a Narc — probably just an unemployed ex-CEO from the States.

We found that shopping in the Thamel district of Kathmandu, a popular tourist destination, could be a little bizarre. We walked past shops and saw raw poultry hanging in the heat in front of stores, overwhelmed by hordes of flies and other unrecognizable winged creatures. I doubt that these offerings would pass USDA

141

approval. Now that I think of it, I never saw many cats on the streets, so perhaps those weren't chickens we observed after all?

One of the most interesting, must-see, eye-opening venues in Kathmandu is to view a funeral, where the cadaver is burned on pyres along the Bagmati River. The family of the deceased washes the body and then places it on a platform covered with wood which is set on fire. As the body burns, any unburned body parts (arms, legs) are pushed back into the fire. When everything is cremated, the remaining bones are pushed out into the river. There is usually a "swamper" standing out in the river to assist the final remains on their journey to the hereafter. You are also likely see some colorful Hindu Fakirs sitting in the area. This is why we filtered all water we consumed. We were definitely not in Kansas now!

Personal experience has led me to believe that spending too much time in Kathmandu is a sure recipe for getting sick from the food or contaminated air or a hundred other things just waiting to strike you down. There's nothing like having the "Nepal quick step" to let you know you shouldn't have left home without extra clean underwear and some anti-diarrheal medication! We spent the minimum time there and then "got out of Dodge."

Our bus ride from Kathmandu took us out of the smoggy megalopolis to our trailhead located in the Kathmandu Valley. The trip was filled with beautiful mountain vistas and lush jungle scenery, a big change from the city. The bus ride itself did, however, have some of its own unique idiosyncrasies. The bus was filled to standing room only, which meant that they would cram three passengers onto a seat designed for two and the aisles and doors were filled to overflowing. At first I was offended by the crowding, pushing, and shoving, but came to realize that this was a normal phenomenon. The bus ride was a real up close and personal adventure. I would rate the sensory overload as living somewhere between a pig farm and cattle feed lot. Thank goodness for the window seat that I grabbed; at least I could get *some* fresh air. Passengers unsatisfied with the accommodations could ride on the top of the bus with the chickens and goats for half fare, but you had to be cognizant of those low road overpasses and hope it didn't rain.

At the trailhead, we met our porters who engaged in their usual debate regarding who got which load, how heavy the loads were, and how much they were being paid. This discourse usually ended up with the porters going on strike for more wages and cigarettes which were part of their daily pay. They knew we were too lazy or out of shape to shoulder our own loads and carry them for miles and miles for the next thirty days, so their strike amounted to well-deserved blackmail. We wouldn't have been willing or able to work for the daily pittance they received. These bargaining sessions are just part of doing business in foreign countries and are usually settled amicably.

Our journey would take us into the Annapurna Sanctuary followed by a technical climb of Fluted Peak. As I said, this was a time of peace and tranquility in Nepal with throngs of trekkers coming and going, going and coming. We passed one particular group several times during the first few days of our trek. The group consisted of a bunch of hippies, obviously stoned out of their minds and appearing to be wandering aimlessly. They didn't seem to be bothering anyone and seemed to be a very happy group. I should mention that marijuana grew wild in Nepal and it wasn't a crime to smoke a "J" every once in a while, for medicinal purposes of course. I sure did like that eastern philosophy.

As we left our trailhead in the Kathmandu Valley, the temperatures were tropical, but as we travelled up and over Thorung La ("La" is "Pass" in Nepali) at 17,771 feet it became cold and snowy. Unfortunately, our porters had only been equipped with the type of clothing normally worn at the lower elevations, so it wasn't long before we were supplying them with hats and gloves, warmer coats, and sunglasses for snow blindness protection. It was interesting the next morning to see the trading of items that had taken place among the porters since they received some of these items. We might ask a porter where his hat was, and he would reply either that he was saving it for later (probably to sell) or it had already been bartered for cigarettes.

Occasionally, one of the porters would stub a toe on a rock or lose his balance and fall, resulting in a minor injury. We would treat the injury with antiseptic and a small bandage, then send the injured party on his way. Later in the day, the bandage would have disappeared. "What happened to your bandage?" we would inquire. "Here, mister," he would reply and out of his pocket the used bandage would appear, to be saved and used another day. I guess we're just a bunch of western wimps.

Once over Thorung La, we descended down toward the Hindu/Buddhist town of Muktinath where we realized that two of our porters were missing. We inquired about their whereabouts with our Sirdar, the manager of our trekking party. He responded, "Many porter die each year on Thorung La." Several of us went back up over the pass and located the missing porters sitting in the snow where they surely would have died from hypothermia if we hadn't gone back for them.

Muktinath is one of the most important pilgrimage sites of Nepal for both Buddhists and Hindus. Pilgrims come from all over Nepal and India to worship there. We witnessed a Hindu ritual of washing away negative karma by walking nearly naked under a series of boar's heads spewing icy cold water from the mountains above. The pilgrim would make several rounds under the flow to wash away his negative karma. I didn't try this, as I didn't think I would have enough time to completely do the job!

Pilgrim washing away negative karma

When you leave the US and travel to third world countries you need to adjust your thinking of what constitutes "normal." During our trek in Nepal, we occasionally stayed at "tea houses," which are single-room dwellings with dirt floors. They had no electricity or running water and contained a small fire pit in the middle of the room used for heating and cooking. The smell of dried animal dung, which is used as fuel, permeated the air and became a permanent part of our clothing. The smoke is mostly vented through a hole in the ceiling or out the sheet-covered door. These houses may be primitive by our standards, but the rural Nepalese have successfully lived this way for centuries. I wouldn't call these structures the Motel 6s of Nepal, but they are where the locals stay during their travels. My hiking partner, Burt, woke up one morning with a chicken standing on his chest!

Most "tea houses" have a primitive toilet located behind their structure which consists of a hole in the ground with "starting blocks" — usually raised, footprint-shaped features which are used to give the occupant stability during toilet functions. Sitting beside the pit toilet would be a bucket filled with water and a ladle which is to be used for dipping and washing away anything which didn't make a clean escape into the toilet. One can only hope that some "newbie" trekkers didn't think the ladle was to be used as a drinking convenience while taking care of business. Occasionally, we would encounter a sign along the trail which advertised "Western Toilets." My first use of a "Western Toilet" proved to be a little mysterious as well as somewhat frightening. The toilet turned out to be a series of wood planks leading out to a wooden box with a "western" toilet seat attached to the top. This contraption was suspended out over the river so all "deposits" went directly into the water! I guess these western toilets made for a nifty porthole for fishing if you don't mind what you catch! If you didn't like the accommodations and were brave enough to go off into the bushes to do your business, you were almost always assured of bringing back several black, icky-looking leeches attached to strategic areas of your body. I hate it when that happens. Removal of these parasites can be accomplished by placing a lit cigarette against the beast, causing it to drop silently to the ground to wait for the next unsuspecting victim. If you're smart, you'll probably want the extrication procedure done by someone you trust. Most folks just seem to back up to the edge of the trail and, well, you know. That's how we could usually tell we were approaching the next village.

Our trek took us along primitive jungle trails which could become very treacherous when it rained. And it didn't just rain — it would literally *pour*. At one point, I slithered off the trail, nearly going over a forty-foot drop-off. At the last moment, Burt reached out, grabbed me by my backpack, and saved me from a very nasty fall.

Our climb of Fluted Peak went smoothly with our Sirdar replying, "No problem" or "Thirty minutes" to any question we asked. I don't think English was his first, second, *or* third language. "Do you think the sun will come up in the West?" "No problem." And so it went. We're not talking Copernicus here.

On the last leg of our trip, we stopped in beautiful Pokhara where we took a boat across an idyllic lake to a lodge in a beautiful setting with outstanding views of Annapurna and Machhapuchhare Peaks reflected in the water of the lake.

At the lodge, we were able to get our first hot showers in weeks and, believe me, they felt heavenly. After the showers, we gathered in the café for what we hoped would be a pleasant, sit-down meal. We had hardly been seated when suddenly the lights went off and the whole place was enveloped in darkness. Shortly, the waiter came over to our table with a candle and explained, "Lights rest now." They apparently only had enough generating power to run the electricity for a few hours each day. We ended up having a very quaint and delicious candlelight dinner.

One of the highlights of this particular trip was a sightseeing flight we took to the Mount Everest area. Our plane circled around the peaks at an elevation of nearly 20,000 feet, yet we were still 9,000 feet below the summit of Mount Everest! This gave me a new appreciation for the effort required to climb such a monster of a mountain.

Wait, the trip wasn't over yet! Our final adventures occurred at the airport in Kathmandu when we attempted to check in for our flight home. We had overstayed our visa permits by a day and were informed that we would need to pay a "fine." A few "portraits" of U. S. Grant exchanged hands and the officials were again happy campers. Getting a flight from Kathmandu to the US is always a touch-and-go thing as the airlines always have a waiting list for seats. If you don't get on the flight you booked a month ago, you may have to stay in Nepal for a few weeks longer until a seat becomes available. I mention this because now that we had renewed our visa, it was brought to our attention (by the same person who "fixed" our visa problem) that our baggage was grossly overweight. If you don't want to pay the "fee" for being overweight, there are several potential passengers just waiting to claim your seat and tender a small "gift" to the purveyor. The official was more than helpful as he knew someone who knew someone and, for another nominal fee, the overweight charge could be overlooked and we would sail through customs. More US dollars exchanged hands and finally we breathed a sigh of relief as we arrived in the passenger waiting lounge looking forward to returning home.

2nd trip - 1999

On my second trip to Nepal, I was accompanied not only by some of my regular climbing partners, but also by my wife, Diane. Our plan was to hike into the interior of Nepal where we would attempt climbs of Gokyo Ri (17,575 feet) and Parchamo Peak (20,293 feet).

Our trip started in Kathmandu followed by a short but thrilling flight to Lukla aboard a twenty-passenger, Twin Otter aircraft. Once at Lukla, we would retain porters for the remainder of our trek which would be on foot.

A description of the Lukla airport is in order. Forget Dulles International or Chicago O'Hare. The airport runway, which is canted uphill at an angle of around twelve degrees, begins at the edge of a cliff with a 2,000 foot drop-off where the planes first touch down. The angle allows aircraft to use gravity to help them decelerate, since there isn't sufficient length on the runway to coast to a normal stop. There have been several notable fatal crashes during the landing procedure. Taking off involves revving up the engines to full throttle and then literally launching the aircraft off the edge of the cliff at the end of the runway. Needless to say the whole procedure is not for the faint of heart.

We departed Lukla and followed the standard hiking trail which climbers and trekkers use to access the Mount Everest base camp. That first day, we hiked down into the village of Phakding, where we spent the night. This gave everyone a taste of what camp life would be like for the next month. The camp staff (porters) would set up our tents while the cook staff (Sherpas) made "milk tea." They would set up a table for our before-dinner snack of tea and biscuits (cookies). A very "British" flair, if I say so myself — quite civilized.

The next morning we awoke to the singsong sound of "Tatopani" (hot water) being called by the Sherpa staff. Then someone would appear at the door of your tent with your private hot water pan, soon to be followed by the delivery of "morning tea." Shortly thereafter we would be called to breakfast, which was served in the open, unless it was raining. Those "open air" breakfasts were quite invigorating. You could usually see your breath, it was so cold. While we were eating our breakfast, the camp staff would take down all the tents and race ahead with them to set up our next camp. This routine became the norm for our entire trip.

After breakfast, we hiked up to the entrance to Sagarmatha (Everest) National Park where we paid our entry fee.

We were somewhat surprised to find many varieties of food and soft drinks available at the local stores along the way, but then many trekking groups made this same journey every year. It was noticeable that the farther we hiked from Lukla, the more expensive items became.

The pace was always easy, giving us time to slowly acclimatize to the difference in elevation, enjoy the scenery, and absorb some of the local culture. The views changed dramatically with every passing hour. Before long we had our first glimpse of several major Himalayan 8,000 meter peaks, including Mount Everest. A few hours later we arrived in Namche Bazaar, one of the primary trekking destinations in Nepal and the primary trading center for the Khumbu region. Every Saturday, people arrive from as far away as Tibet to sell their wares, creating a kaleidoscope of colors.

Once at Namche Bazaar, we took a rest day to further acclimatize and purchase additional supplies. Our "rest day" consisted of hiking up to the Everest View Hotel located at 12,500 feet. We thought we were in decent shape having done a lot of hiking in Colorado, but we found out otherwise. We literally staggered up the last few feet to the hotel. The view of Mount Everest, Lhotse, and Ama Dablam from the hotel patio made the approximately 1,500 foot gain worthwhile.

While we were strolling around enjoying the scenery, we saw some folks with a telescope watching their friends climbing Ama Dablam, one of the notable Nepal peaks. As we walked past later we heard them exclaim, "There he goes!" as they looked through the telescope. "What happened?" we inquired. "Our friend just para-sailed from the top of Ama Dablam, and he's headed up the valley toward Everest base camp." Even without the use of the telescope, we could see the "bird-man" was circling high above the valley as he winged his way to whatever destination he had chosen. Hmm, I sure would have liked to have known how to parasail back when I was locked up in prison!

After leaving Namche Bazaar, we made the multi-day trek over to our next destination, Gokyo Village, which would be our base camp for climbing Gokyo Ri (17,575 feet).

The village still had about three feet of snow from a recent unusual November snow storm, but it made the scenery something out of a postcard. The lakes in this area are turquoise in color and the snow/water contrast was absolutely breathtaking.

The next day, we climbed up to about 17,450 feet on Gokyo Ri, which was Diane's personal best high point. From our vantage point we had an outstanding view of Cho Oyu, Everest, Lhotse, and Makalu, four of Nepal's ten 8,000 meter peaks (over 26,246 feet).

After leaving Gokyo Village, we retraced our steps back down to Namche Bazaar and several of us hiked back up to the Everest View Hotel. Wow, what a difference having been up at 17,000 feet made for acclimatizing! We breezed up the hill we had gasped at when we tried to hike up it earlier. This time we were able to dart past most of the other hikers even while we were talking.

After a rest, we all departed Namche and headed west toward our next objective, Marchamo Peak. Unfortunately, this more technical peak didn't get climbed. The deep snow we had encountered earlier at high elevations, combined with respiratory illnesses affecting several team members, conspired to abort our attempt on the peak. Sometimes it's better to cut your losses and accept the fact that you'll never get to the summit of every peak you attempt. So, we slowly made our way back to Namche Bazaar and a more civilized standard of living that included warmer temperatures and no snow on the ground. That sure beat sitting in a cold tent and plodding through snow.

We were not without some modern conveniences during our treks. Our group had its own "toilet tent" complete with a collapsible seat, western style, positioned on folding table legs over a deep pit dug by our porters at each of our camps. This seemed like a luxury compared to the usual "starting block" arrangement found in most remote areas. Not only was this a welcome convenience, it was a sanitary necessity due to the density of the trekkers in any given area where we were camped. Late one night, the toilet tent went under attack by a wandering zopkio while one of our members was using the facility. When we arose the next morning, the toilet tent was lying on the ground and the collapsible seat was residing several yards away. No injuries were reported by hiker or zopkio, and the toilet tent survived to serve us again.

After two weeks of trekking, we retraced our route back to Lukla, and dropped off the runway abyss on our flight back to Kathmandu.

Our last meal in Kathmandu consisted of traditional Nepalese food — Dal Bhat (lentils & rice), chicken, mutton, pork, vegetables and a spicy sauce, and heavy duty rice wine that contained enough alcohol that I was literally able to dip a finger in the liquid and then set my fingertip on fire. It didn't hurt at all, but then again, I had also been drinking the wine. Even Diane, who generally keeps a more level head on her than I do, participated in the fire show. That stuff was sure to clean out your sinuses!

We finished our trip by taking a rickshaw over to the Yak & Yeti Hotel for a farewell drink and a look at how the "other half" travel. Diane was especially enthralled by the ladies restroom: flush toilets, soft toilet paper, three sinks in front of a mirror (although, who really wants to see what you look like after several weeks of trekking?) and a hot air hand drier. Life is good and the wife is a happy camper again!

Next day we flew to Bangkok and our favorite Thailand hotel, the Amari. Diane and I spent several days on the island of Phuket just doing some serious R&R while she tried to recover from a persistent respiratory ailment. While there, we were able to go into a pharmacy and get just about any type of "controlled substance" we needed to cure her cough. They only use doctors when you're very, very sick. Usually the pharmacist just does the diagnosis and doles out a few of these and a bottle of that without any fanfare.

I especially liked the nude bathing beaches until I happened upon the one for older people (my age). Oh, well, the ice cream sundaes were outstanding so one out of two isn't bad. Sadly, I think the place where we stayed was destroyed during the Tsunami of 2002.

Back in Bangkok from Phuket, we gorged ourselves at the scrumptious smorgasbord at the Amari Hotel. I had seven scoops of their rum raisin ice cream before they gave me "the look" and I didn't have the courage to go back for more.

Summit approach on Chopicalqui

Chapter 14 - Peru

Climbs in the Cordillera Blanca

Pisco , Chopicalqui, Huascarán Sur

1988

"Rappel farther off to your right," I suggested to Dave Cooper, a member of our climbing group. We were in the Colorado mountains doing rappel practice on a steep snow slope for an upcoming Peru climbing expedition. Dave moved to his right as I had suggested and started to rappel. "Aiee!" he screamed in horror as he suddenly crashed through a concealed snow cornice which I had intentionally neglected to warn him was there. A torrent of snow cascaded down on him from the now-broken cornice as he finished the rappel. "Why didn't you tell me there was a cornice there?" he demanded, looking at me wide-eyed. I couldn't answer with a straight face after seeing him standing there, still attached to the rappel rope, looking like Frosty the Snowman. "I meant *my* right," I replied after finally regaining my composure.

I didn't know Dave very well other than the fact that he was from the UK. Those English blokes seem to have a really dry sense of humor. This was our first outing together as a group but I had already noticed that Dave seemed a little more reserved than the other guys. I thought that I could add a little levity to his day by convincing him that it would be easier if he rappelled off at a different place than I had. I certainly hoped that he could take a joke or I was going to be in deep trouble. Thankfully, he laughed after he realized that I had tricked him. I knew that was going to cost me a pint at the pub later in the day.

Unfortunately for him, Dave has been the recipient of several other of my dirty tricks over the years. He still hasn't forgiven me for forgetting to tell him about the two large rocks I stuck into his pack when he left it unattended briefly during one of our hiking trips. Honestly, I *really* did forget they were there!

We began our trip to Peru with flights from Denver to Miami and on to Lima. From there we took the eight hour express bus to Huaraz. Huaraz is an amazing place, located close to the Cordillera Blanca range, which is home to over twenty 6,000 meter peaks (mountains higher than 19,684 feet). It would become our base of operations during the trip. Our plan was to climb Pisco (18,870 feet) and Chopicalqui (20,817 feet) followed by the highest peak in Peru, Huascarán Sur (22,132 feet).

We started the expedition by climbing Pisco, as it was the lowest and easiest peak on our itinerary. Even an "easy" peak requires good conditioning, route finding skills, and some technical ability. This ascent would give us an opportunity to work the "bugs" out of our climbing routine as well as provide us with a period of acclimatization prior to going for the higher peaks we were planning to climb. If anyone was going to get sick from food or altitude, it would usually show up during the first climb of the expedition. We were lucky and everyone appeared to have avoided picking up Montezuma's Revenge on the flight down to Peru or during our brief stay in Lima.

Our approach took us up to our base camp at 15,600 feet where we spent an additional day arranging our climbing equipment and becoming acclimatized. Some of the group hiked up higher on the mountain to get in even more acclimatization elevation.

Dave wasn't the only expedition member I managed to put in the "trick bag." During one of our rest days in between climbs, we were lounging around camp waiting for our cook to deliver the daily lunch bags. When the bags arrived, I noticed that one of our climbers, Lulu, was nowhere to be seen. Being the helpful soul that I am, I offered to keep her lunch bag until she returned. No sooner had the delivery person departed than I decided that things around camp were a little too subdued. *I wonder what I could do to liven things up? Perhaps a little surprise in Lulu's lunch bag could do the trick. Get it? Trick + Bag!*

It didn't take long for me to hatch up a really mischievous scheme. Why not remove the contents of Lulu's lunch bag and replace it with something which had more fiber? The logical choice was a selection of those interesting-looking, dark brown, desiccated donkey droppings lying on the ground around camp. I quickly emptied the contents of Lulu's lunch into my bag and refilled hers with an even half-dozen of the choicest-looking, dried-up morsels from the ground. I was even nice enough to replace her napkin and dessert back into the bag. What a guy. I thought the finishing touch would be to give the bag to Dave, since he and Lulu seemed to be closer than skin on a snake. All I had to do now was sit back and wait for the fun to begin.

Before long, Lulu returned to camp and noticed me sitting there eating my lunch. "Did they bring lunch while I was gone?" she inquired. I held up my sandwich as proof positive that indeed lunch had been delivered. "Dave has your bag," I explained in between bites of my sandwich. The now-unsuspecting Dave produced the lunch bag for his sweetie and they sat together with the idea of having a nice romantic lunch. Lulu opened her bag, stared inside with a puzzled look on her face, and demanded from Dave, "What the hell is this?" as she reached in and produced one of the briquettes, which by now had become a little ripe after sitting in the sun inside her lunch bag. Lulu then made the mistake of holding the offensive article up to her nose and immediately proclaimed, "This smells like shit!" Hey, she's pretty astute. By this time I had really lost it and was laughing so hard I had to spit out a mouthful of my sandwich. Lulu gave me a dirty look and threw the donkey turd at me. The next thing I knew, she was running toward me, hell bent for election, reaching into the bag, and throwing the turds at me as she went. I allowed her to catch me and confessed that it was Dave's idea to put the turds in her lunch bag. Of course, Dave vociferously denied any complicity in the deed. I returned the rest of her lunch to her and offered up my dessert as a peace offering.

The next morning we got the usual "alpine start" using headlamps to illuminate the way. Pisco was climbed quite regularly, so we were easily able to follow in the footprints of previous climbers. There were already two other groups ahead of us on the mountain, their headlamps looking like fireflies in the distance. The presence of the other groups gave us a perspective regarding the distance we needed to climb.

We made it to the summit about mid-morning and were treated to cloudless deep blue skies and another spectacular mountain vista. We could see the impressive face of Artesonraju off in the distance. I remarked that I knew that I would have to come back and climb it some day.

When I returned to climb Pisco again ten years later, much had changed. Due to the ravages of significant glacial melting, climbing Pisco was no longer as easy as it was in 1988. We found that the slopes which we had easily scaled back then were now much steeper. The summit had separated from the slopes below and was ringed by a significant bergschrund which would have required ice climbing skills to surmount. I imagine that Pisco, as well as other Peruvian peaks, will likely become much more difficult to climb as the glaciers continue to retreat, creating technical challenges.

We left the slopes of Pisco far behind and proceeded to our next destination, Chopicalqui. The climbing on Chopicalqui was rated as moderately difficult, involving 55 to 60 degree angle snow slopes as well as being almost two thousand feet higher than Pisco.

The climb went as planned and was much more interesting as we encountered several crevassed areas as well as some technical climbing. Again, the views from the summit were outstanding, including our next objective, Huascarán Sur.

The only excitement on the climb occurred when everyone on the rope team except me had crossed a large crevasse. I somehow

155

managed to hook my crampon behind me on a piece of webbing which was dangling down from my harness. I immediately did a face plant right on to the top of my ice axe, resulting in a very bloody nose (which I thought I had broken). I hollered at the other members of the rope team to stop where they were as I was momentarily unable to see where I was going. After a few minutes I was able to stem the flow of blood and get my wits about me, and managed to cross the crevasse safely. I took a well-deserved ribbing about being a klutz. The next day we broke camp and returned to Huaraz for a hard-earned rest and some real food.

We departed Huaraz, standing up in the back of a large commercial truck, on our way to the Huascarán Sur trailhead. By the time we arrived, the dust from the truck's wheels had nearly asphyxiated us. Everyone was ready to quit riding and start hiking after that bone-jarring, dusty experience.

We hiked up to an area below the toe of the glacier where we set up camp. The plan was to start out in the early morning as two separate rope teams. It's an interesting exercise to see who doesn't want to be on a rope team with someone else because they think their chance of making the summit might be compromised. We obviously didn't want all the least experienced climbers on the same rope team, so some compromises had to be made. As it turned out, I wasn't that enamored with the experience level of one of the members of my rope team and they were probably not enamored with my bitching about rope team travel.

As we began climbing, our rope team began lagging behind the first team which was comprised of a stronger group of climbers. Our team was suffering from some residual effects of an earlier intestinal bug and didn't have the stamina necessary to make the climb. As a result we did not reach the summit.

We returned to Huaraz and prepared to make our journey back to the US. I hoped to return in a year or so to Peru for another attempt on Huascarán Sur with a team of climbers that I had previously climbed with. Unfortunately, that never happened and I have heard that the mountain is in terrible shape as a result of glacial melting, and the route that we attempted is now impossible to climb.

1998

Artesonraju is one of the most beautiful peaks in the Cordillera Real. Its exquisite pyramidal shape combined with a truly spectacular south east face draw the human eye to its splendor. It is rumored that this is the peak which appears at the beginning of Paramount Pictures movies. I had seen Artesonraju from the summit of Pisco Peak in 1988 and had vowed to return someday to attempt the climb.

Artesonraju

Our plan was to climb Artesonraju (19,676 feet) via the normal south east face route, a 2,000 foot, 50 degree, steep snow slope. Our team, including Randy, Dave Cooper, Ginni Greer, and I, arrived at the starting point for the climb, Laguna (Lake) Parón, where we donned our packs for the hike up to our high camp on the moraine. Within the first few minutes we realized that we had a problem. The water level of the lake had risen and covered the normal hiking path along its perimeter. This forced us to climb over and around numerous large boulders just a few feet above the lake. A slip here would have been disastrous, sending the climber plunging into the water weighed down with a pack like a boat

157

anchor. This obstacle took several difficult hours to traverse, but finally we arrived at a point where the water wasn't covering the trail. When we returned this way after attempting the peak, the water level had dropped significantly and we were able to stroll along the same terrain which had caused us so much difficulty earlier.

We left our high camp in the dark on the second day and hiked across the glacier, headlamps lighting the way. To my dismay, I soon discovered that the glacier had many hidden pockets of water concealed by a thin layer of ice. I stepped into one of these features and nearly went up to my knee in ice water. Not a good way to start a climb. We had to stop while I removed my boot and changed to dry socks. By the time we were ready to continue hiking, it was light enough to see without our headlamps. I think when you have a problem at the beginning of a climb, it's often wiser to turn around and try again the next day. That's probably what we should have done.

We reached the steep face of the climb, where our progress slowed considerably due to more challenging climbing conditions. Because we had not camped at the normal start of the climb which was up on the glacier, we wasted a few hours making the traverse over from our moraine camp. This, along with other delays, prevented us from making the summit. By the time we decided to turn around, it was already late afternoon. The altitude, cold temperatures, and amount of effort we had expended all conspired to make us not be as careful as we should have been. At one point, I was ready to rappel and Dave noticed that I had only put one strand of rope through my rappel device, a potentially fatal mistake. In our exhaustion, everyone was making small, stupid mistakes which could have led to a serious or fatal accident.

Our descent took longer than we had anticipated and all too soon we found ourselves attempting to negotiate our way down the peak in the dark. At one point my headlamp slipped off my helmet and cascaded off into the darkness, causing us to move even more slowly in the dark. Luckily, Ginni had remained at the moraine camp and was able to help guide us down by using our two-way radios. We had been unable to see the dangers which lurked below us in the form of cliffs and crevasses. We finally reached our moraine camp around 10:00 p.m. very tired, hungry, and dehydrated. My water bottle and food had frozen in my pack and had become totally worthless.

We awoke the next morning completely exhausted from our summit attempt. My back, which had required surgery a few years earlier, was causing me considerable pain, and I was unable to carry my pack back out to the trailhead. Thanks to the efforts of my climbing partners and a porter who had accompanied us, I was able to stagger back to the trailhead.

We returned to Lima where I met up with Diane, who had flown down to join us. Diane and I had made plans to hike to Machu Picchu on the Inca trail after the others returned to Denver. We all stayed at the same hotel that night in Lima. Diane brought birthday cupcakes and candles to celebrate Randy's and Ginni's July birthdays. Everything was going as planned until we lit all the candles. It seems that Diane had supplied "trick" candles which cannot be blown out without a lot of effort. The problem arose when they started sending up a column of smoke (there really were a lot of candles on the cakes) toward the smoke detector. Disaster was averted as we were able to open the hotel windows allowing the smoke to escape until we could smother the candles with a wet washcloth. We thought we might have to pitch the flaming cakes out the window.

Diane and I spent several fun-filled days hiking the Inca Trail and arrived in Machu Picchu. Our reservation at Machu Picchu Sanctuary Lodge allowed us to explore the ruins after most of the visitors had departed for the day. This part of the trip was perhaps the most memorable for me. These magnificent structures were even more spectacular in person than we had imagined they would be.

Climbing Condoriri

Chapter 15 - Bolivia

Climbs in the Cordillera Real

Huayna Potosi, Illimani, & Condoriri

My expeditions to South America, as well as to other international destinations, usually begin with weeks and weeks of training on the fourteen thousand foot peaks here in Colorado. This type of training generally provides us the conditioning necessary to climb peaks in the eighteen to twenty thousand foot range. And so it was that I, along with my Bolivia climbing partners, Dave and Stanley, made numerous trips to Pikes Peak, Longs Peak, and other "fourteeners" (peaks with an elevation greater than 14,000 feet) within a day's drive of the Denver area.

At long last, departure day arrived and we were convinced that we could "hit the ground running" in Bolivia due to our advanced state of conditioning. We were scheduled to fly to Miami, arriving in the late evening, and then depart for South America on the "red eye" for La Paz, Bolivia. I can never deal with this staying up all night and all day travel stuff. No matter how hard I try, I can't sleep in those back-breaking airline lounge chairs or the sardine-sized economy airline torture devices they refer to as "seats." Being just 5 foot 4, I shouldn't complain. Dave Cooper is 6 foot 6, and he arrives nearly paralyzed from the cramped seating after a long flight.

We arrived at the La Paz airport around mid-morning, dragging our droopy-eyed bodies through the terminal and eventually out through customs. Thankfully, we only had to experience three time zone changes between Denver and La Paz so it wasn't as bad as flying to Nepal or Africa where you're not even sure what day it is. What we hadn't taken into consideration about our "advanced state of conditioning" was the fact that the La Paz airport is located at over 13,300 feet, only a paltry eight hundred feet lower than one of our conditioning hikes, Pikes Peak (14,110 feet). We probably should have spent more time camping on top of Pikes Peak as we were all feeling the effects of coming from near sea level in Miami to 13,300 feet in the space of just a few short hours.

We arrived outside the airline terminal and were overwhelmed by the view which awaited us. Two of Bolivia's most majestic peaks, Illimani (21,122 feet) and Huayna Potosi (19,974 feet) dominated the horizon. These were two of the peaks we had come to climb, so the view was especially impressive to us. These mountains looked *really, really* big.

Our immediate need was to locate our hotel so we could unload our baggage and then head out for a decent late lunch. We arrived at the hotel, got our rooms assigned, and decided we needed more training so we chose to carry our luggage up the stairs to our rooms on the fifth floor instead of using the elevator. After only one flight of stairs I was gasping like a smoker with a three-pack-a-day habit; that was another "advanced conditioning" wake-up call. Once I made it to my room, I needed to lie down on the bed and rest for several minutes before I could even think about eating. How in the world was I going to make it to the top of a 20,000 foot mountain if I had to lie down after climbing only five flights of stairs?

The next thing I knew, Dave was banging on the door, wanting to get something to eat. We discovered a restaurant close by so I wasn't subjected to more demoralizing high altitude walking.

I ordered a cerveza with my meal in an attempt to mitigate the effects of the dry high altitude air by rehydrating (that's my story and I'm sticking to it). Drinking beer at altitude can be overwhelming, but drinking beer at altitude after being up for nearly 24 hours was nearly a disaster for me. I jerked awake barely in time to avoid doing a face plant in my food, which had arrived while I was zoning out. We finished our meal and made a bee-line back to the hotel for some much needed rest. Zzzzzzzz.

Our first objective was a climb of Huayna Potosi which has easy access from La Paz. We were able to obtain transportation to our trailhead at Laguna Zongo.

This is the point when the shoe leather hits the ground and you stand there wondering if there could possibly be anything still left at home, including the kitchen sink. Our packs were, as usual, enormous. You would think that with all the times we've done big mountains we could cut down the size of our loads. Well, nothing to do but "cowboy up," put on the packs, and begin setting one foot in front of the other while thinking about something other than that fifty pound gorilla riding on my back.

Huayna Potosi

We had decided to camp at the edge of the glacier the first night, which meant that we had several hours and several hundred feet of climbing to go before we could set up camp and get some hot water and food going. The hours seemed to drag on forever as we toiled under the hot Bolivian sun but we arrived at our camping destination just before the sun set. The temperature quickly plummeted out of sight. You've never seen a bunch of white guys set up camp any faster than we did. Brrrr.

The next morning we ate a leisurely breakfast and packed up camp for the hike up to our high camp on the glacier. We spent the remaining portion of the day hiking and discussing tomorrow's climb to the summit.

The night passed all too quickly and the sound of the alarm woke me at our agreed-upon 3:00 a.m. *This is crazy! The sun hasn't even thought about rising and it's colder than hell outside and not much warmer inside the tent.* I pulled my sleeping bag up higher around my head in an attempt to drown out the annoying noise of the alarm and conserve what little warmth I had captured inside my sleeping bag. I needed to get my clothes inside the sleeping bag so they wouldn't be freezing cold when I put them on. Did I mention that this is a crazy sport? I lay there for several minutes hoping against hope that Dave would be the first one to get up and start the stove so we could have a hot drink. What a rat — I know he just pretended to be asleep.

We eventually got on our gear, boiled water, ate, and rolled out of the tent under one of the most brilliant, star-filled skies you'll ever see. Perhaps this isn't such a crazy sport after all. We roped up and started the long, slow climb up the glacier. Each of us was in his own little circular setting which was the area illuminated by his headlamp reflecting back from the snow. *Crunch, crunch —* our crampons made a distinctive noise as we carefully placed one foot in front of the other on the still-frozen surface of the snow.

Dave was our climbing leader and was at the front of the rope team. He had climbed the peak before and knew where some of the crevasses were located. Occasionally I could hear Dave shout "Crevasse!" as he encountered one of the gaping slots. Until I arrived at the crevasse, I was never sure just how monstrous it might be, so I always had to be ready to catch the climbers in front of me should they plunge into its depths. I always hoped that, once the team member in front of me had passed the crevasse, he hadn't forgotten that I was still in danger of falling!

After what seemed like an eternity, the sun finally peeked over the horizon as we crested a long section of the climb. We were finally able to take our first break of the morning. It hadn't warmed up much since we left camp and our feet were frozen. We all sat down on our packs and removed our boots in an attempt to restore some warmth to our numb feet.

Shortly, we resumed the climb over easy snow slopes until we finally reached the long summit ridge. I wasn't paying much attention — just watching the climber in front of me — when I noticed a hole in the snow right at my feet. I looked down through the hole, stopped abruptly, and just about fainted. We were walking along a corniced ridge with about 3,000 feet of air below our feet! The ridge looked well travelled, but it was still an alarming feeling.

As we approached the summit, a guided group of climbers appeared, ascending the slope to our left via a different route than we had taken. Instead of waiting for us to finish reaching the summit (since we were on the ridge ahead of them) they rudely crossed over our rope, forcing us to stop where we were. We were concerned that someone from either group might trip over the rope and fall, pulling everyone down the mountain. One member of our group became greatly agitated about the lack of etiquette shown by the guided group and began hurling insults at them, which they returned. After a short discussion among our team, we concluded that since we were only a few minutes away from the actual summit, there was no real reason to sit there and wait for the guided group to vacate that spot (which they did not seem predisposed to do). We decided that it was time for us to start back down to our camp before the snow bridges across the crevasses became unstable or a fight broke out between the groups. Our descent back to camp was uneventful, and we arrived somewhat disappointed and tired but without any crevasse falls.

The next morning we packed our camp away and began the day-long journey back to the trailhead. It always feels good to get back to town after having been out on the mountain for a few days and to enjoy a more civilized life with a hot shower, cold cerveza, and a soft bed. In addition, your climbing partners usually end up smelling much better.

Illimani was to be our next objective. We had become acclimatized to the higher elevation on Huayna Potosi so we thought we would now be able to climb more efficiently. We had also decided to hire some local porters to assist us with load-carrying, which would make the climbing easier.

Hiking in to Illimani

The hike up to our base camp at 15,500 feet was enjoyable, especially since we didn't have to carry the heavy packs. This time we arrived in the early afternoon and soon had our camp established. Since there were still several more hours of daylight remaining, Dave and I decided to get in a few pitches of waterfall ice climbing. It didn't take us long to realize that ice climbing at 15,500 feet required a lot more stamina that we were used to expending at lower altitudes. After climbing only one pitch, we looked at each other and agreed that the remaining hours of the day could be better put to use by resting.

The next day saw us moving camp up to an area on the mountain referred to as the Nido de Condores (Condors Nest) at

18,370 feet. From there, we were able to study the possible routes for tomorrow's summit bid. I spotted what looked like a very straightforward couloir which appeared to climb directly up to the summit ridge. I pointed this route out to Dave who disagreed with my choice. That he disagreed wasn't unusual, as everyone will see the route that looks best to them. I persisted with *my* choice while downgrading Dave's route as being unimaginative and boring. Mother Nature helped make the decision for us. While I was pointing at my route, it totally disappeared as a massive avalanche swept the face. I conceded that perhaps my route wasn't the best choice after all, but at least it wasn't boring.

As usual, we arose well before sunrise and started up the mountain. We attempted to find our chosen route using headlamps. I say "attempted" because, somewhere along the way, I made a wrong turn and we found ourselves on a very steep, icy slope without wearing our crampons and not knowing which way to go. We later determined that this was in the area where a Chilean group of climbers had slipped and fallen to their deaths a few years earlier. Wisely, we decided to put on crampons and wait until there was enough light to determine the correct direction to proceed. Thankfully, it wasn't long before we were able to continue climbing, this time with Dave pointing out the correct route. This mistake cost us a couple of hours of lost climbing time. This fact would become important later in the climb.

As the morning wore on, we approached what appeared to be a significant ridge leading up toward the summit. I was at the front of the rope team and started climbing up the ridge which didn't look as if anyone had previously climbed on it. I wondered if I was going the wrong way again. I stopped to consider my options and noticed that there were tracks in the snow below me which seemed to bypass the ridge. I pointed this out to the rest of the group and we decided to reverse our direction and follow the track below us.

After about an hour of following the tracks, we suddenly came to a very large crevasse which was blocking our progress. We decided that we could probably go around the crevasse and climb up a steep snow face, then traverse above the crevasse back over toward our original ridge. It was either that or lose several hours by going back to the start of the ridge. Going back didn't seem to be an

166

option, as we didn't think we could make the summit and get back to camp in time to meet our porters later in the day. Our arrangement for the porters to meet us at Nido de Condores in the evening on our summit day was beginning to present us with a time problem.

I volunteered to lead the steep snow face, traverse over to the ridge, and set up an anchor to belay up the rest of the group. The climb turned out to be more than I bargained for. The "protection" I placed while making the traverse above the crevasse was a joke. The only purpose it served was to keep the rope from hanging over the lip of the slope I was traversing; it definitely would not have kept me from going into the crevasse if I had fallen. By the time I realized that I was out on a limb, it was impossible to reverse what I had climbed. The result of all of this was that I was climbing tentatively and took an inordinate amount of time to complete the route. This time lapse, combined with the time it took me to bring up the remaining climbers, ate up several more of our remaining climbing hours. Hindsight is 20/20, so it was evident that we made a bad decision not continuing up the original ridge.

We slowly advanced toward the summit which still loomed about a thousand feet above us. It soon became apparent that we simply didn't have enough time to reach the summit and then return to camp where we were to meet the porters before dark. The decision to turn around was difficult to make, but it made good sense since climbing back down the route in the dark would have been very dangerous. Not everyone was happy with the decision to turn around since we had come so far to get to this point, but you don't always get your summit. It took a lot longer to return to camp than I would have guessed, and it was already getting dark by the time we arrived. Without the navigation errors, we would have been successful in reaching the top. However, we were all back to camp safely and that was the most important thing.

After returning to La Paz, Dave and I decided that we needed a break from climbing before we went to attempt our next peak, Condoriri. Part of our Bolivian agenda was to go to Lake Titicaca on the Peru-Bolivia border. If we thought mountain climbing was where all the adventures lay, then we were in for a surprising next few days.

After Dave and I checked into our hotel room we decided to spend the remainder of the day by taking a small boat ride out to the Isla del Sol (Island of the Sun). The scenery during the trip was everything we had expected and more. After a few hours of exploring the island, we boarded our boat for the return trip back to Copacabana. We were about a mile from shore when the motor started sputtering and then finally quit. Silence. We looked at each other and then at our "Captain" (this was a very small motor boat). "No gasolina," he stated. I pondered our fate, realizing that we were still quite a distance from shore and that I could not swim. "No problema," the captain announced, whereupon he produced a set of oars which he summarily handed to us. "Inicio de Remo" he said with a smile. I think that was the name of a woman I used to date. The Captain made rowing motions with his hands so Dave and I slowly propelled our disabled craft back toward the shore. "No reembolsos" the Captain replied upon docking the boat when I suggested that we get our money back. Well, at least he was still smiling. All I had to show for the ride were some nasty blisters from rowing. Nothing a few cervezas couldn't take care of.

We arrived back at the hotel in time for the evening meal. I'm not sure what they served, but I had to keep my knife in one hand and my fork in the other in order to protect myself from whatever it was that looked up at me with glazed eyes from my plate. Everyone else in the restaurant, including Dave, seemed to be enjoying their meal, but I found mine utterly unappetizing and couldn't convince myself to bring the fork up to my mouth.

I wasn't looking forward to going to bed hungry, so I searched throughout the hotel but was unable to locate a vending machine which might have contained something which might be found in the USDA food pyramid. Perhaps a nice hot shower would help me sleep and forget the dismal meal. OK, the water wasn't hot, only lukewarm. I jumped out of the shower, running across the room on my tip toes. By this time I was shivering uncontrollably. I think I was in the first stage of hypothermia. *I need to find the thermostat and turn on the heat. Oh, oh, these rooms don't have thermostats; in fact they don't have any type of heating device. If*

I don't want to freeze to death I'll have to put my down jacket on to get warm. The hell with it, I'm going to bed.

I didn't get much sleep and ended up wearing my down jacket to bed with a bath towel wrapped around my head in an attempt to keep warm. I think I spent the night in the fetal position. Dave thought I looked like someone from India. Very funny. I shivered so much I think I lost five pounds over the course of the night. Dave, being from the UK, thought the rooms were too hot. Those Brits — go figure.

We couldn't leave Copacabana soon enough the next morning and we definitely didn't have the courage to confront the breakfast fare. Mountain climbing was beginning to look better with each passing hour.

We'd had enough of "city" life, so we resupplied, hooked back up with Stanley, and headed for the third peak we hoped to climb, Condoriri (18,530 feet). We established our base camp in a beautiful valley near the edge of Lake Condoriri at 16,000 feet. In the evening we were treated to the silhouette of llamas outlined along the ridge crest. This place was a far cry from Copacabana and Lake Titicaca.

During the night we experienced a minor wind and rain event which proved cataclysmic for one member of our party. The tent which I had loaned Stanley suffered a terminal zipper failure, which caused him to freeze his ass off all night. The next morning he declared that he was done with the climb and hiked back to the nearest town where he found someone with a motorcycle to give him a ride back to La Paz. He later told us that he thought the motorcycle driver was either crazy or doing hallucinogenic mushrooms because of the insane way he drove.

The following morning, Dave and I began the climb by ascending a long, steep couloir which would lead us up to the main Condoriri snowfield. When we were about half-way up the couloir, we were startled to hear the sound of rocks cascading down from far above us. We immediately took cover to avoid being struck. We began to wonder if the gully was too dangerous to ascend. As we cautiously resumed our ascent, we heard the faint cry of "Rock!" which was followed by another volley of rocks. Apparently there was another group of climbers above us who were causing the rockfall. We shouted back up to them so they would know we were in the line of fire, and then continued climbing up the couloir as rapidly as possible. The other group waited for us to catch up to them. After that, we all kept close together to avoid anyone being struck by rockfall.

Upon reaching the main snowfield, Dave and I were able to put some distance between ourselves and the other group which had stopped to rest at the top of the gully. Soon, we ascended over a ridge and approached a steep snow slope which allowed access to the long summit ridge. A couple of the faster members of the other group came into sight not far behind us. We didn't want to be subjected to another round of falling objects, so we pulled out our ice tools and started soloing the snow slope. I can't remember when I've had so much fun climbing a snow slope. The snow was a perfect consistency, so the only problem was our lack of oxygen at this altitude. We had to stop occasionally just to catch our breath.

We reached the base of the summit ridge and paused for a rest break before getting out our rope for the final climb up a rock rib and on to the summit ridge. But then we made a critical mistake. The two climbers from the other group arrived at our rest spot and decided to continue on up the rock rib in front of us. In the process they again showered us with rocks by not climbing carefully. We retreated back out of the danger zone to keep from getting pummeled. By this time, the remaining members of their group arrived and they immediately began to climb the rock rib, sending down yet another barrage of rocks. All of this activity took an inordinate amount of time, while Dave and I sat twiddling our thumbs waiting for them to get their group up on the summit ridge so we could climb. By the time they were all up on the ridge, the weather had started to look questionable. We decided that, given the weather and the fact that this large group was again in front of us, it would be smarter and safer to retreat.

In retrospect, we should have continued up the rock rib instead of allowing the larger group to get in front of us. We were soon to learn that European climbing groups routinely shove their way in front of other climbing teams without hesitation. I think this mentality results from the greater concentration of climbers where they come from. It's a "take no prisoners" form of climbing.

Perhaps that is why they are more successful on peaks than we seem to be. My personal preference is to climb in areas where you are unlikely to encounter another group, but that's getting harder and harder to find these days. The net result was that we allowed ourselves to lose any chance at the summit. We again downclimbed the steep snow slope and made our way over to the couloir and down to our base camp by the lake, thankful that the other group was not above us in the gully.

We had just crawled into our tent and were enjoying the comfort of our down sleeping bags when Dave declared, "Man, would I like to have a cerveza right now!" "Yeah, dream on," I replied.

I'm not kidding – five minutes later we heard, "¡Señor! ¡Señor!" followed by the sound of someone scratching on the tent door. We unzipped the tent and looked out. Here's this guy kneeling in front of our tent with a case of cold beer in front of him that he's carried from god-knows-where and he's selling for a buck a can. You talk about a cheap date — a half can of beer at 16,000 feet and I could hardly sit up. Dave was kind enough to finish my beer and his too. Hey, what are friends for?

We returned to La Paz with the intent of climbing some other peaks near the town of Sorata. Fate again intervened as I began to have a recurrence of my back problems. We spent a couple of days playing tourist in Sorata before returning to La Paz.

Looking back, it seems we rolled "snake eyes" on almost everything we attempted. We did, however, have fun rolling the dice.

Ascending Grossglockner

Chapter 16 - European Blitz

Climbs in the Alps

Matterhorn, Mount Blanc, Grossglockner

I had planned to return to South America for a climb of Huascarán Sur, the highest mountain in Peru, but the Sendero Luminoso (Shining Path) Terrorists blew up the hotel in Huaraz where I was planning to stay, so instead I ended up going to Europe with my longtime friends Burt Falk and Jim Scott. We rented a Mercedes station wagon for our in-country transportation and I think we had more fun with a lot less pain than the Peru expedition would have involved. See, there is a silver lining to those dark clouds.

Our adventure took us to Switzerland where we planned to climb the Matterhorn, then on to France for an attempt on Mt. Blanc, over to Germany for a hike up the Zugspitze, followed by a climb in Lichtenstein. After that, we headed to Yugoslavia to climb Triglav Mountain (now the highest mountain in *Slovenia*) and finally Grossglockner in Austria. Each of these mountains is the highest point in their respective countries. Burt was "collecting" country highpoints at the time, so that's how our itinerary developed.

We initially headed to Zermatt for the Matterhorn but were foiled by inclement weather, so we buzzed through the tunnel and ended up later that evening in Chamonix, France. It's best not to show up late in Chamonix without a hotel reservation on a Friday night. You guessed it, no rooms available. We inquired at numerous places and were finally directed to a "rooming house" way off the main drag where it might be possible to obtain a room. Using our best French (of which we had none) and our worst English, we managed to communicate our desperate need for accommodations to the proprietor. "No problem," he replied. We paid our francs and were each given a bucket and directed to our dingy abode. The bucket was to be filled with water to be poured down the loo after you did your thing. I suspect these rooms were normally rented by the hour for nefarious purposes. Well, it beat sleeping on the cold street.

Our next problem was getting something to eat. We weren't too picky, so our expectations were fairly low. Good thing. Our meager dinner consisted of cheese fondue in some funky bar; not really the ideal kind of meal to prepare to go out and climb a big mountain like Mt. Blanc.

Early the next morning, we were out of the hovel before first light and on our way to catch the téléphérique (cable car) to the Aiguille du Midi where we would begin our climb. This not-to-be-missed ride rises more than 9,000 feet in less than half an hour, almost faster than a speeding bullet.

Once at the Aiguille du Midi, we donned mountain climbing equipment and set out from the ice cave at the top of the téléphérique to begin our climb.

Things seemed to be going well until Jim, who was roped to Burt at the time, slipped while ascending a steep snowfield which Burt had just crested. Burt's initial reaction was to drop his ice axe and grab Jim's rope, intending to arrest his fall. Needless to say, both climbers slid down the slope, coming to a rest in a safe spot at the bottom. Later we discussed the event and Burt was stunned that he didn't go into self-arrest position with his ice axe — something he had often trained to do — instead of grabbing the rope. Just one of those reflex things.

Ice cave at the top of Aiguille du Midi

The remainder of the climb went without incident until we got high up on the mountain and encountered jet-stream-force winds and horizontal snow which encouraged us to beat a hasty retreat back to the Aiguille du Midi. We caught the last cable car back down to town and returned to the backstreet hovel. We departed Chamonix the next day for a quick trip back to Zermatt, Switzerland and the Matterhorn.

Conditions on the Matterhorn had improved dramatically, so we made plans for an attempt two days hence. We visited the local guide's climbing office and made our arrangements for our climb. While we were there, a Japanese climber arrived who had apparently been told he would be able to climb the Matterhorn with a guide the following day. As it turned out, the following day was a "guides holiday" — no climbing. The Japanese climber was absolutely incensed about this development. He suddenly slammed the top of the counter very loudly with his open palm and screamed, "This office," (another slam), "This office promise me I climb!" Another loud slam of the counter top at which time the woman running the office looks up at us in despair as the climber begins screaming in Japanese. You could just imagine this chap with one of those long Samurai swords getting ready to cut off someone's head. Cowards that we are, we disappeared out the door faster than my paycheck on a Friday night. We never heard how this disagreement was resolved.

The next day we made our way up to the Hornli Hut on the flank of the Matterhorn in preparation for our climb.

Our climb of the peak started before daylight (along with a couple of thousand other climbers, or so it seemed) and had us back at the hut in time for lunch. This turned out to be a very crowded climb, exacerbated by a logjam of climbers attempting to ascend and descend a fixed rope above what is called the "shoulder" of the peak. It was a take-no-prisoners free-for-all. From the shoulder, it was only a short scramble to the summit. The Matterhorn is one of the "must do" mountaineering peaks. Even with the crowds, it is a peak that you can take pride in having climbed.

Matterhorn

One of the more interesting, or I should say ghoulish, venues we visited while in Zermatt was the local cemetery. The description on the headstones of the graves gives you a picture of the dangers of

175

climbing the mountain. According to local climbers, there have been several hundred deaths on the mountain caused by everything from rock fall to freezing to death in blizzards or just plain falling.

I need to mention a truly decadent dessert we happened to discover while we were in Switzerland. This treat was called a "Coupe Denmark." It's a large serving of vanilla ice cream topped with real hot chocolate sauce (*Swiss* chocolate, of course) and whipped cream. It comes served with a "gravy boat" containing *more* hot chocolate. I would like to be able to say that my friend Jim, who was avoiding all things decadent, didn't get weak and join Burt and me in overindulging in multiple Coupe Denmarks, but alas, that is not the case. I've been able to keep Jim's secret all these years, but now the cat is out of the bag. Sorry, Jim.

We were able to take the Autobahn during our drive in Germany for our climb of the Zugspitze. I had never driven on a road where they didn't have a posted speed limit, so this turned out to be exhilarating, to say the least. As I mentioned, we were driving a large Mercedes station wagon with a powerful engine. I was tooling along at about 110 mph, passing another vehicle, when I looked in the rear view mirror to see a vehicle rapidly approaching from behind, flashing its lights for me to get out of the way. I put the pedal to the metal and was just barely able to get out of the passing lane when someone in a Porsche absolutely blew the doors off the Mercedes. They must have been going 150 mph!

The climb itself got off to a "rocky" start since we were not permitted to ascend the peak using a trail under the ski lift. Our timing was a little off as it was summer and a major ski lift construction project was in progress where we wanted to hike. What to do? We drove around to the other side of the mountain for an attempt up a different route the next day. As we were about to start our hike, a major rainstorm developed which caused us to question our ability to reach the summit. No problem; I purchased an umbrella and we were able to do the hike, albeit a little damp for the experience.

Our plan for Liechtenstein was to climb Grauspitz Mountain (8,527 feet) located along an easy ridge with breathtaking views. The best of plans don't always work out and ours suffered from not doing our homework prior to attempting the climb. We put in the necessary effort only to find out that we didn't actually climb the highest peak in the country — we missed it by one more peak along the ridge. By the time we discovered our error, it was too late in the day and a storm was approaching. At least we enjoyed a very beautiful hike in one of the smallest countries in the world.

We were able to climb in Yugoslavia prior to the Bosnia-Serbia conflict, while it was still a single country. Our goal there was to climb Triglav, the country's highest point. There is a well-trodden path up to the summit complete with cables that act as guard rails so there wasn't much excitement involved in the ascent.

The entertaining part of the trip occurred at a local guest house where we stayed prior to making our ascent. I ordered something from the menu which proved to be quite delicious, while Burt ordered something that turned out to be a mysterious soup dish. The problem was that, with the exception of a local nine-year-old girl, there wasn't anyone else in the building who spoke English and we didn't speak any of the local languages. After finishing the first course, Burt decided that he would like to try what I had eaten since his meal left a lot to be desired. We went through the pantomime of ordering that occurs when you can't communicate verbally. After all was said and done, Burt ended up with the same soup that he had originally ordered, only a larger portion. They must have thought he *really* enjoyed it. Of course, I made no effort to conceal my pleasure with my meal while he sulked through his second bowl of gruel.

After the questionable meal we ate in Yugoslavia, we were overjoyed to find that our accommodations in Austria would be at the five-star Franz-Josef Lodge just across the glacier from where we would start our climb of Austria's high point, Grossglockner. The meals were absolutely wonderful and the ambiance was charming. And, how could we ever forget our hostess, the charming Frau Blücher?

Who could have asked for a better environment in which to reside prior to a climb? You could have asked that question to a group of three Polish climbers who couldn't afford to stay in the hotel and had pitched their tent on the concrete floor of the hotel's parking garage. They certainly weren't enjoying their pre-climb accommodations in the unheated garage. Frau Blücher had given them permission to use the garage until they could hook up with another group of climbers for the ascent of the peak. When we arrived, she immediately recognized an opportunity to be rid of the Polish squatters and arranged a meeting with us in the bar. I must say, even though these guys were short of funds, they showed extreme generosity by buying us all a beer, an expense which probably caused them to skip a meal somewhere along their travels. It wasn't long before we were all old comrades and another round of brews produced a viable climbing plan for the next morning.

As the sun rose, we sat on the front steps of the lodge putting on our crampons and bid a sad farewell to our luxurious accommodations. From there, it was a matter of descending a path over to the garage and joining our new-found friends for the climb.

The climb started by dropping down a steep slope to a glacier crossing and then beginning a long ascending traverse up the flanks of the mountain itself. As we got higher on the peak, we began to be subjected to ground blizzards which obscured our view of the upper portion of the mountain where we expected to find one of these huts which Europe is famous for. Late afternoon found us literally lost in the blizzard, lying on the ground to keep from being blown off the mountain. We knew we had to be in the vicinity of the hut but, due to near-zero visibility, we were unable to find the building. After lying there for a short period of time, we were lucky to have the winds abate for just a second and — lo and behold — there was the hut not a hundred yards in front of us!

It didn't take us long to get to our feet and struggle over to the hut. Once inside, we were greeted with the warmth from a pot-bellied stove, hot food, cold beer, and a safe place to spend the night. The evening ended on a mellow note with singing (in several languages), beer, and more new friends.

The next morning dawned calm and clear, so we were able to finish our ascent of the peak. Late afternoon found us again back at the lodge and looking forward to another night in luxury. The Polish climbers returned to their home in the garage.

Climbing in Europe proved to be a very enjoyable experience. The ease of access to the peaks, the hut systems, and the diverse cultures combined to leave us with fond memories. The only minor downside was a blowout on the Mercedes while I was winding around one of those narrow mountain roads. The vehicle swerved into the side of the mountain, causing us to throw rocks and debris in the air which narrowly missed an unfortunate soul on a motorcycle who had been drafting us for several miles. He gave us the "one finger salute" as he passed. Guess he couldn't take a joke.

Charlie at the Arctic Circle

Chapter 17 - Scandinavia
Land of the Midnight Sun

"Do you remember where I put my passport?" I shouted as I sat up in bed, startling my soundly-sleeping wife. "What?" she answered groggily. "My passport, where is it?" It must be in the firebox in the basement, I surmised. I literally leaped out of bed, pulled on my pants, and dashed through the house turning on every light available as I scrambled down the basement stairs. Retrieving the suspect firebox, I realized that the keys were stored in a drawer upstairs. Back up the stairs two at a time, found the keys, hurdled down the stairs back to the firebox. By now my heart is beating like a fourteen-year-old teenager looking at the centerfold of his first Playboy magazine. Ah, ha. The contents are finally revealed. Car titles, insurance papers, a family bible, marriage license and ... the bottom of the box! No passport. Diane has now joined me, ready to perform CPR in the event I expire.

"Okay, it must be in the safe deposit box at the bank," I exclaim. It's Saturday – well, it will be in a few more minutes – so I'll go the bank and get it. "Put all that stuff back in the box and let's go back to bed. I'm cold and I'm tired," she grumbled. We slowly retraced our steps back through the house and not a creature was stirring, not even a mouse.

Of course the damn bank was closed on Saturday – they have "banker's hours." The problem was that my airline ticket was for tomorrow, Sunday. No passport, no flying to Iceland where my friends were already awaiting my arrival. "Murphy's Law," "the luck of the Irish," and my stupidity combined to create one of the international traveler's greatest nightmares: attempting to travel without a valid passport.

It was the early 1990s, and I was supposed to be heading to Scandinavia with friends to climb to the highest points of Iceland, Norway, Finland, and Sweden.

"Hello, I need to purchase a one-way ticket to Reykjavik, Iceland for Monday," I informed the airline booking agent who answered the phone. I explained the whole debacle to her in the hope that I could get a refund on my useless ticket for Sunday's flight, or at least a reduced fare. No luck. She probably thought I was too stupid to be flying unaccompanied.

Monday morning, 9:00 a.m., I'm the first person entering the bank where I attempt to nonchalantly stroll over to the safe deposit desk and request entry into my safe deposit box. I now have paid for two tickets to travel to Iceland and am hoping against hope that the passport is indeed in the box. The attendant attempts to engage me in insipid conversation until I interrupt her and describe my dilemma, whereupon she proceeds to deliver the lecture from hell about people who don't have their act together. My theory is that she doesn't currently have a functional lover.

Yes, there it is, lying serenely in the dark confines of that cold metal box just awaiting my warm sweaty hands. "Come to daddy," I think as I reach in, grab the damn thing, close the box and flee the bank lobby as rapidly as possible, hoping that no one mistakes me for a bank robber as I leap into my vehicle and begin my race across town to the airline terminal.

Parking is a bitch because someone in front of me got the last close-in parking spot. Thankfully they didn't see me give them the finger. I finally arrive at the terminal, find my airline's check in counter but there's a long line and I'm at the wrong end of it. Surely this isn't the line for the flight to Reykjavik; perhaps they're giving away something free. I look at my ticket and realize that I'm scheduled to go through Logan airport in Boston. My stress level is about to red line on the stress indicator. This is probably why people have heart attacks.

Two hours later and I'm finally about to board the aircraft. I've notified my friends about my delayed arrival so everything should be okay even though it's going to take an extra day to get to my destination.

I arrived in Reykjavik, sleep-deprived and jet-lagged. My climbing partners had already rented a van and were ready to depart for the mountain we've come to climb, Hvannadalshnukur (6,922 feet). They all looked a little the worse for wear, having just arrived yesterday and not gotten much sleep themselves, but off we went. It's about a fourteen hour driving trip from Reykjavik to our campsite near the peak. I don't remember much about the trip as I was in a state of altered consciousness most of the time.

We arrived at the campground, set up our tents, and piled in for some much-needed sleep. It doesn't get very dark in Iceland this time of the year so my sleep mechanism didn't want to cooperate, but after a sleeping pill I finally started to doze off. Suddenly, I sat up in my sleeping bag, aware of an awful commotion outside my tent. It sounded like we were being invaded by the German Wehrmacht. They were obviously setting up camp right next to me. It was still light out, although it was nearly midnight, and the Germans proceeded to do some serious heavy drinking and singing. So now I'm awake, I'm suffering from drug-induced sleep intoxication, I'm still jet-lagged, and I just want to go home. By 2:00 a.m., I'd had all I could take so I got out of my tent to rouse my companions and we gathered our gear for an alpine start on the climb.

We soon left the drunken singing behind and proceeded to speed along in our van toward the mountain. All went well until just as we pulled up where we needed to park. The gear shift rod broke off at the floor. The vehicle lurched a few times to a sudden stop, awakening anyone who had had the nerve to go to sleep. Our driver was just sitting there holding the now-detached gear shift rod up in the air like he was giving a toast. It took a minute for us in our bleary-eyed condition to figure out what had happened. We decided that there was nothing to be done about the problem until after we climbed the mountain, so we threw the gear shifter into the back of the van, donned our climbing equipment, and headed off in the brightness of a fine Icelandic morning.

The way things were going, we should have known that we would experience trouble climbing the mountain. First of all, no one could pronounce or spell the name of the peak. Secondly, the trip had been a snafu since before we left the States and now here we were caught in the middle of a blizzard high up on the mountain. No one knew exactly where or how high up the summit was located. After all that had happened, it was disappointing, but the only safe choice was to abandon our summit attempt and return to our broken-down van.

Our luck finally changed. During our descent, we encountered a skier with a Satellite phone who was able to contact our rental car company in Reykjavik. They arranged for someone to deliver another vehicle to where our van was parked.

We slowly made our way back down to the parking area and, just as we arrived, our replacement vehicle drove up. The rental car company must have had a depot somewhere close since it had only been a few hours since we called. We quickly unloaded the remaining gear from the disabled van, loaded everything in its replacement, and prepared to set off for the drive back to Reykjavik. As you can imagine, by this time we were all nearly total zombies from lack of sleep, jet lag, climbing exhaustion, hunger, and general malaise. No one was willing, or was capable of driving the replacement vehicle, so we finally elected one of our group who showed the widest eye slits as our driver.

Off we went, leaving the mechanic alone with the disabled van. Everyone soon fell asleep. Did I say *everyone*? Yep, everyone, even the driver. We were all rudely awakened as the van veered off the road, bumping wildly across some ruts and small bushes, stopping only after the engine died of natural causes. I think I heard every variety of curse word, but possibly the most prevalent was "Oh, shit!" A now wide-awake crew exited the vehicle to determine the extent of any damage, but there was none. We managed to push

183

the dreaded machine back on to the highway and re-entered the vehicle just as the mechanic passed us with the no-longer-disabled van. He waved us a fond farewell as he passed. Then his head disappeared from our view only to pop up again after he shifted gears by using a pair of vice grips in lieu of a shifting rod. Good thing he didn't show up a few minutes earlier when we were sitting off the road.

After all that excitement, the drive back to Reykjavik was pretty boring. And that's how our first peak-bagging adventure of the trip unfolded.

Our flight from Reykjavik to Norway began innocuously enough. I stood in one of those never-ending lines at the airline counter with the other passengers and, after an inordinately long wait, the ticket agent asked me for my passport. She looked up my booking information and stated, "I'm sorry, there are no more seats left on that flight." How can that be? I confirmed my reservation and the rest of the group has already headed for the boarding area. My original dark thoughts included the ticket agent's unborn children and a flush toilet. "We'll have to put you in business class at no extra charge," she said with a big smile. What a wonderful person; I hope she has a nice large family. So, instead of being in the "cattle car" with the rest of our group, I was seated in luxury, eating like a king as the great silver bird winged its way across the Atlantic.

Upon our arrival in Oslo, the other members of our group complained that they were hungry. "Oh, I just couldn't eat another thing," I remarked with a smirk on my face. This statement, of course, led to my being called everything that either ran on four legs or slithered along the ground. I would have let out a loud belch at this point if I could have managed it. Where were they when you actually need them?

Galdhøpiggen, the highest point in Norway, was to be our destination. We rented a large SUV and departed for the hut at the base of the mountain.

We soon discovered that there was no lodging available at the local mountain hut. No problem. Let's all sleep in the large SUV. Sleep might have been a word in Webster's dictionary, but it didn't occur in the SUV that night. In the morning, we joined a literal cast of thousands of Norwegians as we made our way up toward the summit. A few uneventful hours and we were on top where we enjoyed a pleasant meal in the mountain haus. All in all it was a relaxing and fun round trip. It looked like this European peak-bagging portion of the trip was going to go without problems.

Next up: Halti, the high point of Finland, which stands at only 4,355 feet. It was unique because we arrived near our trailhead in a seaplane, a rather unusual method of approach. The climb itself was very straightforward. I did find it odd that one could sit out on the porch at 2:00 a.m. reading a book and have it be total daylight. So, not only did I have jet lag, I was diurnally challenged! Years later, I learned from Wikipedia, "A quarter of Finland's territory lies north of the Arctic Circle and at the country's northernmost point the sun does not set for 73 days during summer." However, that means that during mid-winter the sun doesn't appear for over two months! If that scenario wouldn't give you depression, nothing would.

Our next stop was Kebnekaise, Sweden's high point at 6,973 feet. While in Sweden, I was to learn some interesting facts about the country. We travelled to a very opulent and recently-constructed lodge near the mountain where I engaged in conversation with one of the local residents during lunch. "So," I said, "I'll bet this place (the lodge) is really busy with skiers during the winter." "Actually, we're closed here during the winter," the resident replied with a snide smile. "Really? Why?" asked the stupid American. "Well, it's dark here during the winter," he said and then laughed. Maybe we should talk about climbing or something else that I know a little about.

Later that day, we drove over to the climber's hut nearer the mountain and prepared for our next day's climb. The following morning we were able to purchase a spartan breakfast at the hut for a nominal fee. The walls had several signs which explicitly prohibited patrons from departing with any "doggie bags." *Read my lips* — do not attempt to take food from the premises for the purpose of creating a "free lunch." Förbjuden! Since no one appeared to be looking, one of our group attempted to furtively sneak a couple of breakfast rolls into his jacket pocket. The swinging doors going into the kitchen area suddenly burst open with a resounding crash and Hitler's mother came racing across the room shouting and pointing her finger at the culprit. BUSTED! I wasn't sure what this woman said, but her intent was very clear. My friend sheepishly placed the two stolen rolls back on his tray where they were quickly rescued from their kidnapper. We later learned that Frau Hitler would routinely position herself so she could peek through the crack in the kitchen doors, just waiting for someone to break the rules. We were happy to depart the premises without having to deal with Interpol for our alleged crime.

After narrowly escaping the clutches of Frau Hitler, we geared up for our summit attempt under threatening skies. Soon we were joined by several large, guided groups of Swedes which were also making the hike toward the summit. After about an hour, the guided groups split off, obviously knowing something we didn't about the route. We continued merrily along our way, just dumb and happy, having a great old time. All too soon we encountered a line of insurmountable cliffs blocking our intended path. Now we knew why the Swedes turned away from our path. It was time for a quick powwow to discuss an alternate route. No problem, let's just hike up over the easy, snow-covered peak to our left. Up we went and were then confronted with a descent of 500 feet into the next valley before we could regain our intermediate objective some 900 feet above. Things seldom go wrong one at a time and this hike was proving no different. The wind picked up, the clouds began lowering, and lo and behold, moisture appeared out of nowhere.

A couple of hard hours later we arrived at a hut which we were told was only thirty minutes from the summit. Let's just ditch the packs and make a mad dash for the summit! Fifteen minutes later, we were back at the hut for more clothing. Neither rain, nor snow, nor . . . you know the rest of the story. By the time we finally got to the summit, we were slogging through deep snow, assailed by blowing snow, and we all looked like Frosty the Snowman.

We didn't linger on the summit as there wasn't any view due to the inclement weather conditions, but we did linger in the hut on our way back down the mountain. Nothing like a lucious hot chocolate to rejuvenate the soul. Back out into the elements we went and beat a hasty retreat back to our vehicle, glowing in the aura of success.

186

One thing we discovered on this trip was that everything is very expensive in Scandinavia. I was going to purchase your basic cheese sandwich in Oslo and was astounded that they were going to charge me $12 US for the measly thing.

Atop the Devil Peak

Chapter 18 - El Picacho del Diablo

A Devil of a Peak

El Picacho del Diablo (10,154 feet), located some 100 miles south of the US border, is the highest mountain in Baja California. It's a very remote and devious peak with a sinister name that frequently lives up to its reputation. With a name like "Devil's Peak" you're sure to be in for an epic adventure and epic ours was, in more ways than one.

My climbing partners for this south-of-the-border journey were my old friends Burt "the Falcon" Falk, Jim "Seismo" Scott, and David "Remedial" Reeder. This was to be Burt's and Jim's fourth attempt at the peak, having gotten lost once, having a vehicle mired in the mud on the drive to the trailhead another time, and finally having a team member with a serious heart problem necessitate terminating the trip. These previous attempts date back to 1974; it's currently 1990 — now that's what I call dogged perseverance. We were all a little apprehensive about being able to make the summit due to all of those previous misadventures.

Driving through Mexico can be an adventure in and of itself. Would this trip finally put all those demons to rest?

We departed the US and quickly passed through Tijuana and then on to Ensenada and San Vicente, a small, dusty town located along Mexico Highway 1. We were finally free from all the congestion and garbage that you see near the US-Mexico border, or so we thought. We rounded a sharp bend in the road and were about to go under an overpass when, to our surprise, we encountered the burned-out skeleton of a large tour bus sitting in the middle of the road, obviously having crashed into the overpass. Guess we weren't on the safe side of Mexico yet. We never did figure out what had happened to the bus or its passengers, but it gave us reason to be concerned about our driving.

Out in the countryside, we passed numerous small villages and ranches on our way toward the small farming hamlet of San Telmo de Abajo. Here we would exit Mexico 1 on a road leading to the Astronomical Observatories located in the Sierra San Pedro Matir National Park. What a great place for an observatory; there wasn't any light pollution within miles.

After entering the National Park, we finally reached our destination, a place called the "Llanitos Shack," a point where the trail toward Blue Bottle Peak began. No more of this sissy automobile travel stuff, now we had to put the Vibram soles on the ground and put some miles between us and the last form of civilization we would see for several days. We had planned on a four day round trip to bag this devil of a peak. Four days out meant four days of food, climbing equipment, sleeping bags, tent, and so on. You get the picture — very large and very heavy packs, but we were much younger and dumber then. OK, much younger.

From the area of Blue Bottle Peak saddle, the plan was to split into two groups. Burt and Jim would do the "standard route" dropping down 3,100 feet into Canyon del Diablo to Camp Noche and then ascending nearly 3,900 feet up Slot Wash to the summit. Sounded straightforward to me. Dave and I would attempt a route along the notoriously convoluted fifth-class-rated Pinnacles Ridge which had a mere net gain of 2,000 feet as it traverses over to the summit of Devil Peak — how hard could that be? Why would anyone want to descend 3,100 feet, regain that elevation plus 800

189

additional feet, lose it again, and then regain the 3,100 feet a second time when there is this perfectly nice ridge leading over to the Peak? Including all the ups and downs, the "standard route" would have you hiking what amounted to 7,000 feet of elevation gain. I'm not a math major but 7,000 minus 2,000 equals 5,000 feet of unnecessary elevation gain. Go figure. Dave and I should be back in camp enjoying a siesta in the shade by the time Burt and Jim would arrive, struggling back up from their ordeal like two apparitions, tired, hot, dust-covered, and thirsty.

Several hours of hiking brought us past the first waterfall on the trail and on to the Blue Bottle Peak saddle. We established our camp and readied our gear for an early morning departure on our chosen routes. Dave and I discussed the merits of which gear would be necessary to successfully climb Pinnacle Ridge. I always take more gear because I have less ability than Dave. My motto is always "What if?" Dave's is "Improve your skills and lighten your pack." I've had back surgery using my motto, he hasn't, so let's throw out some of this junk. OK, we're down to one bottle of water, a little food, no flashlights, no matches or other fire starter, and the bivy sack I slipped in the pack when Dave wasn't looking. We'll wear the slings, harnesses, and helmets and Dave will carry the rope. I could see how we could easily move faster through the technical sections without all that extra weight. It's obvious why Dave is successful climbing more difficult peaks than I am. I'm beginning to get the hang of this climbing stuff and it's only taken me 25 years.

Morning arrived and before the sun even had much time to warm up the chilly February day, I had finished breakfast (real climbers don't bother with such vacuous activity) and we were off and running. I wasn't sure why this ridge was classified at difficult fifth class, 'cause we were making great time. *We don't need no stinkin' rope! What wimps we were to bring it along.*

About the time I was applauding my superior technical climbing ability, we arrived at the first of what were to be four of the larger pinnacles. Hmm, now I understood why they called this "Pinnacle Ridge." *Bring it on. We're tough guys, we can kick some Pinnacle ass!* A couple of hours later, and several derogatory comments regarding the sexual relationship I envisioned this route having with its mother, we finally surmounted this first obstacle. *That sure took longer than I would have thought* (that's what she said). An easier section followed; then we encountered several smaller pinnacles, eating up more of our morning. Time flies when you're having fun. *Hmm, still have a long way to go and we're about out of water.* But, the luck of the Irish was on our side (Murphy's law would overtake us later) and we found some snow to replenish our diminished water supply. I mixed the snow in with our existing water and recapped the bottle, placing it securely in the pack.

About mid-afternoon, we arrived at a point on the ridge where it appeared that a short downclimb would speed up our progress. I set up an anchor and prepared to belay Dave down an area of steep slabs. Watching Dave slowly progress downward, I came to the realization that I would be attempting this section without the upper belay that Dave enjoyed. "How hard is the climbing?" I called down to Dave. "I think it's probably 5.10," he replied. *Is this guy crazy or what? I can't climb 5.10!* I convinced him to come back up while we discussed our alternatives. I suggested that we perform one rappel down the other side of the ridge and then traverse up and around the offending feature. Dave agreed to give it a try. Well, four rappels later we had lost a significant amount of elevation and were now faced with a lower traverse and the need to regain our lost elevation. Needless to say, we had burned more daylight which we didn't have to spare. *I wonder why Dave isn't speaking to me?*

We eventually made our way back up to the ridge, but the summit loomed as far away as when we started. I hate it when that happens. The afternoon wore on and finally we found ourselves in a gully underneath the south summit. We stashed our packs and made a hurried dash up the gully, arriving on the south summit at 4:15 p.m. *Hmm, the north summit is higher and is separated by more technical terrain. Hmm, it's February and the days are short and the nights are cold and the rope's in our pack down below. Oh, what the hell, let's just get the job done -- shouldn't take us more than an hour to reach the north summit.* More math: an hour over also means an hour back to this point. That's one plus one equals two. That must be that "new math" they keep talking about.

A mere forty-five minutes later we had reached the north summit. Success was ours! However, daylight was rapidly receding as was our ability to see where we needed to traverse back over to the south peak and then head down the gully to retrieve our packs. After several false attempts, Dave finally located the correct gully. We raced downward through increasing darkness but couldn't find the errant packs. *Not good. We're dressed lightly and it's starting to get cold. Got to be here somewhere.* In a moment of absolute brilliance, Dave recognized the rock where we stashed the packs. We were saved, except now it was really starting to get dark. Now, about that flashlight we left behind to save weight. Good mountaineers don't need flashlights to navigate in the dark. Guess that left us out — we'd just have to do the best we could.

Hours passed (or so it seemed) until we found ourselves on a trail leading down to a stream. The nighttime temperature had plummeted, the damn stream was frozen, and we didn't have a clue where we were or where we should be. It's stupid(er) to continue trying to find the trail down in the dark. We agreed to do a bivy until it got light enough to see where we were going. *My, that climbing rope makes for a nice bed to keep us off the cold snowy ground. My, we even have a bivy sack in the pack. Hmm, everything in the pack is soaked. Crap!* The lid on the water bottle didn't get properly seated and most of our water was gone. We didn't need too much water since we didn't have anything left to eat and couldn't build a fire since we didn't have any matches. Perhaps we even left our brains back at the Blue Bottle saddle?

As bivouacs go, this was a long, cold one. We both occupied the somewhat wet bivy sack and shivered the night away. About every ten minutes or so one or the other would ask what time it was.

Dawn finally arrived, and we crawled stiffly out of our cocoon, dreaming of a breakfast of hot coffee and pancakes with hot syrup topped with a scrumptious helping of whipped cream. Actually, I was dreaming about the pancakes. All Dave could envision was the hot coffee. The guy just doesn't have a good imagination.

We gathered our gear together in preparation for the climb down into Canyon del Diablo. A closer examination of the frozen stream revealed that if we had started down it the previous night, we would have slipped on the ice and cascaded over a waterfall to land some 400 feet below on the rocks. At least we had made one smart decision during this trip.

We eventually arrived at the bottom of Canyon del Diablo where we were able to get water and find the trail to lead us back up to the Blue Bottle saddle. Late afternoon saw us arriving at the saddle like two apparitions, tired, hot, dust-covered, and thirsty. I seem to remember that those were the adjectives I used to describe how I envisioned Burt and Jim would appear upon *their* return to camp. And did I mention hungry? I guess the joke was on us. Thankfully, Burt and Jim had waited for us to return. They had begun to think that we were lost or injured since they beat us back to camp by a day and were considering notifying search and rescue. It appeared that they had been crying, but I later found out it wasn't because they were worried about us but rather that they had been laughing so hard about our misfortune that they had tears in their eyes. A couple of real Sickos!

Dave and I hiked back out to our car, arriving just as dusk set in, tired, wiser, and happy that we avoided going to the Devil. Burt and Jim finally had the Devil off their backs.

You would think that our adventure would have ended at this point, but as luck would have it, we were stopped at a roadblock by plainclothes police looking for drug smugglers. We never saw any badges of any kind from this group ("Badges? We don't need no stinkin' badges!"), but they most assuredly had guns stuck in the back of their pants. We finally convinced them that we were *alpinistas*. They released us after interrogating us and searching the vehicle. Tijuana was starting to look better all the time!

Find a copy of Eleanor Dart O'Bryon's *Coming Home From Devil Mountain* for a compelling account of just how things can go very, very wrong in this devilish locale — a true horror story of two hikers lost for a mind-boggling thirty days on El Picacho del Diablo.

Burt near Boundary Peak

Chapter 19 -
High Mountains - Slot Canyons
Boundary Peak & The Subway

Proclamation from the lips of one very disgruntled woman:
"I don't ever want to go on a trip like this one again!"

"Now, honey, when we get home, are you going to tell people about that boring plod up a no-name peak with sparse vegetation and abysmal views, or are you going to tell them about being caught in two flash floods in a slot canyon, spending the night in a cave above the raging flood waters, and later — in the same week — being lost and alone while descending Boundary Peak in Nevada, staying out all night again, and then hiking 25 weary miles back to our campsite?"

Very long pause.

"I'm still thinking about my answer to that question," she replied.

Diane and I are avid hikers. When we set out on a typical two-week trip to Utah and Nevada to climb various peaks with friends, we had no idea what an eventful time we'd have. In fact, after climbing one exceptionally boring, rocky, barren peak, it seemed like this might be one of our less memorable trips.

Zion National Park, The Subway

"Water, water, everywhere, Nor any drop to drink."
The Rime of the Ancient Mariner
by Samuel Taylor Coleridge

Strange as it may seem, reaching the summit of some mountains requires going *down* before you can go up. Such was the case with our attempt to climb South Guardian Angel peak located in Utah's Zion National Park. Zion is a truly spectacular place with its towering sandstone towers and deep, mysterious, sunshine-deprived, flood-prone slot canyons.

Our journey started off with a group of six climbers: Steve and Shane Holonitch, Burt Falk, Jim Scott, Diane, and myself. Our goal was to camp at Lava Point campground, located high above the slot canyons, and begin backpacking the next morning up the Left Fork of North Creek toward a feature named "the Subway."

The Subway is a point along the North Creek where the walls of the canyon become especially narrow, creating the "slot" effect referred to in canyoneering terminology. We made our attempt when you were still able to obtain a camping permit at the mouth of the Subway; camping at this location is no longer permitted by the National Park Service (NPS).

Our group arrived from various parts of Colorado and California in the early afternoon under a beautiful, sunny September sky in 1997. Shortly after cooking dinner, drinking beer, and swapping climbing stories, the sky began to cloud over. The nearby surrounding spires of Zion's peaks limited our view of the sky, somewhat, so no one seemed to notice that clouds had appeared and thickened. Suddenly, we heard thunder and it began to rain. It didn't just rain, it was a torrential downpour. We jumped into our vehicles to wait out a particularly violent thunderstorm complete with wind and hail. Inasmuch as this was September, we hadn't expected a storm of this magnitude, much less *any* rainfall. Looking back, I don't recall anyone saying anything about the canyon being dangerous for tomorrow's hike and subsequent climb. I believe we all thought this was just an isolated, early fall event.

The next morning, we drove down to our trailhead at the mouth of the Left Fork of North Creek where we parked our vehicles. Leaving the parking area, the trail descended steeply down into the stream bed. We backpacked several miles upstream while crisscrossing from one side of the stream to the other. Debris left from the prior night's flood was very sobering and should have been a wake-up call for us, but we were absorbed in our enthusiasm about our journey. After several hours, we reached our NPS-authorized camping site for the night.

After establishing our camp, we changed into wet suits and placed some extra clothing in "dry bags" for the climbing portion of the route preparation which we intended to complete during that afternoon. Heading upstream into a canyon that resembled a subway tunnel, we were soon wading and swimming through deep pools of frigid standing water. In some places where it was too smooth or vertical for scrambling, we attached our climbing ropes to the canyon walls using previously-placed bolt anchors. Our plan was to leave these ropes in place for tomorrow's ascent which would save us some time. Part of our route preparation required us to go through a narrow corridor with walls so high that they all but blocked out the sky and then climb 10 feet up a flowing waterfall. More technical climbing remained after that obstacle.

Just before reaching the last section of the canyon where we would need to use the ropes again, it began sprinkling lightly. We decided to immediately return to our campsite at the entrance of the Subway and finish the technical climbing tomorrow on our way to the peak.

I led the way back downstream toward the waterfall pitch where I waited for everyone to queue up for the necessary rappel. Since it was still raining lightly, I decided to stand under a small rock overhang. A steady stream of water was descending from the overhang where I had taken shelter. Funny that I did not remember water cascading down here before. I looked upstream where the remainder of the group were wading toward me, and all I could see behind them was a wall of water! I screamed out, "Look behind you – water!" From their point of view they could see that a large waterfall had formed behind them, cascading water several hundred feet down from the desert floor above. That was the "wall" of water that was visible to me.

The next few minutes were a cacophony of screaming voices and frightened people running downstream toward me. As luck would have it, we were in the only place in this section of the canyon where there was a narrow, steeply-sloped section of mixed rock and vegetation. I quickly ran toward that area and scrambled up a vegetated slope out of the quickly-rising flood waters. Everyone in the group was able to follow me to the safety of a ledge out of danger.

We sat and waited at our refuge for a couple of hours for the flood waters to subside. When we deemed it safe, we climbed back down into the now tranquilly-flowing stream. Steve scrambled over to an existing anchor just above the waterfall where he attached himself so that he could assist the rest of us in rappelling back down to the next level. As we started over to Steve, I sensed something didn't quite feel right. "Wait!" I yelled, and then realized that the water was rapidly rising up to the level of my knees. "Get back to the ledge!" Everyone except Steve was able to quickly regain our previous spot above the water. Burt managed to lose his shoes as he splashed back upstream through the rushing water. We perched up on the ledge for an hour or so while the torrent raged through the canyon for a second time. During this time we weren't able to see or hear Steve who, thankfully, was keeping his feet up out of the water by hanging on to the anchor. It's a good thing the water didn't rise any higher or he would have been in serious trouble.

Within a couple of hours the flood waters again receded somewhat. Steve unhooked himself from his anchor and waded and climbed up to where we were all huddled together. It was getting dark by now and no one wanted to attempt a return to camp and risk another hair-raising flood event so we decided to remain where we were for the night. Steve located a small cave

197

slightly above where we were positioned, and everyone scrambled up to that area.

The temperature was dropping and some of the group had not brought enough warm clothing, so we shared whatever we had with one other. We didn't have much food or water remaining and everyone was a little hungry and thirsty. During the night, the people lying near the back of the cave kept sliding forward on the sloping rock surface pushing those in the front out into the damp, cold night. Curses would fly through the air and then everyone would squirm back into the cave. Jim, who was at the rear of the cave, suggested that he believed he was lying on Hantavirus droppings, which we found to be hysterically funny at the time. All in all, it proved to be a long, cold, sleepless night.

As soon as it was light enough to see, we quickly scampered back down into the water and over to the waterfall area where we reversed our route. We climbed down and back through the extremely narrow section below the waterfall and out to camp where we arrived cold, hungry, and wet – but alive. We were all shaken to think what would have happened had we been in the narrows just below the waterfall when the flood waters came through. Only a few short minutes separated us from being killed.

Any enthusiasm to go back and attempt the climb was decidedly lacking. Everyone just wanted to eat and drink something and get out of their wet clothes. We broke camp and started the long hike back out of the canyon to our waiting vehicles, all the while thinking of hot pizza and cold beer. We found Burt's shoes a couple of miles downstream from our camp hanging from some debris. We had dodged another bullet.

Boundary Peak, Nevada

During this period, Diane and I were writing a hiking and climbing guide for the highest spot in each of the fifty states, *Highpoint Adventures*. The summit of Boundary Peak (13,143 feet) is located on the border between California and Nevada with the summit barely sneaking over to the Nevada side of the state boundary, making it the highest peak in Nevada.

Jim Scott, Diane, and I started off in the early morning light under a beautiful, cloud-free, Nevada autumn morning. We decided to take the Trail Canyon approach to the summit and then Jim and I would continue on over to the higher peak along the ridge, Montgomery Peak, which is located in California. An interesting side bar is that Montgomery Peak is actually 200 feet higher than Boundary Peak and is located on the same ridge. However, Montgomery Peak is located in California, so while it is visually and technically higher than Boundary Peak, it is just another California high peak.

The actual climb of Boundary went without incident. The trouble began *after* Jim and I started our traverse along the ridge toward Montgomery. Diane wasn't interested in bagging Montgomery, so she decided to descend back to our camp at the trailhead. Here is her description of the ensuing events.

It looked like such a straightforward hike. Who would have guessed that I'd end up lost, and spend the night curled up in the fetal position under a tree, with a garbage bag as my shelter?

As my husband Charlie, our friend Jim, and I drove toward our campsite below Boundary Peak, the highest point in Nevada, we could see our objective for the next day. As its name suggests, Boundary Peak lies just on the Nevada side of the boundary between California and Nevada.

We started out at 6:00 a.m. along an easy trail that quickly brought us into a wide-open valley leading directly toward our destination, which was in clear view. The trail through fields of sagebrush gradually gained elevation until we reached a bowl. We climbed a steep, 2,000 foot scree slope toward the saddle. From there, we made our way around two rock outcroppings and up the final slope to the summit, arriving at 10:00 a.m.

After this obvious, but tiring hike of 4,200 feet elevation gain, Charlie and Jim (peak-baggers extraordinaire) wanted to "run" across the ridge to Montgomery Peak in California. The wind was chilly on the summit, so the boys decided to hurry across to the other peak (about a 45 minute trip each way) while I headed back to camp.

As I followed one of many trails back around the rocks on the ridge, I noticed one that sloped down the scree at an angle that looked like it would cut some distance off my descent. I headed down and across. I reached the bowl below, and decided to wait for my companions there.

After 1½ hours, there was no sign of Charlie and Jim. Another hour went by . . . still no sign of the two strong, fast, highly-experienced climbers. I blew my whistle, hoping they'd respond so I knew their location. Silence.

[Jim and I completed our climb of Montgomery and returned to the summit of Boundary at 11:20 a.m. We continued down to the trailhead and, not finding any signs of Diane there, left a note on our car that she was presumed missing and that we were going back up to look for her. That was about 1:00 p.m.] –

I concluded that they had come down some other way, and I had missed them. But I had a clear view of the entire slope and ridge! Could I have come down the wrong way? No – look: there are the rocks we rested at just below the saddle, and over there is the light-colored stripe of scree we thought would be the easiest line of descent. But, I really don't remember those trees over in the next drainage . . . or that patch of snow way off to the left.

I started looking for the trail we had come up . . . and the terrain seemed all wrong. Still, I convinced myself that I was simply on the wrong side of a small ridge. "If I just follow this trail over here, I'm sure it'll join up with the trail we used. After all, I can see down the valley all the way to the highway that led to this area! I must be very close to our trail."

So I headed down. The trail disappeared, so I climbed over a small ridge in the direction I thought our original trail might be, and found another trail. And followed it down.

My brain finally kicked in and said, "You are lost." I turned around and studied the ridge between Boundary and Montgomery above me . . . perhaps 3,500 feet above me. A little voice said, "I don't have the stamina to climb back up there now. I messed up." So, I decided to stay put so others could find me. For 2 hours I waved the end of my silver emergency bivy sack in the air like a flag, and blew my whistle. Nothing.

200

[Jim & I continued our search. I climbed the peak again and encountered another hiker who had a set of binoculars. We scanned the surrounding terrain for Diane with the binoculars, all the while yelling out her name. Jim and Burt Falk (who had joined us after attempting to climb another peak in the area) continued searching the valley and the approaches to the peak. At 6:30 p.m. the decision was made to send Burt and Jim to the nearby town of Dyer to call for Search & Rescue (SAR). It had been 8½ hours since anyone had seen Diane. The SAR folks arrived around 11 p.m. amidst an armada of rescue vehicles and clouds of dust. They quickly set up a communications network and dispatched their members out into the field to look for Diane. As quickly as they had arrived, they had all departed and a heavy silence descended upon the camp. I attempted to sleep in the front seat of my vehicle but my concern for Diane's safety kept me awake. At approximately 3:00 a.m. I heard a strange *thunking* noise and looked out to see a military helicopter swoop past, two red lights glowing from the front of the fuselage. I later learned that they had forward-looking infrared radar equipment which can be used to detect heat sources. By the time daylight arrived, the "cavalry" had returned from the field empty-handed. After a quick discussion, I gathered that they were planning to bring in horses and fixed wing aircraft to aid in the search. Diane's story continues.]

Miles down the valley, I could see the highway and dirt roads that led to campsites. I decided to continue down. If I could find a road, then I could find people.

I made my way through thick vegetation, across small streams, and over hills. At 5:00 p.m. I neared a jeep road, and bushwhacked my way to it. I spent the next 5 hours hiking down the road, and exploring its side roads, hoping to find "our" road, or an occupied campsite. I blew 3 blasts on my whistle every few minutes . . . silence. Finally, in the light of the full moon, I chose a tree next to the road as my shelter for the night. I hung my yellow raincoat on the tree at headlight level, put on more layers of clothing, and crawled into my silver-foil bivy sack, exhausted.

The night turned colder and windier, the bivy sack began tearing into shreds, and I added more layers of clothing and a

201

garbage bag from my pack. Finally, I saw a faint red glow on the eastern horizon. I got up, ate a cookie, decided I could allow myself 2 gulps of my very-limited water supply, and set off down the road again. It was 6:00 a.m.

After finding a familiar road sign, I finally understood where I was. I had walked all the way down Middle Creek Canyon, in the valley south of Trail Canyon where we had camped. I now had about 9 miles to hike up the correct valley to our campsite. Finally, 24 hours after I had last seen another person, I spotted a jeep driving down the road toward me. I jumped up and down, shouted, waved wildly, blew my whistle, and generally acted like a wild woman. "Are you the lost hiker?" the driver asked. "Can I give you a ride to your campsite?" Obviously a rhetorical question.

What was the worst part of this experience for me?

Being lost. I cried a little, mad at myself for being so determined to convince myself NOT to climb back up to that saddle – the last place that I knew where I was!

Seeing all those Search & Rescue people near the trailhead, who had been working since 11:00 p.m. the previous night looking for me. Yes, I felt guilty.

Thinking about what Charlie was going through trying to find me and figure out if I was lost, injured, or lying dead somewhere. This was by far the worst part of the experience. I don't ever want to put him through something like that again.

We have since purchased compact two-way radios, a SPOT Satellite Messenger device, and a GPS unit (most of which weren't available to us in 1997). Some of you may grimace at "high tech" gadgets making their way into the wilderness. But, long-distance communication could have saved Diane from spending a night out in the cold. It could have saved me from climbing Boundary a second time that day (I climbed nearly 10,000 feet within a twelve hour period!). It could have allowed all those wonderful Search & Rescue volunteers to spend their night (and morning) at home with their families. And it could have saved us from some tremendous emotional upheaval. Someday, it may save someone's life.

Boundary Peak - the high point of Nevada. That's a "straightforward" climb that we'll <u>never</u> forget.

I wonder why Diane has never answered my question about her preference for predictable (a.k.a. "boring") trips versus "adventurous" trips.

Maybe that helps explain why I've been married four times.

Ama Dablam - Nepal

Chapter 20 - One Last Time

Ama Dablam & Ishinca

2002 - Nepal - Ama Dablam southwest ridge

I never thought I would return to Nepal after having been there twice previously, but when my close friend Randy decided to attempt Ama Dablam using Dan Mazur for his logistical support, I knew I couldn't pass up the opportunity to climb this beautiful mountain which had always been on my "wish list." We were joined on the climb by our friend and frequent climbing partner, Dave Cooper, who I first met in 1988 on an expedition to Peru.

Our route up the Southwest ridge would require us to be in Nepal for about a month and necessitate placing five camps in strategic locations on the mountain. The terrain on the route included technical rock and ice climbing at altitude. A month in Nepal, technical rock and ice climbing — these are the words that climbers live for.

Ama Dablam is locally referred to as the "Mother's Necklace" and the hanging glacier — the "dablam" — is known as the "Mother's Charm Box" among other names. The Charm Box shed some of its charm in 2006, totally wiping out Camp 3, sweeping six climbers to their death.

This was Randy's and Dave's first trip to Nepal, so it was fun sharing my many stories with them from past trips. We followed the same route from Lukla to Namche Bazaar as I did on my 1999 trip to Nepal with Diane, so I was familiar with the villages and peaks we would be seeing. I was anxious for Randy and Dave to hike up to the Everest View Hotel when we arrived at Namche Bazaar where they would get their first good view of Mount Everest and Ama Dablam. They weren't disappointed with the view, and we spent several hours sitting on the hotel patio, enjoying the atmosphere and whetting our appetite for the coming climb.

After a rest and acclimatization day at Namche Bazaar, we continued our hike toward Ama Dablam base camp, passing through the villages of Thyangboche and Pangboche. At Pangboche we departed the standard Mount Everest trail and headed east to Mingbo which would be the last village we would encounter on our approach. Once at Mingbo, we left the trail and slowly hiked up to Ama Dablam base camp at about 15,000 feet, all the while feeling the altitude. When we arrived at base camp, the porters had already set up our tents. Each climber had his own tent, so we could be as messy with our belongings as we could stand.

One of the historic sites we passed on our trek to base camp was the Tengboche monastery. This is one of the most famous and beautiful monasteries in Nepal and a popular tourist destination.

I'm always a little "out there" when it comes to what is termed "normal" behavior and I seldom pass up an opportunity to entertain my fellow climbers. While we were at one of our approach camps, I noticed a group of people hollering with glee as they ran out to greet an attractive woman trekker approaching the camp. They formed a line and she gave everyone a big greeting hug. This looked like an opportunity not to be squandered, so I joined the line. After my hug, the woman asked, "Who are you?"

"Oh, I don't know you but the hugging thing looked too good to resist!" and it was. Everyone got a good laugh out of that and I didn't get slapped for taking liberties.

With the exception of a few hours each day, base camp was a cold, uncomfortable place to stay. The sun didn't reach camp until about 9:00 a.m. and it (as well as the temperature) plunged by about 6:00 p.m. each evening. Most nights we got an inch or two of snow. We would go out to the stream near our camp each morning to break through the ice so the cooks could get water for preparing meals. Eating in the dining tent required wearing a down jacket, a hat, and gloves. I wondered if I would ever be warm again. Having to go to the toilet in the middle of the night was one of my (and probably everyone's) worst fears. The toilet was located about a quarter of a mile from camp at the top of a windy hill. It took an extreme set of circumstances to cause you to get out of a warm sleeping bag in the middle of the night and put on all your layers of clothing to make the journey. I guess the one positive thing about the bathroom trip was that you had a chance to enjoy the brilliant night sky. Otherwise, thank goodness for the pee bottle for less serious interruptions — you just wanted to make sure you didn't spill the bottle in the tent or, perish the thought, mistake it for your water bottle in the middle of the night!

Someone apparently caught a cold on their flight over to Nepal and proceeded to pass it around to almost everyone else in camp. I was the last person to get sick and, as it turned out, I was unable to recover from the effects during our trip. I eventually managed to move up to Advanced Base Camp (ABC). From ABC I made a "carry" to Camp 1. By the time I reached Camp 1, I was coughing so hard that I had to have someone hold my hand to keep it from shaking so I could get a cup of hot tea. I left Camp 1, returning back to Base Camp, and was never well enough to climb back up to ABC.

During one of our rest days, the group tried out the life-saving "Gamow bag." I volunteered to be the "victim" of high altitude edema. The Gamow bag is a hyperbaric chamber which allows climbers experiencing acute altitude sickness to be placed inside the bag, which is then filled with air using a foot pump to simulate being at a much lower elevation. I volunteered to be the "sick" climber and got to experience what the oxygen level would feel like several thousand feet lower by being sealed up inside this device. Ah! Life is good!

After meals, our cooks would put left-over food scraps into a 55 gallon drum for later disposal. One night, after everyone had gone to bed, one of the yaks decided to have a midnight snack. He managed to get his head into the barrel, but it became stuck on his horns which totally freaked him out. Here we have a 1,500 pound beast running amok through the camp with a large blue barrel completely covering his head. We're lucky he didn't take out some of the camp tents (and their occupants) during his rampage. Someone was finally brave enough to grab the barrel and pull it off the yak's head, thus ending his adventure.

One of the climbers had brought along a parapente, a paraglider which allowed him to jump off a cliff or high hill and use his "wing" to fly to a safe landing somewhere down the valley. At the end of the climb, the porters were dismantling the tents when the flight took place, with the paraglider circling over the camp. This bizarre scenario had two immediate effects. It freaked out the yaks, who rushed for safety, and it thrilled the porters, who picked up some of the dismantled tents and ran around the camp with tents flapping along behind them screaming, "Bird-man, bird-man." All in all, it was quite a spectacle. We all laughed until we cried.

Randy was successful in reaching the summit of Ama Dablam. Dave reached camp 2 before he became incapacitated with a sinus infection, causing him to abort his summit attempt. I told Dave it was "all in his head" but he failed to see the humor in my statement. Those Brits.

What an invigorating feeling it was to be back in Namche Bazaar and civilization after so many weeks of being at 15,000 feet! Hopefully, now I could recover from the hacking cough that had plagued me for the past couple of weeks.

Dave and I checked in to one of the local Inns where we were able to secure a room for two with toilet facilities down the hall for the paltry sum of seventy-five cents per night. No TV or telephone service, but for seventy-five cents, how could you complain?

One of our first requests was for a hot shower, which cost one dollar. The cooks would heat up a large container of water, carry it across the road to the roof of a building with a small shower cubicle, then dump the contents into a water dispenser which the occupant activated by pulling down on a chain. The cubicle consisted of a concrete room about 5 by 5 feet with no place to put your clothes except on the cold, damp floor. Dave swears that he had a nice hot shower but mine was tepid at best. Those Brits don't understand the meaning of the term "hot."

The next morning, I was somewhat appalled to see one of the cooks walk out to the cobblestone sidewalk, scoop up recently-deposited yak dung with his bare hands, and fling it over the nearby fence before returning to the kitchen. I can guarantee you that I didn't order hot cakes for breakfast that morning.

My trek back to Lukla was filled with reflective conversation regarding my failed attempt on Ama Dablam. The only positive thing I could have done differently was not getting sick. I'll always wonder if I could have made the summit.

Back in Kathmandu, while waiting for the plane back to the US, I decided that I would make one more international trip somewhere to climb a big mountain, one where I could end this segment of my climbing life with a successful ascent.

Approaching Urus Este summit - Peru

2006 - Peru

After many years of climbing high peaks all around the world, I decided that carrying heavy packs and getting sick in foreign countries wasn't what I most enjoyed about mountaineering. My previous high peak adventure was the attempt on Ama Dablam in Nepal which ended when I got sick and was only able to reach Camp 1, a big disappointment for me. My goal was to finish climbing high peaks on a high note — a successful summit. When I heard that Randy, Dave, Ginni, and several of my other regular climbing partners were planning an expedition to Peru, I decided to join them for one last fling. The plan was to climb Urus Este (17,782 feet), Ishinca (18,143 feet), and Tocllaraju (19,790 feet), all to be accessed from a base camp in the Ishinca valley.

We arranged to have our climbing equipment packed in on burros, which made the hike to our base camp more enjoyable. The older I get, the less I like being a beast of burden! We arrived in the Ishinca Valley mid-afternoon under a deep blue, cloudless sky. The view of the surrounding peaks, some of which we were intending to climb, was something out of a picture postcard. After establishing our camp at about 14,000 feet, we decided to do a short acclimatization hike up toward Ishinca in preparation for our climb of Urus Este the following day. Everyone made it up to about 15,000 feet, although we had to stop a few times to catch our breath. This was a wake-up call for most of us. We were going to climb almost 4,000 feet tomorrow to get to the Urus Este summit. We were attempting to apply the "climb high, sleep low" routine that helps the body acclimate to elevation, so we returned to our camp for the night.

We awoke to another of those star-studded skies that are almost too brilliant for the eyes. We departed for the climb after the usual grumbling about how early it was, how cold it was and "I hardly got any sleep last night" banter. It didn't take long before everyone was stopping to take off a layer of clothing as we ascended the rocky slope up out of the valley.

The time just seemed to pass in a flash and before long the sun had made its appearance, which was the signal for everyone to take a well-deserved rest break. We had left a talus field far behind and were now climbing on firm snow slopes. The remainder of the morning was absolutely perfect — no wind and cloudless, cobalt-blue skies. We couldn't have asked for more ideal climbing conditions. Everyone was climbing at their own pace and reached the summit with a big smile on their face. We arrived back at camp tired but happy. It had been a successful day, indeed.

We spent the next day getting our climbing ropes dried out and packs ready for the climb of Ishinca which we planned to do the following day. Ishinca would be a longer climb with more technical difficulty than our climb of Urus Este.

As usual, we were off hiking long before the sun made its appearance on the eastern horizon. The group seemed a little more subdued than when we started out on Urus Este. Perhaps we all realized that we were going to be required to work much harder, plus we probably had some residual lactic acid buildup in our muscles. I started out before the main group of climbers so I could hike up to the edge of the glacier at my own pace. I hoped this would allow me to be rested for the more strenuous section of the climb. I didn't have long to wait until the rest of the group joined me at my rest spot.

Everyone put on crampons and their "game face" and got down to the business of climbing the steep snow slopes which led up to the summit. Ever wondered what the term "game face" relates to? I think it's something that encompasses your whole mentality, your body language, as well as the intensity with which you are approaching a climb or whatever activity you are undertaking. I'm more focused and absolutely "in the zone." I know where I am and why I am there. I'm not thinking about work, relationships, or anything other than the task at hand.

We worked well as a team and the anticipated climbing difficulties were ironed out with little effort. By noon we had all successfully reached the summit.

Another rest day was in order as we prepared for the more technical climb of Tocllaraju, which would require extensive planning and equipment checking. It was during this day off that I met three young climbers from the US who were preparing to climb Ishinca, following a more technical route than we had taken. They asked if they could borrow several ice screws for their ascent. I had several ice screws with me that we wouldn't need, so I gave them to their group to keep.

We saw them again the following evening at the hostel located in the Valley. They remarked that they made "good use" of the ice screws I had given them. Little did any of us know that we would never see them alive again. Several days after our last encounter, their group was making an ascent of the difficult face of Artesonraju when tragedy struck. All three climbers fell to their death down the mountain while roped together. I had no knowledge of this incident until I returned back to the US. Accidents like this leave me at a loss for words, wondering what had happened and what could have been done differently to prevent the heartbreak and loss that was surely felt by their family and friends.

Prior to our attempt on Tocllaraju, I visited with a couple of climbers who had spent the last several days attempting to climb the mountain. They described miserable conditions up high on the peak — freezing temperatures, high winds, and deep snow. I gave this report a considerable amount of thought and decided that I had finally reached my last high altitude summit. My goal of finishing big mountains with a success had been realized. I informed our group that I would not be joining them for the

211

Tocllaraju attempt the next day. This was the right choice for me after experiencing international mountaineering adventures over the course of a quarter century. I was at peace with just hanging around base camp while the others climbed. I'm sure I'll miss the camaraderie that goes along with high altitude mountain climbing expeditions, but not the jet lag, cold, and sickness aspects. Still, I'm not ready to hang up my crampons just yet — perhaps they're just resting for the time being. There are certainly more than enough peaks of lower elevation in the US which will occupy my time for years to come.

Chapter 21 - Here, There & Everywhere

or, Adventures for the Criminally Insane

A collection of vignettes — some humorous, some serious, some simply pathetic.

♦♦♦

A response from a neurologist who was treating me for a herniated disc upon my request to be allowed to go climbing at a local climbing gym: "Why can't you just be normal?" Normal? Never was and probably never will be.

♦♦♦

During one of my trips to Mexico, we stayed in a climber's hut located close to the mountain we were climbing. I had been nursing a slight cough so I had brought along some individually wrapped packages of cough drops. On the morning we were to climb, we arose at "O dark thirty" (that's when most people are experiencing deep REM sleep) to begin putting on our harnesses and other climbing gear. Looking over in the dim light of the hut, I noticed that one of my climbing partners — let's call her Janet — was also experiencing respiratory difficulty, a common malady at higher altitudes due to the dryness of the air. I peeled off several individual packages of cough drops and handed them to her saying, "Here, you might need these." Janet immediately put the packages in her pocket without comment. Shortly, we all took off for the climb and nothing more was said regarding the transfer of the cough drops.

Several weeks later, after returning to Denver, I was visiting with one of the other team members who related a conversation she had with Janet on the day of our climb. Janet told her, "When we were in the hut the morning we were going to climb Popo, Charlie walked over and handed me these small flat packages. I stuck them in my pocket, all the while wondering why he would give me condoms since he knows I am a lesbian!"

♦♦♦

While in Moscow, I was staying at an unnamed hotel near Red Square. As was common in many hotels in the USSR during that time period, each guest was required to check in and out with the room monitor on their floor. She would give you your key and usually inquire if you needed any assistance or supplies.

One evening, upon my return to the hotel, I retrieved my key from the woman in charge and went on to my room. I had hardly closed the door when the telephone rang. I picked up the phone and, lo and behold, it was the room monitor. She spewed a verbal concoction of Russian and English, none of which I could comprehend. I asked her to repeat what she had said, thinking that perhaps I could make heads or tails out of the oration. Finally I replied, "No thanks, I don't need any." A period of silence followed. Then, in heavily-accented English she said, "But they are very young and pretty." Oh, oh, it wasn't towels she was trying to help me out with, it was Russian girls. I quickly hung up the phone, dashed across the room, locked the door, and lodged a chair under the doorknob fearing that the young lady bringing me "towels" might have left her underwear at home.

♦♦♦

Sometimes when I'm out hiking alone, I have an idiot for a climbing partner. Such was the case during one of my solo attempts to bag three separate summits in Colorado in a single day. Knowing that I would likely be out after dark, I made sure I had the requisite headlamp with working battery, matches, map and compass, as well as an altimeter (this was before GPS technology was available).

As I came down from my last peak, I realized that, sure enough, I was going to finish the hike out in the dark. My only concern was that the Forest Service had been rerouting some of the trails in the area so the actual terrain did not match my USGS topographic map.

I continued down the trail until finally it was too dark to hike without a headlamp. Setting down my pack, I retrieved my trusty headlamp. Now I'm not your average "I just got off the boat" hiker — I'm very experienced. So, what do experienced hikers do? Experienced hikers take the headlamp's battery (this was before LEDs) out of its compartment and turn it around to prevent the light being unintentionally turned on while in the pack. No problem, out comes the battery and it's a simple task to reverse the polarity and reinsert it back into the battery compartment. Oops! The battery just shot out of my hand and is now hiding somewhere in the vicinity. I'll need the headlamp to successfully navigate my way back to my vehicle.

Perhaps a small controlled fire will illuminate the area sufficiently to enable me to see where the misbehaving battery might possibly be lying. Out come the matches. I pull together some kindling, strike the match, and presto — we have light! Well, we had light for about five seconds. Hmmm, perhaps a larger blaze would be more helpful. Not a good idea, might set the forest on fire. Let's go to Plan B.

Plan B includes the matches and the map. Apply one to the other and you have the caveman's torch. Those cave guys were pretty smart dudes. Okay, here we go, let there be light. And there was light, and burning shards of map hurtling their way up into the night sky. The map's burning faster than I could have imagined, so I had better find that stinking battery soon. Ah ha, a slight hill near where I was attempting to replace the battery. Good choice – I see the battery. Yeah!

The nasty little son of a battery is soon safely positioned again in its proper resting place and we have light. By this time, the map has been reduced from its original 7.5 minute format to something resembling a space ship upon re-entry into the atmosphere. Amid a column of smoke and ash, I attempt to straighten out the smoldering remains. Hmmm, I can still see the name of the map but very little is left of the geographic detail. I guess it has served its purpose and earned its place in map heaven or hell — whatever the case may be.

I gather my belongings and prepare to dash off down the trail. The question is, which trail? Nothing to do but try to keep going as straight as possible until I reach what I know to be my starting elevation and then work it out from there. The big question is, what time does that hamburger joint in town close because it's already 8:30 p.m.

Ten-thirty, and I finally locate my vehicle after two very nasty hours of bushwhacking. I'm so dirty from the brush and trees (and ashes) that I'm not sure anyone will allow me to get something to eat. What an idiot!

Looking back, it's interesting to note how much equipment has changed since this experience. Now we have cell phones galore, inexpensive two-way radios, GPS Navigation Systems, very lightweight, long-lasting LED headlamps, and SPOT Messenger Devices to let people know you are okay or need assistance. All of this technology takes the fun out of the adventure.

◆ ◆ ◆

A group of us were in Russia staying at a Dacha, a country villa, at the end of a trip to climb Mt. Elbrus. On our last evening there, several large, black Mercedes automobiles arrived amid a choking cloud of dust. When the dust cleared, out piled a group of Russian businessmen along with an entourage of quite lovely young ladies. They quickly took over the ground floor of the Dacha and proceeded to party hard all night long. We know because we didn't get much sleep with all the singing and other noises resulting from their connubiality (you know what I mean).

Come morning, as we were preparing to load our climbing gear onto our bus for transport back to the airport, some very tired-looking Russian businessmen and their nymph-like companions appeared in the courtyard.

One member of our group who had more balls than sense casually walked over to one of the burly Russians and asked, "What kind of business are you in?" We all cringed, thinking the climber was going to end up floating face down in the river or some other such catastrophe. The businessman smiled and casually replied, "Commerce." I wonder if the concrete business comes under the heading of "Commerce."

They quickly loaded themselves into their Mercedes, and roared happily off to pursue their "commerce" businesses elsewhere. It's probably better not to ask a question if you don't want to know the answer.

◆◆◆

As you head up north of Sundance, Wyoming on US 14 in the northeastern corner of the state, you are likely to see a sight that will literally take your breath away. No, it's not a cowboy with Velcro gloves passionately pursuing a terrified sheep. You're about to have a *Close Encounter of the Third Kind*. We're not talking here about *you*, the cowboy, and the sheep — that *would* be a close encounter. You're going to be looking at our country's first National Monument, the monolithic formation called *Devil's Tower*.

The Tower means many things to many people. On the one hand, it is sacred to Native American Indians, and on the other it's revered by dirtbag climbers for its unique geologic structure and climbing routes. There is no consensus about how the Tower was formed, but it is composed of a type of magma rock called phonolite porphyry. It has those really cool, symmetrical columns that make climbing lots of fun. The Tower is something that's on every climber's "to do" list. I've climbed it several times with different climbing partners; the last time was with my wife.

Devils Tower

After Diane and I rappelled down from the climb, we threaded our way through the hordes of tourists that usually jam the parking lot. We looked a sight, adorned with our ropes, hands still taped from climbing, and bandoliers of climbing equipment jangling away. As we made a bee-line for the drinking fountain, we could see curious heads turn in our direction. Children were wrapping their little arms around their mothers' legs and peeking out at us with those inquisitive eyes you see on the little ones. Adults, however, were not so shy. Predictably, the first question asked is, "Were you climbing?" immediately followed by, "How do you get those ropes up there?" The crowd gathers. "Did you have to pound in those stakes?" Now the fun begins.

Diane responds, "Yes, we climbed all the way to the top." As she turns, she points over toward The Tower. "No, you can't pound in those stakes, because when you pull them out the water inside the tower will shoot out," she adds. At this point the tourists are unsure whether we're pulling their leg or telling the truth and no one is going to show their ignorance about climbing techniques to ask another question.

Then they usually want their picture taken. We hang all the climbing gear and ropes on them, tie a bandana on their head, and press the shutter; now they have a souvenir photo to take back home to Kansas. They've got a smile a mile wide, we've made some really happy campers, and it's made our day even more enjoyable. "Oh, did you have film in your (digital) camera?" I innocently inquire.

◆◆◆

During one of my South American trips, we were staying in a semi-luxurious downtown hotel which had a gambling casino located on the lower floor. After a nice dinner, our group decided to go in and spend a few pesos gambling. We headed over to the casino, only to be stopped by the doorman who informed us that we would not be allowed to enter the premises unless we were wearing a tie. A sport coat and a tie would be preferable, but at the very least a tie was required. Well, here we were, just a bunch of dirtbag climbers, so the tie thing presented us with a big problem. How to get everyone a tie so we could go in and gamble?

We may be a little slow, but we are definitely a devious bunch. We went back up to our hotel rooms and dug through our climbing equipment until we were able to locate and fashion enough climbing webbing to make the obligatory ties.

We returned to the casino with everyone wearing a big smile and the gaudiest selection of climbing webbing this side of Joshua Tree National Park. One of our members wore a "daisy chain" and convinced the doorman that it was a North American form of bow tie. The doorman just shook his head and waved us inside. That reinforces the idea that necessity is the mother of invention.

◆◆◆

"You light up my life" — or was that "you light up my wife?" Diane and I were out with a group of friends on a training climb on one of Colorado's 14,000 foot peaks when we experienced an "electrifying" event.

We started up the peak just as the late September sun peeked over the eastern horizon. Along with the sun came some high, wispy clouds gently fluttering their way across the morning sky.

Hiking at altitude is hard work, and we soon started taking off layers of clothing. We were making good time until suddenly the sun began to dim as those wispy clouds were quickly being replaced by a lowering fog layer. It was time to stop and put some of those clothes back on. A few hundred feet farther up the mountain, as we neared the summit, the fog became denser and the humidity level, which had obviously been increasing, turned surprisingly into a light snow. We quickly tagged the summit and signed our names in the register, ready to proceed down the mountain before the snow, which had temporarily quit, should return.

By 11:00 a.m. we were well down along the exposed ridge when someone said they thought they heard distant thunder (it was probably my stomach grumbling from that Mexican food I had last night). Best thing to do was to continue our descent as rapidly as possible.

Next thing I know, I was sprawled on the ground and, off to my left, Diane was also on the ground. She turned to me with a dazed look on her face (she later told me she thought I had hit her on the head with a rock). I must have looked equally as dazed, as she kept saying over and over to me, "Are you all right? Are you all right?" Since I don't remember much of the next few minutes, I'll let her tell what she witnessed.

I had no idea why I had sunk to the ground, and was even more baffled when I turned and saw Charlie down as well. He was muttering something about "lightning," however, so I was inspired to get up quickly and get down off the ridge. I asked Charlie, "Are you all right?" He didn't speak, but instead began removing his backpack. "Charlie, are you all right?" He slipped the pack back on again. I got to my feet. "Can you get up? Do you need help?" He slipped his pack off. "Charlie!" He put the pack on again.

He continued in this silent "loop" of the on-again, off-again backpack as I became more insistent. Suddenly, he snapped out

*of it, jumped up, and began running down the slope toward safer
ground, shouting encouragement to everyone to "get out of here!"*

*As we ran, we saw and heard a lightning strike in the valley
below us. We quickly assumed the "lightning crouch," even while
realizing that we were doing much too little, much too late. I was
on the verge of hysteria by then, but all I could do was charge
down the slope as quickly as possible behind Charlie, and hope
we wouldn't be killed.*

When we reached safer ground, we exchanged breathless stories
with our friends. Some described witnessing a fireball pass
between them and the rest of the group. Diane and I were at the
rear of the group and were the only ones to find ourselves on the
ground. Several people described a sensation like being hit on the
back of the head with a heavy book or a bat. I've heard this from
several other people who have found themselves suddenly on the
ground during a thunderstorm. Usually they jump up and look
around for who might have hit them. I think perhaps it was the
Grim Reaper taking a shot at us.

Later that evening, Diane and I rehashed what we had been
through. She had a bump on her head and hearing loss for a
couple of hours. I remember seeing what appeared to be a
cantaloupe-sized, sparkling ball coming off my right shoulder. I
had been hiking with a trekking pole in that hand. I also had what
looked like a horsefly bite on that shoulder. Perhaps we dropped
too much (or not enough) acid in college?

◆◆◆

This story is nothing to "Snicker" about. An unnamed female
hiking partner I'll call Lucy (not her real name) and I decided to do
a winter ascent of a peak in Colorado's San Juan Mountains.
Winter ascents require additional time due to snow-covered roads
leading to trailhead access as well as the amount of effort required
to reach the summit. That being the case, we decided to drive as
far up the road toward the trailhead as possible and then camp in
the back of my pickup truck. As night fell, so did the temperatures
until it was probably around zero degrees Fahrenheit. As we lay in

our separate sleeping bags discussing the plan for tomorrow's climb, the talk turned to food. We had already eaten dinner and now it was too damn cold to get out of the sleeping bag for a midnight snack. Lucy proclaimed that she had a Snickers bar that she would share with me. That sounded like a good idea, except Snickers bars turn to iron when exposed to extreme cold like we were experiencing. "No problem," she said as she handed me half of a very warm and pliable Snickers bar. "Wow!" I said, "How did you manage to keep the bar that warm?" A sly smile appeared on her lips. "You probably don't want to know," I ravenously devoured my portion of the delectable treat and went sound to sleep with visions of sugar-plums dancing in my head. I've never been able to eat a Snickers bar after that without remembering that incident. Lucy, if you're reading this now, I want you to know you made my night!

◆◆◆

How I almost "screwed" up.

Those of us who have flown since the events of 9/11 have come to realize that the government takes the issue of passenger security very seriously. You don't even want to *think* about making innocuous jokes about anything relating to security or play tricks on your fellow travelers which might result in the authorities finding a reason to make *your* life a living hell. I, for one, fully appreciate their diligent efforts and make every attempt to make their job less stressful. However, on one occasion *prior* to 9/11 when I was traveling to New Zealand to do some technical ice climbing, I did have a lapse in sound judgment. I decided that I would transport my ice screws onto the aircraft in my carry-on luggage, hoping not to take a chance on them getting lost in the mysterious labyrinth of baggage transportation, which has sometimes happened. For the uninitiated, ice screws are used as protection when ascending vertical waterfall ice. At the time my plan seemed like a reasonable idea.

You might imagine the airport screener's consternation when she opened my bag for examination to discover ten, 13cm long, hollow, polished steel cylinders lying serenely at the bottom of my carry-on bag, each with a small red plastic cap covering the "working end" of the screw. The working end is composed of five razor-sharp teeth which, when placed against the surface of the ice and rotated, easily chew their way deeply into the ice. This provides a means of safety for the climber after the screw is attached to a climbing rope with a carabiner.

Could these be explosive devices? The screener quickly realized that these were items which she did not recognize, and became further mystified by my description of how the screws were utilized. My climbing partners and I quickly exchanged nervous glances, realizing that we were about to have a major problem. The screener immediately summoned the assistance of her Supervisor, who, upon examining the screws, was equally as befuddled.

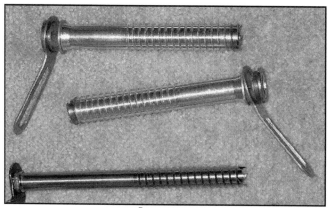

Ice screws

I decided that an exhibition of how ice screws were placed in the ice was in order. I proceeded to take out one of the screws and gave them an animated demonstration of the correct way to place an ice screw. The supervisor took the ice screw from me, carefully examined it and finally exclaimed, "Well at least they're not sharp," as she handed the screw back to me. You can imagine my shock and surprise as I realized that she had failed to remove the red protective cover from the screw, which would have revealed its sharp, jagged teeth! I thought my traveling companions and I exhibited a great deal of restraint by not busting out laughing at her comment. The Supervisor departed, confident that she had successfully accomplished her assigned responsibility. We quickly gathered up the suspect ice screws and made a very hasty exit into the terminal, realizing that we had just dodged a major bullet.

From that day on the ice screws travel comfortably in the dark recesses of my checked baggage.

Reality Check

The Old One-Two Punch
Pardon Me?

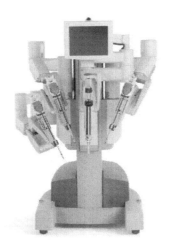

(photo ©2010 Intuitive Surgical, Inc.)

Chapter 22 - The Old One-Two Punch
The Big "C" and Falling is a Catchy Term

One Chance in Six

May 29, 2009: I have just returned from receiving the disconcerting news that I have prostate cancer. I re-read Claudia Berryman-Shafer's courageous words (see Chapter 8, Denali) and they inspired me to try to be as tough as she was.

Let's cut right to the chase. I have prostate cancer. I can lie on the floor in the fetal position, be angry, cry, or whatever. It's not going to help; I still have prostate cancer. The word *cancer* alone is pretty scary but when you add the "I have" it hits you where you live, it takes your breath away. How could I have cancer? I'm climbing better than I ever have and am in great physical condition. OK, so I am 72, but who's counting?

What does a diagnosis like this mean to me as a climber? As a person, a husband, a lover? Maybe there's something here that could answer that question for someone else experiencing these same questions. Guys, let's face it, if you live long enough, there's a one in six chance that you'll get prostate cancer; that's 100% if you're the *one*.

Does this mean I'll never be able to climb again after having whatever treatment option I choose? Is this going to kill me? I wonder if the Grim Reaper is going to be my next climbing partner. Should we tell our friends? Who shouldn't we tell? I'm in the midst of planning an ambitious climbing trip to the Washington Cascades; should I still go? These were my questions. If you get diagnosed with prostate cancer or cancer of *any* type, you're sure to have your own questions.

Let's turn back the clock a little. About fifteen years ago, my brother was diagnosed with prostate cancer. *Bong!* That puts me at twice the risk of getting prostate cancer. OK, maybe I shouldn't have eaten so many pints of that artery-clogging, high fat ice cream, or those irresistible pieces of creamy frosted carrot cake that melt in your mouth. Fat is supposed to be bad for the prostate, but it's good for the brain. Who knows. "They" say testosterone fuels prostate cancer cells; perhaps I just had too much testosterone! All this is pure conjecture on my part, as no one really knows why some men get prostate cancer and some don't. If they do know, they're not telling. See, I'm already attempting to rationalize away what is happening in my body. It's time to get past the "what ifs" and move on to something that I *can* do something about. I *do* have prostate cancer.

The information that follows is simply my understanding of how all this works and should certainly <u>NOT</u> be substituted for the advice of a physician.

Statistically, my PSA numbers weren't off the chart for someone of my age; they were 4.1 ng/ml. However, two years ago my PSA had jumped up by 1.5 ng/ml. My primary care physician wasn't comfortable with the spike, which is referred to as a "change in velocity," so he prescribed a different PSA test which is monitored by a urologist, a specialist in male human plumbing (women see a gynecologist). The velocity of change, rather than the current PSA measurement, seems to be the real warning sign for the probability of prostate cancer. In retrospect, I should have requested the advanced testing procedure at the time I initially noted the change in velocity.

I still didn't feel that I had prostate cancer because I didn't have any "symptoms." That's a good question: what are the symptoms? Guess what — early stage prostate cancer is asymptomatic; there are no symptoms. A very insidious disease.

I received a call from the urologist's nurse and she began by asking me how my day is going – a *very* suspect way to begin this conversation. The results of my free-PSA test had come back at 19%. That's good – a low score, that must mean I don't have prostate cancer, right? *Bong*, again! The lower the score, the higher the chance that you have prostate cancer. A score above 25% *usually* indicates no cancer present; below that, watch out. Low scores only count in golf. Ouch!

The next step in this whole process was the dreaded prostate biopsy procedure. No one adequately described to me what I would experience during this procedure, so I'll try to draw you a picture. Ever been driving along out in the country and see that big bull with a raging erection? Well, he's going to be the one giving you your biopsy. Having a flashback of that picture when you're in the urologist's office waiting to go in for your procedure should make you break out in a cold sweat; if not, you're a better man than I am. Yeah, and if you see some guy coming out of the urologist's office walking like Charlie Chaplin, he's probably just finished *the procedure.*

Actually, it's not that bad. Really. Trust me. (How many times have we told women that line?) You go in to the examination room, disrobe from the waist down, and sit on the examination table with a sheet over your lower body and wait for the urologist. Take your time to look around. You look off to the side of the examination table — what's *that* device? Jesus, it looks like the dildo from hell! Even more disconcerting, it's got a condom on it. Whoa! Get Back! Maybe I should have smoked a joint before I came in for my appointment. Isn't that a great use for medical marijuana?

You can feel the sweat starting to run down the crack of your ass as you visualize all of the bizarre possibilities confronting you.

Then, just when you think it can't get any worse, the urologist walks in, *smiling*. Running down the hall and out the door without your pants is *not* an option. It's time to cowboy up! All joking aside, the biopsy procedure is fairly standard and only results in mild discomfort. There are plenty of descriptions of the procedure on the Web so I'll spare you the gory details. Bottom line: imagine someone sticking a shotgun up your ass and pulling the trigger. (Sorry, couldn't help myself.)

If the biopsy comes back positive, you could be in for mental hell trying to decide which treatment option to choose. People have written complete books on this subject, and believe me, Diane and I read a bunch of them over the next several weeks. Inasmuch as I apparently have early stage prostate cancer, my options are just about anything available.

We devoted hours and hours of research on the various prostate cancer treatments and finally came down to two viable options, surgery or radioactive seed implantation. How to figure which treatment is best suited for us (considering the side effects) and my active lifestyle? Let's do it scientifically. We enter the pros and cons of each treatment into a spreadsheet and give a point value to each item. We crunch the numbers. Bottom line: the results come up within 1% of each other. Not much help in making a decision using that method. Let's apply a more scientific method to solve our dilemma; let's flip a coin twenty times. Heads it's surgery, tails it's seeds. OK, here we go. Six straight heads, then three tails; seven heads, five tails; and finally — you guessed it — ten heads and ten tails. Go figure. Back to square one. I guess we'll have to gather more information, so it's off to see another cancer specialist.

Brachytherapy — the radioactive seed implantation treatment — is not as invasive as either radical or *da Vinci*® robotic surgery. It doesn't take long to insert the seeds and you're home the same day. Not too bad a treatment. You may still have both of the prostate cancer treatment bad boys, erectile dysfunction or ED (a.k.a. Captain Midnight is playing Rip Van Winkle), and incontinence (something akin to the Chinese water torture treatment). Longevity is about the same as if you had surgery. Brachytherapy is looking better since it seems to have a shorter recovery time than surgery.

Since the prostate cancer treatment decision is very important, we seek even more advice. It's time to visit a *da Vinci*-trained surgeon. If you've never heard of *da Vinci* robotic-assisted surgery, check it out on the web. It's Star Wars stuff.

We went to visit the urologist in Denver who had operated on my brother and was recommended as being the "gold standard" of surgeons in the area for using the *da Vinci* surgical robot for prostate removal. I asked him how many prostatectomy procedures he had performed. His answer: "Fourteen hundred radical procedures [traditional surgery] and six hundred *da Vinci* procedures." I think I just found the key to the *da Vinci* code. Signed up then and there for the procedure. The outcomes were close to being the same as the Brachytherapy procedure but I felt that just getting the cancer out of my body was the most important thing to me.

Now it's scheduling time; August 19ᵗʰ is "D" day. Two months away . . . plenty of time to go out and play some more. This is *supposed* to be a slow growing type of cancer. Now that the decision has been made, Diane and I are once again able to sleep at night.

For the next two months, I backpacked and climbed hard, finishing another of my peak-bagging lists and keeping thoughts of my cancer mostly at bay. But then it was time to get ready to go under the knife — and the five robotic arms.

Two weeks prior to surgery and counting. Nothing to eat in the six hours prior to the tests I'll take today. I went in for the prescribed stress test where I was hooked up with wires for an EKG and breathing monitor as well as a pulse oximeter to measure the oxygen saturation in my blood – 90% or more is good, and that's where I remained during the testing. At the end of the test the doctor declared, "I want your genes!" They were impressed that I wasn't breathing very hard. Since I had just returned from a lengthy climbing trip where I carried a heavy pack, the stress test hadn't seemed stressful at all.

Diane and I drove the five plus hours from our home in western Colorado to Denver two days before my scheduled surgery. We met with the PA (physician's assistant) in Denver, who gave me some of that industrial strength stuff they use to clear out sewers. Wonderful way to spend my last days of freedom, shitting my brains out. I think I've already killed most of mine climbing, so I didn't find this to be as bad as I expected.

S-Day (Surgery Day)

The big day arrives. Up at 4:30 a.m. and over to the hospital by 5:30 for admission. At 6:30 they come to get me for the trip to pre-op. Now the real fun begins. Off with my clothes. Next, plenty of needles and connectors stuck in my hand. The anesthesiologist arrives to discuss what he is going to do and inquire about any pre-existing conditions which might kill me during the operation. They hate it when that happens.

The next person to visit is the operating room nurse. Again, a few short questions regarding my expected longevity (since I'm already an old guy of 72) and she's gone. I'll never see these people again while conscious.

My final visitors are the surgeon and his assistant; the second surgeon is there in the unlikely event the primary surgeon has a cardiac arrest during the procedure. They give me the old "trust me" talk and toddle down the hallway.

Some unknown person arrives to hang another drip bag into my IV and they start to wheel me down the hall – good night. That's all I remember. Next thing I know, it's about noon and hopefully I'm in the recovery room and not on a slab. Thankfully, I never did figure out where the morgue was located.

The recovery room nurse asks how bad the pain is on a scale of one to ten. I told her, "Seven" and she shot me up with some more liquid morphine. Everyone from here on out asks me my pain level before dispensing any narcotics. They don't say, "where Ten means suicidal" anymore; I guess they had a few bad outcomes with that question.

That first evening mostly goes along in a fog. The nurses come in about every two hours to check my vitals during the night. Diane, who has been awake since 4:30 a.m., dozes on a daybed in my room, but is awakened every time they enter. At least I'm still heavily drugged — I fall asleep again quickly. During surgery, I

231

was fitted with a catheter, which I'll get to keep for ten days, so peeing is a no-brainer.

S-Day + 1

Had a restless first night and felt worse than yesterday afternoon. Still getting the liquid morphine diet. That kills the pain but leaves me feeling like crap. They normally release patients around 3 p.m. but I need another day to rest prior to our long drive home. I take a peek at my belly. The *da Vinci* robot has left a series of one inch, horizontal slits that look like a dotted line across my abdomen, intersecting my belly button. I look for instructions that say "open at the dotted line," but they must have removed them after my surgery.

S-Day + 2

Finally, discharge day! I was up at 5 a.m. walking the halls. Had a lot of fun joking with the night nurse. "Nice purse," she said, complimenting me as I was carrying my catheter bag down the hallway. I replied that I was running away from home.

The PA came in and dictated my discharge papers. Free at last! The PA wanted us to drive for 45 minutes and then get out of the car and walk ten to fifteen minutes each hour. We followed his directions and it took us about eight hours to drive home.

The surgeon called the next morning. The pathology report showed that the cancer had been "attempting to escape" from my prostate and the cancer looked a bit more aggressive than originally thought. Glad we opted for the surgery as this gave us a better look at the cancer potential. He said that my results weren't perfect but I should *hopefully* be cancer free for the rest of my life.

S-Day + 30

The surgeon's nurse just gave me the "no restrictions" message on any activity I wanted to pursue. She just said "if it hurts quit doing it." It hurts when I have to use the vacuum cleaner so I guess I'll never be able to vacuum the carpet again – ever.

Three months after my cancer surgery, Diane and I participated in a two week rock climbing trip to El Potrero Chico near Monterrey, Mexico. My performance far exceeded my expectations and I climbed longer and harder routes than I ever had in the past. I hadn't expected to be very strong or to have much endurance, but thankfully I was wrong on both accounts.

I went out hiking shortly after a two-foot snowfall in the San Juan Mountains in Colorado. I enjoyed back-to-back days of achieving nearly 3,000 feet of elevation gain while breaking trail most of the way in knee-deep snow on the first day. My recovery totally blew away my expectations.

It seems that my hiking and climbing ambitions weren't thwarted by the prostate cancer surgery. In fact, I think I became even more inspired and determined than prior to the surgery. Those thirty days of total rest did wonders for my body.

Now I can focus on the remaining side effects of the surgery.

Incontinence status: most prostate surgery patients are "dry" within three months of surgery. At first, during day-to-day "normal" activities, I had a very minimal problem with incontinence. Due to my active lifestyle, I had some problems after completing a long hike (ten miles) and coming back downhill. That must have something to do with the jarring the bladder experiences as the body comes down on each foot. But, good news! By four months after my surgery, I conquered the incontinence entirely. No more pads!

Erectile Dysfunction status: after a year, the jury is still out. I've been using ED medication, but Rip Van Winkle is still AWOL. The *fun* is in our effort trying to coax him awake. See, every cloud *does* has a silver lining!

My PSA tests in the following year have been excellent. Looks like smooth sailing from here on out.

OK, I *had* prostate cancer, it's gone now, time to get on with living a full productive, healthy life. I was lucky.

Guys, get your PSA tested at age 50. Gals who love your guy, make sure they get their tests! That will give you a baseline measurement for PSA comparison in later years. Look for a change in the velocity or doubling of your PSA reading. Be proactive and get the tests *you* need.

If cancer strikes, don't try to be stoic and go through the surgery procedure alone. Involve the people who care the most about you; you'll need and welcome the support.

Get a second or third opinion before selecting which treatment is right for *you*. There are some really draconian treatments out there!

A parting thought: "Old at the hips, young at the lips." I'm not dead yet!

Ouray Ice Park

Ice Climbing 101 - The Shit House Wall

"Talk to me, talk to me!" my belayer Randy kept shouting to me as I hung on the rope in the fetal position 60 feet above him, out of breath, staring at the sky, wrapped up in a tangled mess of ice screws, rope, and ice tools after taking a fall. Did I mention I had the ass pain from hell?

I'm 72 years old, with 25 years of ice climbing experience under my belt. I had prostate cancer surgery four months ago, and have come back strong. The "Women's Room" ice climb located on "The Shit House Wall" in Ouray Ice Park was one that I had done many times in the past, but I guess today just wasn't my day, as I peeled off and fell ten feet, landing on my back on the edge of an ice-covered, rock ledge. We always said, "If you can't take a joke you shouldn't climb," but I failed to see the humor in my current situation.

After being lowered back to the ground amid a lot of cursing and moaning, I made a feeble attempt to stand with the help of my friends. Arrrg! %$%^@#! Well, you get the picture. "I can't walk," I declared. "We'll need to call for a rescue," Randy stated. "I don't want to be rescued!" "I'm going up to call for a rescue," and off he went. Meanwhile, my other climbing partner, Dan Blake, carefully removed my crampons and other climbing equipment in preparation for my being lifted out of the canyon in a litter.

It wasn't long before I was surrounded by members of the excellent Ouray Mountain Rescue Team. They professionally wrapped me up in an inflatable full body splint, placed me in a litter which had been lowered from the top of the cliff, and began the process of hauling my sorry ass (and all other parts) up from the bottom of the climb. "You guys should be thankful that I only weigh 125 pounds," I quipped. "Yes, we are. Manhandling someone who weighs 200 over this type of terrain can be a bugger of a job."

I didn't want to be transported to the hospital by ambulance, but by the time I arrived at the top of the climb, I wasn't ready to jump behind the wheel and drive myself there. I had Randy call Diane to tell her that I had fallen and severely bruised my ass, which is all I thought I had done.

Incidentally, while I was experiencing my own misadventure, one of my other climbing partners, Dave Reeder, was having an adventure of his own just upstream from where I had fallen. Dave managed to break through the ice into waist-deep water at the bottom of the canyon while looking at a climb he was interested in leading. Dave said it took him several minutes to get out of the water as the ice kept breaking when he attempted to climb out. Do we ice climbers know how to have a good time or what?

It was about an hour's ride to the hospital and by the time I arrived, Diane was already there. The first thing I heard from her was, "Carlitos, you've been bad again." The next thing was the ER doctor saying, "I worked on you last year." "Rib or chin?" I asked. "Chin. Someone else must have done the rib at another time." It's not a good thing when the ER docs start to recognize you.

The net result of this misadventure was two fractured ribs, bilateral fractures of the sacroiliac, bilateral fractures of my L5 vertebra transverse processes, and severe damage to my ego. Well, I guess that adequately describes my statement that I bruised my ass. I just hadn't mentioned breaking my back.

After reviewing my X-rays and CT scans, the Orthopedic Surgeon explained to Diane, "You might hurt him, but you can't

236

damage him any more." Her prognosis was that I'd be hiking again in about four to six months. In the meantime, I'll be missing some great winter and spring hiking and climbing.

I was released from the hospital after 24 hours of observation and pain management. Randy had asked Diane to call him on his cell phone to let him know when I would be released. She called him mid-afternoon on the day of my release. He was in the middle of an ice climb when he answered her call. "Hang on a sec," he said, "I need to get my other tool in the ice before I can talk." And so goes the insanity of waterfall ice climbing.

An important footnote to this whole story is that my wife, Diane, was my savior, my nurse in training (for when I get older), literally waiting on me hand and foot during my recovery from my back-breaking fall. I awarded her the "Wife of the Year" for her efforts, but then I happily stuffed the ballot box.

One of the biggest challenges I encountered after I was able to get up and about using a wheeled walker was my inability to gain access to the bathroom due to the fact that our bathroom doorways weren't wide enough to accommodate the walker. Our next house *will* have ADA-compliant doorway widths! This experience gave me a big respect and empathy for people who are handicapped and need a wheelchair or walker to negotiate public and private accommodations. And, while I'm on the subject of disabled access, I would like to express my intense dislike for those uncaring people who park in handicap spots because they're "in a hurry" to get something from the store. Be considerate of others. On the positive side my friend, George, and his son-in-law built me a nifty handicap ramp so I could get in and out of the house without having to negotiate any stairs.

Two months after my accident, I could walk again without using a walker for assistance. At four months, I was able to join Diane and many old friends rock climbing at Joshua Tree. Life is good!

健康和幸福

Chapter 23 - Pardon Me?
Resolution & Rehabilitation

How did my life finally turn out after such a wretched beginning? Well,

> *The Moving Finger writes; and having writ,*
> *Moves on: nor all your Piety nor Wit*
> *Shall lure it back to cancel half a Line,*
> *Nor all your Tears wash out a Word of it.*

The Rubaiyat of Omar Khayyam

That translates into "Don't live it up if you can't live it down."

Fifty years is a long time, and it's taken me that long to finally sit down and write my story. Try thinking about all the things that may have passed in your life during that amount of time, or project where you think you will be or what you will be doing fifty years from now.

I didn't know if I would ever start writing this book, and if I did, I had serious reservations about it ever being finished. There was a lot of history here that was locked away in my subconscious for many, many years. People who have known me may be shocked by my "coming out" with the truth about my past as I didn't readily share that information. I'm still the same person I was yesterday, and I don't intend to change the way I've decided to live my life.

Verbalizing my thoughts by putting them down on paper has been therapeutic as they kept arising from time to time to torment me. I could call some of these "demons," but they weren't driving me to do anything. They were just a constant pain in the ass — or pain in the past — reminding me who I used to be.

Hopefully you've stayed the course throughout all of my adventures, so you deserve to know how some things turned out.

We'll start with the oldest mystery first.

My Mother's Disappearance

As you may recall, my mother abandoned me (and my sister) when I was eleven years old. We never saw or heard from her again and — truthfully — I had effectively erased her from my mind. Later in life, I just assumed that she was dead or she would have attempted to get in contact with us. Girls often change their names when they get married but boys rarely do. Our last name "Winger" was not all that common, so I believe that she could have located us if she had wanted to. I really wonder if the authorities back in Chicago didn't have more information about her disappearance than they released.

In the early 2000s I became interested in our family's genealogy and decided to pursue my mother's whereabouts. I never knew her social security number, and she had a puzzling history of using different first names and even different maiden names, so that made any attempt to trace her very complicated. Diane and I started looking through the Social Security Death Index on the internet for someone with my mother's presumed name and approximate date of birth without much luck. If we did get a possible match, we would request a copy of the form that she would have completed upon receiving her social security number to see if the signature matched the ones on my grade cards, which I still possessed.

One day we received a form in the mail which looked like it might be the real deal. No luck again, wrong race. So, we kept trying until — there it was without a doubt! — my mother's signature at the bottom of the form. Now we had her social security number and were able to search the death indexes armed with more pertinent information. Bingo! We established that she had died, but not until fairly recently. She had apparently remarried somewhere along the line and her death notice was filed under a different name than any we had used in our searches.

Our next task was to request a copy of her death notice from the county where the death was recorded, since it might contain the name of the person reporting the death. This took some doing, but eventually we received the long-awaited document and had a name to contact — let's call her Hazel Johnson. Again we used the internet to locate the person of interest and I made a call I had been waiting over 50 years to make.

I explained who I was to the woman on the phone and gave her some background information about why I was calling. I could tell she was very suspicious about the call (turns out my mother never told her she had any children). After a few more minutes of conversation, Mrs. Johnson told me that she had recently gotten home from the hospital from having heart surgery and perhaps I could call her the next day, to which I agreed.

By now I was very excited about what I might find out. I had not relayed the news to my siblings, deciding to wait until I had more information to share with them. I called Hazel again the next day and it became apparent that she believed me. She gave me the telephone number of another woman who had worked with my mother and had been a good friend of hers. It didn't take me long to dial the other number and begin a conversation with perhaps the last person to know my mother before she died.

My mother's friend revealed that she knew my mother had

children and that Mother told her, "They were going to kill me" (whoever "they" were) if she didn't leave and never contact her kids again. I didn't believe that explanation for a minute, but it didn't matter much now as I couldn't confront my mother with that information. I also found out where my mother had worked before she went to the nursing home where she died.

I finally had enough information to share with my siblings, and you can just imagine how stunned they were. We made plans to go to California where my mother had been working and where her friend lived to attempt to get some first-hand information and possible photos of our mother. It turns out that where she had been working was only about 50 miles from where I had been going rock climbing for the last fifteen years. If only I had known. I would like to have been able to sit down with her face-to-face and find some answers to my questions, but she took the answers to her grave.

We were able to talk to some of the people my mother worked with and obtain some photographs which they had taken on an outing. Frankly, I didn't recognize the person in the photos as being my mother, but then it had been sixty years since I last saw her.

We at least had some closure on a disheartening period in my life, but still had many unanswered questions. I decided to pursue the matter further. I discovered that a relative of a deceased person can obtain their earnings records from the Social Security Administration (SSA). I was shocked to find out that my mother remained in Chicago for many years after she abandoned us there. What a shame that she never even notified the authorities that we had been left alone. I'm still pissed, but that isn't going to change anything. At least we know where she ended up and what she died from. Now when I get to one of those questions about my mother's cause of death, I don't have to write "unknown."

A further discovery which I made was that if you know the social security number of a missing close relative, you can send a written request to the SSA asking that that person contact you. Apparently they can, at their discretion, pass that request on to the person you are attempting to contact to see if there is any desire on their part to reply to your request. Unfortunately, I didn't know about this procedure or have my mother's social security number, so I missed the opportunity to possibly get some answers to my questions before she died.

I guess I could have pursued this quest earlier but, as I said, I had erased her from my consciousness and considered her dead, which, for all practical purposes, she was.

Prison and Life Thereafter

I survived prison and came out a better person for the experience. Thankfully, something in my personality had dramatically changed for the better. The day I left those forbidding prison walls behind me was the day I stepped into a new world, one that held a bright new future for me. I wouldn't recommend my experience to anyone as a way to improve oneself — you might consider one of those self-improvement courses as a better choice. The computer skills which I learned in prison have been the mainstay of my life, providing economic security and an occupation which I have thoroughly enjoyed. Enough said about that period of my life, as I've covered it extensively already.

Fifty years have passed since that dark day when I first walked through the prison gates and they still slam shut now and then when I least expect it. This year I decided that my life since that time was an example of how the system is designed to work. You get sentenced, you do your time, you get paroled, you get released from parole, and that should be the end of that. Unfortunately, you have a large "F" (for felon) figuratively carved into your forehead. The "F word" could stand for "F***ed" but I've sadly come to realize that it stands for "have you ever been convicted of a Felony?" — no matter how long ago.

I have much to offer, and I'm frustrated because my criminal record keeps me from participating in some of the activities I enjoy. There are so many young people today who could benefit from my mentoring, but some volunteer organizations are freaked out when they learn about my past, even though it was fifty years ago. They see me as only one step better than Osama Bin Laden as a person you don't want children to associate with. I consider this a waste of good resources — mine — in a time when they are critically needed. President Obama and former President George H. W. Bush recently held a seminar at the Points of Light Institute urging us all to volunteer for community service. How can I do that?

What should I do about this problem? If the system can convict and lock me up, there must be some way to reinsert that key back into the lock. So, why not apply for a Pardon? Did I deserve to get the lengthy sentence which I received? Yes, and then some; my behavior was certainly unacceptable. Have I earned a Pardon? Who knows; perhaps Omar Khayyam was right, the moving finger has writ and has moved on.

Obtaining a Pardon is not an easy process and not one that parole boards and Governors take lightly. It can take several years for an application to pass through the system. The parole board usually has to recommend you for a pardon based on a multitude of factors like the nature of your offense, how long it's been since you were released from parole, numerous letters of recommendation from friends and community members, and a host of other factors. In fact, you have to be squeaky clean, even cleaner than the average citizen. That's all well and good and as it should be.

Just getting a pardon wouldn't clear my record; my next step would be to petition the State to have my record expunged, locked away from the prying eyes of persons other than law enforcement authorities.

After fifty years of exemplary behavior, I foolishly thought that I would be a good candidate for a Pardon from the state where I was incarcerated, but perhaps things just don't work that way. Eighteen months after submitting all my paperwork and hearing absolutely nothing from the parole board, I contacted them to ask if they had a timeframe for processing my request. The impression I got was that Pardons are very low priority, and that it would be years — if ever at all — before they would even look at my application.

No problem, let's fall back and regroup. The Canadians will be more understanding, eh? Not so fast. Send in the address of every place you've lived and every place you've worked in the past fifty years along with a state police report from every state you've ever had contact with the police. It will take up to three years to process all of this information at which time it will probably need to be updated to make it current, then you send that in and . . . well, you get the picture.

So that's how the story ends, no runs, no hits, but plenty of errors on my part. The good old USA is looking better every day. Any Pardon I'll ever receive will have to come from within.

On the plus side, however, I was deeply touched by the letters of recommendations for a Pardon written by my friends. At Diane's urging, I have included some of their comments:

◆◆◆

I have known Charlie for 30 years. When I first met him, he became a business mentor to me as I began my own independent software consulting business after being employed by a small corporation for several years. He had a well-deserved reputation with his own software clients as being highly skilled and exceptionally trustworthy. He taught me that if I always treat my clients right, and exceed their expectations by delivering everything I promise to them and beyond, they in turn will remain good customers for many years. He was quite an inspiration to me in building my own successful business, and the loyalty of his clients spoke volumes about his character.

◆◆◆

Charlie's huge enthusiasm for life is infectious, and he has readily shared that enthusiasm with literally thousands of people. Through his passion for all aspects of mountaineering, Charlie has volunteered countless hours to teach and mentor several generations of climbers, passing along his wisdom and knowledge to allow those people to enjoy, in a safe manner, the joy and self-discovery that can accompany this pursuit.

◆◆◆

When you share a climbing rope with a person, you must absolutely trust your partner – your life is literally in their hands. *There is no one I trust more than Charlie, either when tying into a rope with him or with regard to everyday matters.*

◆◆◆

...He is an example of true honesty, sincerity, trustworthiness, truthfulness and integrity. The errors that he made as a much younger man taught him to be a leader in his life and work. He lives his life with dignity and self respect.

◆◆◆

Charles Winger has been in my life for over 40 years and I have never known him to do anything that is any way dishonest. He shows care and respect to other people in his life and always finds time to help anyone in need. He has always had a positive influence in the lives of people he has met as a teacher and as a mentor.

◆◆◆

In 1982, Charlie disclosed to me that earlier in his life he had been in prison. I was shocked; it seemed so out of place and character. I had come to know him as an honest and honorable man. His warm and cheerful demeanor impressed me ... He is, and has been for the thirty years I have known him, a man of integrity, kindness, and honor.

◆◆◆

And, finally, a letter I found in my files about an incident I had nearly forgotten:

Dear Charlie,
On behalf of all the members of the Colorado Mountain Club, I would like to thank you and commend you for your part in the rescue of ____ and ____ on March 24th [1985]. Your quick thinking and calm, deliberate, well-executed action together with the other BMS instructors and assistants was clearly instrumental in saving the lives of the victims. Your actions bring great credit to the Colorado Mountain Club and are an excellent example and inspiration for all members.

245

Thanks, everyone. The "officials" may never process my requests for forgiveness of my early transgressions, but knowing that I have a circle of caring friends who accept me for the man I am today is priceless.

While I was incarcerated, I earned my high school diploma and years later went on to complete my college education, receiving a Bachelor of Science Degree in Computer Information Systems, graduating summa cum laude. I owned a successful business. I finally figured out the marriage thing and have a loving, stable relationship. I've survived a bout with prostate cancer and a serious climbing accident and I've lived my life in an honest and productive manner that I can feel proud of. I'm still alive and have plenty of exciting adventures planned for the next twenty years. That will take me into my nineties, and by then I will surely be able say "I've been rehabilitated!"

I sincerely hope you've enjoyed my story, and that it gives you the inspiration to overcome any obstacles which life might throw your way, or the motivation to find a better path so that you can go out and climb your own mountains, whatever they may be.

"There is only one success . . .
To be able to spend your life in your own way."
Christopher Morley

◆◆◆

Glossary of Terms

Adze A slightly rounded, axe-like blade normally used for chopping steps in ice or snow. (See *Ice Axe*)

Arete A somewhat exposed ridge between two gullies or **couloirs**.

Ascender Usually a mechanical device which can be used to
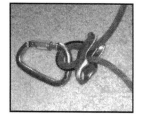
ascend a climbing rope which had previously been "fixed" to an anchor at the top of a "*pitch*" or climb. Ascenders will slide up on a rope but will lock in place when weighted, keeping the climber from sliding backward down the rope.

Belay The process of controlling the climbing rope from the belayer to the *lead climber* by using a *belay device*.

Belay Device A mechanical safety device attached to the *belayer*. The climbing rope passes through the belay device in such a fashion that friction may be applied when necessary to arrest (stop) the fall of the *lead climber*.

Belayer The person performing the belaying function.

Bergschrund A giant *crevasse* or split formed where the moving

ice of a *glacier* separates from stationary ice. The lower edge can be much lower than the upper edge of the gap.

249

Bivy (short for **Bivouac**) A primitive campsite usually without the benefit of a tent for shelter. A "bivy" may be planned or unplanned depending upon the circumstances. A climber may do a planned bivy by sleeping under a tree at the *trailhead* to enable an early start the next morning. The climber may find himself too far from his vehicle or campsite to be able to complete his climb before dark and decide to bivy (spend the night) wherever he can find suitable natural shelter.

Bubble Gum Machine The effect created by the red and blue flashing lights on top of a police vehicle.

Bushwhacking The process of making one's own trail from point A to point B, often by climbing around and through bushes and branches or easy rock outcrops. Basically, off trail hiking.

Cache Usually means a place where hiking/climbing equipment which will be used later is stored temporarily.

Cairn A pile of (usually three, but possibly more) stones or rocks erected as a trail marker. Sometimes called a *"Duck"* in California.

Carabiner A mechanical safety device used to control the

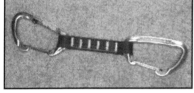

climbing rope or to attach climbing *slings* to climbers, belayer, etc.

Couloir A steep *gully* or chute which usually contains snow and rocks or ice.

250

Crampons  Used for snow/ice climbing. Spiked metal "platforms" which attach to the bottom of hiking/climbing boots. Crampons usually contain 10 bottom points/teeth and 2 front points/teeth.

Crevasse A deep crack or separation in the glacier which can be hundreds of feet deep.

Crevice A narrow crack or opening. Some people incorrectly refer to "*crevasses*" as "crevices." Not a mountaineering term.

Denali The local native name for Mt. McKinley.

Divorce The processing of recycling spouses after their warranty period has expired.

Downclimbing Climbing down a steep section of rock, snow, or ice. If the downclimb is too difficult or dangerous, climbers will **rappel** down that section of the climb instead.

Duck See "*Cairn*"

Exposed A spot or section of the hike/climb where tripping or stumbling could result in a serious fall.

Exposure Hiking or climbing on ridges, cliffs, etc. where a fall could result in serious injury or death. Also used in the context of "he died from exposure," which actually refers to death as a result of hypothermia.

Fumarole A hole in a volcano from which hot sulfuric gasses and smoke are emitted.

Gendarme Pinnacles or towers of rock on a ridge which can vary in height.

Glacier A permanent, slow moving snow/ice field.

Glissade Sliding down a steep snow slope in a sitting, crouching or standing position.

Gully A lower-angle vertical depression formed by erosion on the side of the peak or mountain.

Headwall The steepest portion of a rock face or snow field.

Example: The "headwall" on the West Buttress of Mt. McKinley/Denali which is pictured here.

Ice Axe A long (70cm to 75cm), straight-shaft, technical climbing tool. A mountaineer will usually carry one of these when snow or glacial travel is anticipated. It is used for ascending steep snow, *self-arresting* a fall, or probing for *crevasses* on a *glacier*.

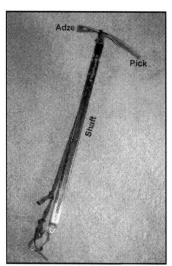

Ice Tool A short (50cm to 55cm), curved-shaft, technical ice climbing tool. An ice climber usually carries a pair of these to be used when ascending frozen waterfall ice. The head may contain either an *adze* or a hammer. "Adze" is a great Scrabble™ word.

Knife-edge Ridge A ridge that falls away steeply on both sides, with a very narrow area on top. The top can literally be the sharp edges of rock or could be up to a few feet wide.

Lead Climber The person being *belayed*. The lead climber is the first (and usually the highest) person on the climbing rope.

Leader See "*Lead Climber*"

Moraine, Lateral The debris deposition zone formed along the sides of a *glacier* as it moves downhill.

Moraine, Terminal The debris deposition zone formed where a *glacier* terminates its movement.

Pass The lowest spot between two adjacent higher peaks, sometimes called a Gap.

Pitch A climbing term which refers to the length of a section of a climb. The length of a "pitch" is variable and can be anywhere from several feet to the maximum length of the climbing rope being used less the amount used by the climbers to tie themselves in to each end of the rope. Modern ropes are usually 50 to 70 meters in length (164 to 230 feet).

Protection Safety devices of various sizes, shapes, and  configurations used by climbers to secure themselves or their climbing ropes to climbing surfaces.

Prusik A *sling* tied from cord which can be used as an ascender. The sling is wrapped around the climbing rope with a special knot referred to as a "prusik knot." See *"Ascender"*

Ramp Usually a ledge which has a tilted profile.

Rappel (*or* **Rap** *for short*) A method of lowering oneself down a steep area using a climbing rope and (usually) a mechanical device to add friction to slow the descent.

Ridge A long, narrow, elevated strip of mountainous land.

Ridge Crest The horizontal top of the mountain prior to the **summit**.

Runner See *"Sling"*

Saddle The lowest part of a *ridge* between two peaks.

Scrambling Climbing that requires using your hands and/or feet to make progress. "Scrambling" is usually more difficult than *"bushwhacking."* Ropes are sometimes used when scrambling.

Scree Small, marble-sized pieces of rock which have decomposed from larger rocks.

Self-arrest A technique used by climbers to stop themselves using an *ice axe* when they slip and fall on a snow-covered slope. Not to be confused with turning yourself in to the police after committing a crime.

Serac A free-standing ice tower formed when a *bergschrund* starts to disintegrate.

Sharp End A colloquial expression used to describe the end of the rope tied off to the *lead climber*.

Sling Usually a piece of variable width and length webbing sewn or tied together to form a circle or rope. May be a piece of rope.

Snow Bridge A natural snow accumulation which spans a *crevasse* providing the means for a climber to hopefully cross from one side to the other.

Summit The highest point on the peak or mountain.

Switchback A portion of a trail which forms a zigzag pattern as it ascends up the side of a hill or mountain.

Talus Large chunks of rock which have exfoliated from the side of a mountain and formed a slope.

Trailhead The starting point for hiking along a trail.

Traverse To move in a mostly horizontal direction along the side of a hill or mountain.

USGS United States Geographical Survey. Purveyor of various types of geographical maps and related information.

Wand Used for delineating climbing routes. Usually a thin bamboo stick approximately 3 to 4 feet long (1 meter or so) topped with a piece of brightly-colored tape. Also called a "flag."

Yosemite Decimal System (YDS) A numbering system which uses "classes" to define the difficulty of hikes/climbs. Class 1 is generally considered easy hiking on a trail, *"Bushwhacking"* would be considered class 2, *"Scrambling"* would be considered class 3 or 4, technical rock climbing normally requiring ropes would be considered class 5. Fifth class climbing is rated from 5.0 to 5.14. The higher the number after the decimal point, the more difficult and serious the climb.

About the Author

Charlie Winger is a prolific mountaineer with a passion for climbing lists of peaks: the 200 highest mountains in Colorado, the 50 state highpoints, over 100 USGS-named peaks in Death Valley, the 57 ultra-prominence peaks in the lower US, the highest mountains in North and South America, Europe, Africa, and Australia, and many more lists few people understand.

He and his wife, Diane, live in Colorado and are co-authors of several guidebooks on outdoor recreation.

Charlie makes killer Belgian waffles, numerous sick jokes, and enjoys telling climbing stories almost as much as he loves actually getting "out there."

http://wingerbookstore.blogspot.com

Made in the USA
Charleston, SC
08 October 2010